BONDING WITH THE LORD

BONDING WITH THE LORD

Jagannath, Popular Culture and Community Formation

Edited by

Jyotirmaya Tripathy
Uwe Skoda

B L O O M S B U R Y
NEW DELHI • LONDON • OXFORD • NEW YORK • SYDNEY

BLOOMSBURY INDIA
Bloomsbury Publishing India Pvt. Ltd
Second Floor, LSC Building No. 4, DDA Complex, Pocket C – 6 & 7,
Vasant Kunj New Delhi 110070

BLOOMSBURY, BLOOMSBURY ACADEMIC INDIA and the Diana logo
are trademarks of
Bloomsbury Publishing Plc

First published in India 2020
This edition published 2020

Bloomsbury Academic
An imprint of Bloomsbury Publishing Plc

ISBN: HB: 978-93-88414-51-7; eBook: 978-93-88414-53-1

2 4 6 8 10 9 7 5 3 1

Typeset in Minion Pro by Manipal Digital

Digitally Printed and bound in India by Replika Press Pvt. Ltd. In 2019.

For Hermann Kulke

CONTENTS

LIST OF FIGURES

FOREWORD

I congratulate Jyotirmaya Tripathy and Uwe Skoda on their fascinating anthology *Bonding with the Lord: Jagannath, Popular Culture and Community Formation* and for inviting me to contribute a foreword to it. This takes me back to my own sustained engagement with Odisha and Jagannath studies that defined me as a scholar. As a member of the two Orissa Research Projects (ORPs) of the German Research Council from 1970 to 1975 and from 1999 to 2005, it is alluring for me to reconsider their history in view of the present volume. It makes me see the present anthology as a logical expansion of some of the issues that my colleagues and I delved deep into.

One observation is particularly noteworthy. Looking back to the preliminaries of the second ORP, the subject of a few chapters in this anthology reminds me strongly of the conference with a very similar title 'Jagannath Revisited: Studying Society, Religion and the State in Orissa', which had been organised jointly together with Prof. Burkhard Schnepel in June 1997 at the South Asia Institute at Heidelberg. The German Research Council financed the conference. The subsequently published conference volume with the same title was presented to the Chief Minister of Odisha, Naveen Patnaik in 2001. In fact, the inducement to organise this conference was the expected presence of several Odia and Indian scholars of Odisha studies at that time at Heidelberg such as Gaya Charan Tripathi, Gaganendra Nath Dash, Prasanna Kumar Nayak, Ishita Banerjee, Saurabh Dube and Subrata Mitra. What would have been more obvious than to invite together with them also the former German members of the first ORP to a conference for a kind of stocktaking about ongoing new research on Odisha about twenty years after the end of the first ORP. No exact plans about future cooperation existed yet at that time, although Burkhard Schnepel and I had toyed already with the idea of trying to apply for a second ORP. But the successful course of the conference and the consent and approval by the participants led to the clear decision to apply for a new project as the second ORP.

But it took more than a year to define in detail the new research agenda of a second ORP in view of the results of the first project and the individual and general accomplishments of Odisha studies during the last twenty years. As well documented by its major publication, *The Cult of Jagannath and the Regional Tradition of Orissa*, published in 1978, the first ORP had focussed primarily on Puri and its Jagannath cult. The result of the intensive debates about follow-up studies was to apply in 1998 for a successor project with the title *Various Identities: Socio-Cultural Profiles of Orissa in Historical and Regional Perspectives*. Its major idea was to extend the studies beyond Puri and its Jagannath cult into its hinterland and its 'various identities'. The outcomes of the studies of the second project were anthologies like *Periphery and Centre* edited by Prof. Georg Pfeffer and *Centers Out There? Facets of Subregional Identities of Orissa*, which I edited with Georg Berkemer.

It is interesting and fascinating to read the 'Introduction' of this anthology 20 years after the end of a great project on Odisha studies. But again, as in the case of the beginning of ORP II, the present volume rightly intends not only a visiting and revisiting of Jagannath; it reveals a clear progression and further advance of Odisha and Jagannath studies. Already the sub-title of the book 'Jagannath, Popular Culture and Community Formation' and of its introduction reveal three such significant advances. They focus on 'community formation' and not state formation (the subject of both ORPs in different ways), on 'popular culture' rather than Brahmanical or tribal culture, and finally, not only in but also 'beyond' Odisha.

To quote from the 'Introduction': 'Jagannath is metonymic of Odisha's life-world', but what matters in this context to my knowledge is the fact that so far only very little genuine scholarly work has been devoted to these essential but neglected issues. Without going into details, but looking at the contributions to this anthology, I have the strong impression that it fulfils the necessary requirements to be a noteworthy intervention in the way Jagannath is understood and will inspire new projects on, in and beyond Odisha.

Hermann Kulke
Professor Emeritus, University of Kiel, Germany

ACKNOWLEDGEMENTS

When a non-resident Odia academic and a European scholar of Odisha meet and choose to work together on topics of mutual interest, Jagannath, the Lord of the Universe, is always an inescapable presence. With a dose of self-reflexivity we may say that Jagannath as a scholarly pursuit is perhaps the most authentic (or should we say the easiest) way of being an Odia and the most legitimate way of being a scholar of Odisha. Or so we thought, and embarked on this journey after working together for close to ten years.

Given that giant leaps have already been taken in terms of Jagannath's institutional history by scholars associated with ORPs as well as other independent researchers, the volume presents perhaps mere baby steps. However, they traverse a new ground by exploring Jagannath in popular culture and tracing His relevance in community formation. The nature of our enquiry demanded an involvement of scholars of various disciplinary backgrounds who approach the research questions from within a framework that is multidisciplinary.

Being an anthology, the book belongs to all the contributors who had to grapple with our endless demands and were open to multiple suggestions at various stages. It also belongs to those scholars who provided an ocean of material which helped us to identify questions that we felt had not been addressed. We fondly remember Hermann Kulke, G.N. Dash, Georg Pfeffer, Jakob Rösel, Roland Hardenberg among others. We also benefitted immensely from our interaction with Jagannath Tripathy, B.N. Patnaik, Sumanyu Satpathy and Jatindra Nayak. But for their guidance and support this project would have been impoverished. Finally, we are thankful to Mr R. Chandra Sekhar of Bloomsbury for his commitment to this project.

As we write these lines, we are filled with gratitude and humility. We are equally fired with hope and excitement that the anthology will find engaged readers, both sympathetic and critical.

Jyotirmaya Tripathy
Uwe Skoda

INTRODUCTION: EVERYDAY BONDING WITH LORD JAGANNATH IN AND BEYOND ODISHA

Jyotirmaya Tripathy and Uwe Skoda

Few other Hindu gods guide a regional consciousness or define the collective psyche the way Lord Jagannath does in Odisha and contiguous areas. Though Lord Tirupati or Padmanabhaswamy may command similar adulation and a lot more revenue, Lord Jagannath is a metonym for Odisha's life-world, arguably much more than any other god for a particular geography or its peoples. Though, occasionally and perhaps increasingly, challenged by subregional deities, such as Ma Tarini or Ma Samaleswari or a competing Shiva as in Lingaraj or Loknath temples, He remains the ultimate reference point (both sacred and secular) for what constitutes Odia-ness and Odisha's sociocultural life, and provides the glue for non-resident Odias as well. There is hardly any facet of Odisha's social world which has not been shaped by histories and narratives around Jagannath, His abode at Puri and the symbols associated with His name. Needless to say, His impact on people is not limited to particular registers within the religious sphere but is overdetermined in different social contexts. His deployments are not confined to the quest for a metaphysical realm outside the material and social but are integral to them.

His sway over people spills beyond modern Odisha's borders and commands cross-regional affiliations around temples in West Bengal, Tripura, Tamil Nadu, New Delhi or various parts of the Western world that leads to a multi-region sacred, evident in several Jagannath temples far away from what we know as Jagannath culture area. This spillage complicates the idea of a regional tradition that conventionally distinguishes itself from other regions on the basis of some underlying principles underpinning each region. Perhaps, we can never be sure if such spillages dilute the epistemic and experiential specificity of a regional tradition or strengthen it by building networks of such affiliations across the globe. But more than anything, these networks take us from the institutional and structuralist Jagannath to a popular and culturalist[1] Jagannath and the focus, thus, moves from what Jagannath is to what Jagannath means in everyday contexts. This culturalisation of Lord Jagannath deals with artefacts, objects and experiences in our daily lives—what we hear, watch, eat or the temples we visit or the way we fast and pray. This meaning-making process shifts our attention from Jagannath to His sociocultural usage and guides the chapters in this anthology.

Towards Jagannath Praxis:[2] *Culture, Materiality and Agency*

Though religious and mythological literature on Jagannath grows virtually every day and hundreds of new books on Jagannath *leela* (divine play) and *mahima* (glory) are produced every year to be consumed by an ever-expanding number of devotees, they are mostly in Odia language and cater to the devotees' religious universe. The same is the case as far as films, video/music albums or *prabachana*s (religious speeches) are concerned that provide a sense of purpose in an Odia's life, not just a guideline for rituals but as a guide to everyday social conduct. Scholarly attention to Jagannath in English (also in German) language only partially responded to the constantly evolving culturalisation of Jagannath faith, while this volume contributes in novel ways to the existing but often dated literature with a focus on the Lord. The two major Orissa Research Projects (ORP I and II) funded by the German Research Council, while offering path-breaking insights, had limited space for a sustained engagement with everyday Jagannath. ORP I had focused on the evolution of Jagannath worship through the ages and the religious/political aspects in the context of kingship. *The Cult of Jagannath and the Regional Tradition of Orissa* edited by Eschmann, Kulke and Tripathi (1986) was the most prominent outcome of this project.

The second project (ORP II) in the 2000s concentrated on a bottom-up approach and discovered links between a dominant centre and various peripheries or 'little' traditions. It led to a range of publications like *Jagannath Revisited* edited by Kulke and Schnepel (2001) and many others (Kulke and Berkemer 2011;

Malinar 2007; Pfeffer 2007) concentrating on aspects such as texts and contexts, periphery and centre thereby bringing Jagannath to the international English language scholarship. Additionally, there have been occasional attempts to engage with the memory of Jagannath's desecration and its effect on modern sensibilities (Banerjee-Dube 2018), Jagannath temple as an inclusive metaphor (Mohanty 2008), Jagannath's influence in Odia literary and performative practices (Behera 1999; Das 2006; Pattanayak 1992), *Kanchi Kaveri* legend vis-à-vis Odia identity (Mohapatra 1996) or rath yatra (procession of chariots) in colonial narratives (Ghosh 2018). Yet, while there have been substantial shifts in the study of Jagannath including a calibrating of attention towards demotic practices, there is still relatively little critical material in the English language on the linkages between the Lord and His significations vis-à-vis everyday expressive activities and questions relating to contemporary community formation.

While not derecognising the historical Jagannath, what is attempted here is a novel look at the deployment of Jagannath in contemporary and popular cultural practices involving the sensorium in the widest sense. The project of culturalising and vernacularising Jagannath, in a very substantive sense, not only materialises Jagannath in people's everyday practices but also democratises Jagannath scholarship, hitherto confined to institutional and textual articulations. It also goes beyond existing studies on the peripheral Jagannath culture (Kulke and Schnepel 2001) by delinking and de-hyphenating Jagannath practices from the logocentric Jagannath at Puri. The expansion of the scope of Jagannath research to such expressions rather than confining it to religious/literary sources makes Jagannath an everyday presence and significantly enhances His sphere of influence. This cultural materialisation involves bringing critical material on Odia/ Indian popular culture to converse with Jagannath praxis and to see how the latter helps people in weaving narratives of belonging.

Jagannath's tribal origin, his association with Buddhism and Jainism, his present *avatari* (being treated as Vishnu's avatar) status, His multiplication through various media and new temples contribute to His democratisation as well as vernacularisation and negotiations around these markers make Him a treasure trove for multiple interpretations and a multilayered symbol. As Kulke has shown (1986),

Jagannath can be a very slippery, multivalent site and so can be used even in contradictory ways or as Dash (1986) has shown, He can be a veritable metaphor of secular practices alongside His being a religious anchor for Odias. On top of that, we have an ocean of relatively untapped material (primarily in Odia language as films, music albums, posters, religious speeches, performances like *jatra*s (folk theatre), *osha*s (religious fasting) as well as food habits, etc.) that make Jagannath a potent source of scholarship hitherto not brought into the previous English language scholarship (refer to the first six chapters in this volume). An important expression of this culturalisation is the Jagannath metaphor as the gateway to realise what people are, where do their core values come from and what are the everyday strategies used to reiterate and negotiate with that distinctness.

Jagannath as praxis shifts our attention from scriptural/textual codes to the popular and everyday meanings. It also means a parallel weighing of the people who make sense of Him—not just priests and devotees, but all mediators and value adders. Here 'people' do not come as pre-packaged and predictable in their values and attitudes but as carriers of an array of opinions and positions that keep evolving and transforming. As can be seen in any other public culture,[3] the agentic participants appropriate and contest existing values and in the process constantly alter what they consider a multi-meaning space. This project involves conception, production, circulation and consumption of Jagannath images, memorabilia, videos, albums, etc. or other affiliating sites as in popular *osha*s and even research communities, their economic imperatives and their social functions. That said, the attempt to take Jagannath beyond the divine and spiritual has its pitfalls as in desacralising Jagannath and reducing devotees to consumers, something that may appear as an Orientalist project or may reduce bhakti to a false consciousness. But not doing so after decades of Jagannath scholarship would mean the poverty of such scholarship and limit its appeal to a nativist constellation of scholars working within predictable trajectories. Our objective is to expand the scope of Jagannath research by moving out of ritual-based, institution-sanctioned registers to the value-laden processes and the people associated with them, thus, ascribing them subjecthood that so often elides them.

Such praxis, we believe, is an appropriate way of doing Jagannath, both as a word and as the world. Thus, all players operating in various knowledge and performance fields are inscribed and mainstreamed as Jagannath subjects who in turn materialise Jagannath and create conditions through which He can be experienced. Thus, the person preparing and selling the sacred food is as important as the person consuming it to experience divinity, which means imagining Jagannath outside history and materialism is a limited exercise, particularly at a time when mediation of experience (on top of cultural conditioning) has led to a situation of authenticity itself being constructed. But does this approach rob Jagannath of His power? Are devotees being duped into believing in His existence? These questions are not any more or less important than asking if a bhajan (devotional song) regulates devotees' responses or the priests control ways of knowing Jagannath. This consciousness of Jagannath as a social and material imaginary, something not always discussed when we speak of Jagannath's Odia-ness, is a necessary though disruptive approach. If praxis is a mechanism for change, the latter can be wrought by giving new directions to scholarship and by expanding the scope of Jagannath as knowledge and experience. It is an active way of pushing theoretical debates and material realities so as to move beyond normative clichés. An engagement with how things happen or being attentive to the process of experience making can make Jagannath a multivalent habitus.

Thus, Jagannath in the Puri temple is authenticated and mediated by Jagannath as a sticker on a cellphone cover or as a refrigerator magnet or as a movie poster. This may sound like trivialising Jagannath and reducing Him to a consumer durable good. Also by delinking Jagannath from Puri, we may be seen as diluting the place-ness of Jagannath. But we must understand that Jagannath believers create their sacred environment (Sahney 2016: 282) with these decorations and paraphernalia and create Puri in their own homes. His images outside puja rooms create subject positions for their users when they place a Jagannath image in a car or on an office table, thus, deciding how to experience God and in what sort of places. The multiple ways of experiencing sacred and secular Jagannath bring out

His everyday character and highlight people's agency. Quotidian acts such as bringing *prasad* (food offered to god and later shared among devotees) home or carrying a photo to a relative outside Odisha makes Jagannath the symbol He is.

The Culture of Bonding: Bhakti, Affect and Reciprocity

This volume is attentive to both the material and sacral Jagannath and how they intersect each other. While being constructed through cultural performances, inside the temple(s) and outside of it, through devotional songs or posters or food, He remains a presence, almost omnipresent. However, such constitution through cultural processes does not make Him an invention. Being an important god and perpetuated in literature, sufficient to command the adulation He gets, His mediation through popular media such as television, cassette and film industry and related practices such as religious discourses, sale and consumption of *prasad* consolidate His power (see the chapters 'In the Eyes of God: Jagannath Iconography in Popular Cultures', 'Worldliness of the Otherworldly: Dissemination of Devotion from Early Modern to Cassette Era', 'Syncretic Jagannath Culture and Popular Odia Imagination: Representations of Lord Jagannath in Odia Cinema' and 'Eating with Eyes: The Food Economy of Jagannath Culture'). The iteration and circulation of such performatives create a consciousness among listeners/viewers/participants and produce certain types of subjectivities. Thus, a TV programme on Jagannath rewarding a poor *bhakta* (devotee) or a *bhakta* longing to have a *darshan* is expected to evoke among viewers similar emotions of fulfilment. The making of the consciousness is interestingly iterated through unconscious interpellation of the devotee by media narratives leading to pre-fabricated subject positions. This is to say that devotees are neither duped into believing in something which is only an economic good/service (cassette, CD, movie, etc.) nor that devotion is a planted emotion. These narratives are not always complementary to one another and produce multiple subjectivities that in turn process such information in their own already mediated mindscapes.

Though there is nothing before mediation in a literal sense, mediation, as mentioned previously, acts on something that is always already there, that is Jagannath and 'bhakti'. The pre-existence of Jagannath and 'bhakti' does not make our structuralist/culturalist distinction untenable; rather they mainstream the operationalisation of a taken-for-granted reality (Jagannath) and make ordinary folks the processors of such knowledge. While being sanctioned by religious literature and institutionalised through centuries of practice, the bond between Jagannath and the *bhakta* is conditioned and strengthened by mediation—especially in the Vaishnav tradition to which Jagannath is closely tied to (see the chapter 'Contemporary Bangla Songs on Jagannath: A Hermeneutic for Bhakti and Community of *Bhaktas*'). Thus 'bhakti' is as much internal and intimate as external and guided wherein the magic of knowing and experiencing is complemented by mediation. That brings us to the core of 'bhakti' that is concerned with bhava (emotion) offering alternative ways of knowing. In various stories, Jagannath has been given maximum adulation and has been imagined as a lover, son, friend, etc., the only demand from the devotee being the Lord's company. But no emotion is describable and so the poet/singer cannot communicate with the audience without them experiencing that emotion. Intrinsic to such representation is the entry condition of the reader/viewer as a devotee. This conversion is required for appreciation of the content.

'Bhakti' closes the gap between human and divine: 'the deity seems at once lodged far away in the unattainable realm of lofty ideals and magical powers, yet at the same time it is placed close at hand in a human form' (Paranjpe 2002: 278). This condition leads to a series of reciprocal relationships (no matter how asymmetrical) of affection, love, admiration, forgiveness, compassion and even envy and anger, immortalised in devotional genres such as 'bhajan' and *janana*. In the former, one expects nothing other than His *karuna* or deliverance from mundane life whereas in the latter the poet throws abuses and accuses Him of indifference (Behera 1999: 253). If in one story, Jagannath receives coconut from Dasia Bauri, an untouchable, in another story He stops His chariot during rath yatra so that His Muslim devotee Salabega can see Him. In the

Vaishnavite tradition, there are two impulses at work: one is *dharma* where social norms are confirmed and the other is *parodharma* where social norms are transcended and the materiality, centrality and hierarchy of divine manifestations are relatively downplayed. Schweig (2002: 423) tells us that such embracing and transcending lead to a type of devotional behaviour characterised by humility and passion respectively which again correspond to the idea of God as powerful (*aisvarya*) and intimate (*madhurya*). These emotions are abundantly visible in Jagannath worship, though He is predominantly a *madhurya* deity (Schweig 2002: 425) where devotees role-play as mother or beloved—enacting mutual care. Beyond its etymological meaning, 'bhakti' (derived from *bhaj* that denotes sharing) may convey a sense of bonding. If the worldly use of bonding refers to instinctual attraction or friendship, the sacred use may refer to religious discipleship or the mystic's ecstatic union with the divine (Gupta 2016: 150).

It may be noted here that social bond theory, following its main proponent Travis Hirschi (1969: 16), emphasizes attachment to families, commitment to social norms and institutions, involvement in activities and the belief that all these are important as crucial elements of social bonding. Though the evolving nature of bonding and proliferation of alternative values are social realities today, Hirschi's ideas still have enough strength to understand various ways of bonding. Outside crime theory, bonding offers interesting insights into the way devotees bond with the Lord and their meaning within the commitment to social norms. We must also understand the prior existence of a social/religious normative value system that acts as a glue to keep the individual connected to social conventions. In His uses as both sacred and secular symbols, bonding may range from attachment between mother/son, friend/friend, god/devotee, lover/beloved, etc. to situations of role reversal where the *bhakta* takes care of the Lord when the latter falls sick.

The negotiation of human and divine engenders an interesting possibility, that is, the difference between the feeling of an object and the sympathy with such a feeling. There can be a 'feeling of which the direct object is another feeling' (Bhattacharya 2001: 196), to be distinguished from the understanding of it as a fact. To sympathise with a person is to feel his feelings or to feel him feeling. The devotee is not interested in the food to be eaten by the Lord but in the possibility of He enjoying the food, like the mother enjoying the child playing with a toy. In the Odia film, *Pua Mora Kala Thakura* (*The Dark God, My Son*) released in 1988, the distressed mother sings (*hasa tohara, khusi mohara*) how Jagannath's smile engenders in her immense joy. Similarly, a fruit meant for the Lord is not attractive because it is a mere fruit, but because in a future time, it will be consumed by the Lord that makes the fruit's purpose entirely different. It is quite common in Odisha to send the first fruit of a coconut tree to Jagannath or a nearby deity. The use value of the food/fruit is not absolute and the emotions it evokes while being eaten by oneself and while being eaten by the Lord are non-identical. This attachment with the Lord makes the fruit something more than itself and the devotee's ability to imagine that possible pleasure makes him/her a transformed person.

If bonding is the process through which culturalisation of Jagannath takes place, its experience is realised through affect, something which has been neglected in the existing literature. The regular puja sessions and related practices along with consumption of devotional images and sounds and regular visits to temples create a template of Jagannath praxis that is popular and mundane, something that Appadurai calls 'community of sentiments' (1990: 94). While recognising bonding's emotional dimension, Saroglou treats it as a self-transcendent experience that connects the individual with a transcendent reality, with others and with the inner-self and he also argues that this self-transcendence is common to all religions (2011: 1326). Though this may be true, the idea that self-transcendence is the same like bonding may not adequately capture non-Abrahamic religions where gods come in different shapes and sizes and demand rituals, veneration, engagement not always at a transcendent level but at a very physical and visceral realm. In fact, bonding at a physical level is definitive of Jagannath praxis wherein everyday puja is all about treating the god as human and offering Him bath, fresh clothes, food, etc. This becomes even more pronounced when He falls sick and is treated with medicine.

In this embodiment and affective framework, both god and human play their part and are constitutive of that bonding. Often the emotional bond manifests in corporeal dimensions when the devotee sways, folds hands and closes eyes in response to a relationship that is both physical and psychological. Even emotions shape and constitute the surface of our bodies and their materialisation and meaning in a sacred universe. The body is not *jada* or inanimate but a pathway for the realisation of god; the human body is processual and mediates between the divine body and the human body (Pati 2011: 193). This processual body can be called dividual,[4] a constellation of substances and processes connected to other bodies. The bonding between Jagannath and His devotee collapses the difference between experiencing and losing oneself.

By treating the Lord like a human, the devotee creates possibilities where devotion and care are interchangeable, earthly and ethereal are interchangeable, and also that subjecthood of the devotee is not a cognitive process but an intensely affective one. Crying for the Lord or complaining to Him establishes a link with the divine that is experienced through bodily sensations. Thus, Appadurai sees emotions as grounded in embodied experience (1990: 92) and that such emotions are negotiated with gestures and responses (1990: 94). During prayer sessions, the *bhakta*'s whole body, closed eyes, folded palms and legs, swaying from one side to another get adjusted to the demands of the occasion; they are physical adjustments where the devotees come in contact with one another. Similarly, when the deity is carried in a rath or on shoulders, the sheer physicality of a complex relationship is established. The constant movement of the Lord through pushing and pulling during *pahandi bije* (procession of moving the idols to the chariots) are activities where god and human meet and interact in physical terms. Similarly, fasting on auspicious occasions establish that the body is the medium through which god can be felt.

The intimacy with the Lord's idol is replicated in the *bhakta*'s relationship with Jagannath images present around him in calendars, stickers, or any other electronic images rather than requiring priestly sanction. If devotees wish to see their deities, they also wish to be seen by them, the reason why eyes are so very important in

Hinduism (Eck 2017). No wonder, Jagannath has been imagined and represented as just a pair of circular eyes. The exchange of vision with the Lord adds to the devotee's power of seeing the universe in true spirit (Babb 1981: 389), like Arjun's vision of Krishna's *viswaroopa* (cosmic form). Babb introduces the idea of closure in Hindu worship and how the distance between deity and worshipper is closed through intimacy. Pinney's idea of corpothetics (2004: 158) captures this intimacy. While talking about images, Pinney says the question is not how the image looks but what it can do (2004: 8). For example, to be seen by a deity often has a quality of being touched in an entangled multi-sensorial experience. Western practices privilege a 'disembodied, unidirectional and disinterested vision' whereas in India the emphasis is on 'mutuality and corporeality' (Pinney 2004: 193), that is, seeing and being seen, caring and being cared for, as much as nurturing and being nurtured and the volume provides fresh evidence of how closely visual and popular culture are intertwined around the Lord.

Tripathi provides us details of the daily rituals in Hindu temples and the way they create a web of dependency where care and affect are reinforced. The worshipper, Tripathi tells us, meditates upon the 'mantra' and realises the deity in his heart and later takes the deity's *tejas* (light) out of his heart and places it in the image. Then the *tejas* of the deity is taken back from the image into the heart where it originated (Tripathi 1986: 289). In the shifting of *tejas*, we have a spatial transformation as well because the deity is not where it physically is; it is in the heart of the worshipper. This deterritorialisation of the divine and its location in the worshipper's heart blurs the difference between I and thou, God and human, best captured in the expression *tat tvam asi* (*atman*/self-being identical with Brahman/Ultimate Reality). The Jagannath bhajan '*Asithili kalia to darasan painre; tate chhadi jibaku mo mana balu nahinre*' (having come to see you, I don't feel like leaving) shows how the observer gets caught in the web of 'bhakti' and loses the power to leave; he becomes the observed.

Though conventionally there is a binary of conceptual mediation and affective immediacy, it is analytically untenable. There is a flaw in affect theory in its romantic attachment to fantasy immediacy or immediation (Mazzarella 2009: 294). Supposedly, affective responses to Jagannath may be actually mediated by popular cultural narratives or iterations of cultural cross-pollination. Though affect is progressively evacuated from an increasingly rationalised bourgeois world, popular politics and religion ensure a return of the repressed (affect, emotion) against the discourse of modernity. That partly explains the rise of so many Jagannath temples in recent times which not only mean the coming of age of Odia diaspora, but also the increasing weakness of any other social anchor outside religion.

In and Beyond Odisha: Centre, Region and Diaspora

Being the principal deity in one of the *char dham*s (four principal pilgrimage sites) Jagannath has His fair share of attention from all over India, and as Krishna Jagannath, His power transcends His location in Puri and His *karuna* goes beyond Odisha's borders. But this power is neither confined to guiding individual/public religious life nor is it premised on a transcendent realm of spiritual plentitude; it also covers the everyday world of economics, culture and politics. This extra-religious potential strengthens and at the same time also undermines Jagannath. While being a multipurpose, multi-accentual, cross-regional god, Jagannath loses His distinction as Odia God and defender of Odia interest. The obverse is equally true, every effort to project Him as a symbol of Odia pride undermines His aura as a pan-Indian religious symbol.

The present anthology is a corroboration and interrogation of Jagannath's regional tradition and the chapters mark both convergence and dissonance around Jagannath's Odia character. These chapters problematise the spatial nature of experience and reinterpret regions as conceptual categories that ignore internal inconsistencies within them—earlier political units such as little kingdoms that have been characterised by alliances rather than clearly demarcated boundaries. The ensuing displacement and replacement of Jagannath culture establish the evolving nature of Odias' identification with Him and betray the limits of regions as carriers of culture. Thus, the region becomes the interstice of the local and the global and culture becomes the in-between of the region and sub/supra-region. So, Jagannath as a cultural symbol moves beyond the contiguous areas of Bengal and Jharkhand further to Agartala, Chennai, Delhi and other places and emerges as an experience that does not respect what we know as authenticity; it also revels in multiplication. Such multiplications do not always de-auratise the real and originary nor does it lead to an imaginary relation with real and material, but are pathways to consolidate the real. The following chapters acknowledge the power of the real (Puri Jagannath as centre) as well as the pervasiveness of representation, thereby distinguishing them from a typical constructivist project.

Given that Odias and their ways of being are no longer confined to Odisha's borders, if indeed they ever were, mediatised forms of what constitutes Odisha's culture increasingly find their way beyond Odisha in its current shape and engage with competing cultural expressions. Diasporic Odia experience has created new conditions wherein Jagannath is inscribed through dislocation as in new Jagannath temples or various non-resident Odia associations. This expansion/dilution or circulation/fixity of Jagannath has thrown open new challenges and possibilities to know and understand Jagannath and what He means in the present time. This takes us to the question of diaspora where we bring this literature to converse with the Jagannath experience that would shed light on the processes of community formation around the Lord beyond the supposedly limiting region and would also illustrate the ongoing forms of cultural production.

Since the 1990s, diaspora (literally meaning being dispersed or scattered) has emerged as a key concept in the humanities and social sciences, especially after it had been applied not only to proto-typical 'victim diasporas' but also to communities evolving through the process of labour migration or trade migration (Cohen 2008). While this rudimentary typology already indicates a considerable diversity of such triangular cases—diaspora community, homeland and host society—some common features beyond the mere dispersal are, however, frequently encountered. They include, for example, collective memories and an orientation towards a homeland (real, idealised or imagined), uneasy or troubled relations with the new host society often (re-)enforcing a specific consciousness as a distinct group or a specific cultural creativity and reflexivity tied to the processes of displacement and emplacement—even more so in pluralist societies (Cohen 2008; Safran 2005). Settling over generations in new localities, the conditions and traditions of the homeland and host society often continue to determine the processes of boundary maintenance and boundary erosion—in terms of social relations such as marriage, but also political loyalties or economic opportunities (Brubaker 2005; Vertovec 2000).

Given the relatively recent focus on diasporic situations it may not surprise that earlier scholarship on Lord Jagannath by and large neglected His presence beyond Odisha and this volume explicitly starts filling this gap (see the chapters, 'Becoming Jagannath in Dravidanadu: *Kanchi Kaveri* Legend and Other Possibilities in Kanathur Jagannath Temple', 'Delhiwallah Jagannath and the Odia Diaspora: Notes towards a Social History', 'Jagannath in Tripura: Disappearance and Dissemination', 'A Scholarly Community around the Lord: The Orissa Research Projects'). While the Lord with his claim to universality, can—by definition—never be diasporic in a literal sense, His dispersed devout worldly devotees find themselves in more or less alien environments beyond their 'homeland' Odisha. In cultural encounters in Delhi or elsewhere—vis-à-vis other ethnic identities—their specific Odia-ness may be questioned, (re-) discovered and creatively dealt with in novel ways. Building temples in India and beyond with its concomitant ritual performances but also producing, circulating and consuming popular culture media (images, music, films)—all under specific diasporic conditions—becomes part and parcel of (re-)formulating one's identity with the Lord as a central focus, vehicle and recreation. That said, older Jagannath temples as in Mahesh, Agartala, Ranchi (and many more) but before the wave of migration of Odias to new territories are not exactly sites where diasporic Odias can test their distinctness but are texts of belonging outside ethnicity and region where non-Odias can experiment with a diasporic Jagannath.

Narayanan (2006: 231) refers to Tamil poet Auvaiyar who asked her people to avoid towns where there is no temple, a sentiment not uncommon in other parts of India. We have temples where the deities are believed to be swayambhu (self-emerged) or swayamvyakta (self-announced), but such already sacred places pose problems when one goes on pilgrimage to other *kshetra*s (sacred places) thereby limiting the power of the *kshetra* one hails from. However, Hinduism not being a religion of the book, the difference between sacred and profane is not rigid. It is believed that a place outside one's sacred geography can be regenerated as sacred if people bring their gods either to their puja room or mobilise among themselves to build a temple. *Divya desa*s (holy places or shrines) in Hinduism are multiple and so are *tirtha*s (places of pilgrimage). The *divya desa* for a Shaivite will be different from a Vaishnavite's in Tamil Nadu and entirely different elsewhere. Similarly, every region has its own understanding of *sristi* or origin myth associated with a particular place. That gives the flexibility to Hindus to imagine a new sacred place out of an alien space by building a temple or by installing Jagannath at home. Installing an idol or fixing a calendar on the wall becomes an act of home making which converts an alien place into homeland.

Migration of people has not only created diasporas for themselves but also a spree in temple building in India's urban centres, wherein gods travel out of their *kshetra*s to accompany the devotees, leading to a phenomenon Waghorne calls the 'diaspora of gods' (2004) that she believes is a sign of a post-secular age. Though the difference between home and host places is not rigid within India, some sort of cultural negotiation takes place when the gods are displaced from the old and replaced in a new setting. Jagannath's migration, thus, is linked to the migration of his people. Jagannath travels with Odias when the latter carry Jagannath idols, photos, calendars, etc. to their places of residence. Temple building for Jagannath is only a part of diasporising Him in a temple but this cannot be separated from the migration of people and personal friends and relatives who bring Jagannath with them for use at home. In the international context, migration of Hindu gods happens through transnational networks between the country of origin and the country of residence (Sahney 2016: 280).

Thus, Jagannath is not just a rallying symbol of Odia identity and nationhood (Dash 1986; Mohapatra 1996) but also in a different culture area, a site of self-discovery. Building a temple or visiting an already existing temple is both individual and communitarian acts of place-making that take Odisha outside its borders (Pati 2011). Community mobilisation outside Odisha to build a Jagannath temple is a way of integrating with an alien place where the temple can act as a veritable identity marker. Already existing Jagannath temples outside Odisha also confer novel ways of imagining and offer negotiations around what constitutes authentic Jagannath in Puri and its replication/deviation elsewhere. Studying these different Jagannath sites enriches and relativises the idea of Jagannath and makes Him a contested terrain. The fact that most contributors in this volume are Indians corroborates the experiential and 'culturalist' position we have taken. The objective here is not to produce broad theories on institutional Jagannath but to show the negotiation around Jagannath discourses. That makes Jagannath both given and mediated, one and many, institutional and popular, distant-and-far as well as here-and-now.

D.P. Mukherjee, one of the pioneers of sociology, believed that India is nothing but a cluster of sociocultural regions (Routray 2008: 363), a principle that has been the hallmark of research in religion and culture studies. Understanding the intrinsic link between Lord Jagannath and the regional tradition of Odisha, as the title of the central volume of ORP I stated, was the primary goal of the early scholarly work. The approach has its merits no doubt, but at a time of ever increasing mobility, migration, mass media, standardisation of human wants and emotions and deterritorialisation of culture, we have reached a point what has been called the end of geography (Greig 2002: 229) and along with that, the demise of understanding people and their culture as frozen in their place. Earlier studies analysing the historical evolution of the 'Cult of Jagannath' highlighted historical ruptures, shifting boundaries and competing concepts defining the region (Odisha, Kalinga, Utkal and Kosal) and, thus, at times also critically reflected on the region. However, the contemporary expansion of the Lord's realm has never been the focus of a systematic academic scrutiny and it is here that this volume contributes by advocating a broadening of Jagannath studies.

Design of the Book

The following chapters address that underrepresented space of contemporary Jagannath praxis, communities around Him and their symbiotic relationship with Jagannath. The tentative questions that inform the anthology are: What are the performative practices (religious, sociocultural and economic) that bring Jagannath to people's everyday life? How does Jagannath continue to remain the justification of Odia national narratives while accommodating vernacular expressions? How is Jagannath imagined and mediated with new technologies and how is this effort to visualise Jagannath informed by contemporary economic and devotional apparatuses? How do non-resident Odias imagine themselves and form a community and to what extent such impulse accommodates and resists other prevailing cultural values? How is Jagannath deployed in intercultural spaces and how such representations advance/impede certain types of behaviour?

These questions are not an exhaustive list of trajectories to which the chapters respond to. They are a way of opening up the discussions we have had so far and seeing how the authors engage with various popular cultural sites in their own ways. The eleven chapters are organised in three sections and are concerned with Jagannath praxis and the possible pathways of bonding and community building. However, the tripartite sectioning does not rule out overlaps nor is it imagined as mutually exclusive ways of experiencing Jagannath. It is done for the sake of convenience and with the objective of imposing some sort of order on the chapters dealing with a range of issues. Though all the chapters are intended to be read vis-à-vis the framework created in this Introduction, they can also be read independently dealing with a specific set of questions.

The first section 'Mediating Jagannath' carries four chapters and deals with stages/layers of mediation that establish Jagannath's everyday character. The first chapter 'In the Eyes of God: Jagannath Iconography in Popular Cultures' by Shaswat Panda examines how vision is the most potent medium of omniscience so far as

Jagannath's sway over people is concerned and how His iconic eyes have been used and appropriated in various media for diverse purposes. Keeping the religious and cultural dynamics of such an iconography in mind, the author examines the figure of Jagannath in popular visual cultures and addresses questions regarding production, popularity and use of Jagannath images. The second chapter 'Worldliness of the Otherworldly: Dissemination of Devotion from Early Modern to Cassette Era' by Animesh Mohapatra looks at the circulation of Jagannath *janana*, an immensely popular form of devotional song that did not acquire much prominence in the print domain. It studies the evolution and dissemination of the genre and how it witnessed a revival of sorts in the cassette era as the distinctive tonal character of the *jananas* could be more effectively and emotively communicated through mechanical and professional oral reproduction than was possible beforehand. He suggests how the arrival of modern technology, instead of jettisoning, consolidated a traditional verse form. Through a close reading of select Odia films, especially early Odia mythological films, the third chapter 'Syncretic Jagannath Culture and Popular Odia Imagination: Representations of Lord Jagannath in Odia Cinema' by Amarjeet Nayak showcases the way a popular medium such as cinema reflects on and helps foster the bond between Jagannath and the Odia people who adore Him. The fourth chapter 'The Prabachanas as Performatives: Tracing the Moral Grounds of Spiritual Discourse in the Jagannath Culture' by Ranjan Kumar Panda evaluates Jagannath *prabachan* by Charana Rama Das and highlights the importance of *bhakti-bhava* (devotional feeling) that creates a bond between *bhakta* and *bhagwan*—devotee and deity. It also establishes an uncanny presence of Jagannath in the everyday life of devotees.

The three chapters in the second section 'Practising Jagannath' deal with the performance of rituals and their iteration as sites of experiencing Jagannath and how these sites are negotiated by Odias and non-Odias. The fifth chapter 'Eating with Eyes: The Food Economy of Jagannath Culture' by Umasankar Patra traces the commercialisation of the Jagannath *mahaprasad* that once was locally cooked and made available for consumption in Puri and how it is prepared in several temples across Odisha for sale in the form of *prasad* now. Its limited desacralisation makes it amenable to consumption by Odias (devotees and otherwise) at home or in the temple premises. It argues that the new Jagannath culture based on this food economy of *prasad* has resulted in the democratisation of the culture without compromising its religiosity. The sixth chapter 'Domestication of Jagannath Temple Rituals in Odia Households: A Sociological Understanding of the Pantheism' by Pranaya Kumar Swain explores parallels between the rituals of Lord Jagannath and Odia households to understand everyday Odia life. This is done by digging into the available texts and content analysis of focused group discussions among key informants. The seventh chapter 'Contemporary Bangla Songs on Jagannath: A Hermeneutic for Bhakti and Community of *Bhaktas*' by Sreejit Datta presents a comprehensive survey of Bangla devotional songs that have gained currency among Bengali devotees of Jagannath in recent times. These songs are subjected to critical analysis through close reading with the aim of producing a hermeneutic of contemporary bhakti—a meta-language for interpreting and understanding the economy of pilgrimage, devotional music production and cross-cultural transactions between Bengali and Odia cultural spheres.

The third section 'Re-placing Jagannath' highlights both multiplication and dislocation of Jagannath outside Odisha, what they mean for non-resident Odias and non-Odias and what kind of challenges and opportunities they offer. The eighth chapter 'Becoming Jagannath in Dravidanadu: *Kanchi Kaveri* Legend and Other Possibilities in Kanathur Jagannath Temple' by Jyotirmaya Tripathy unpacks layers of contestation and consensus around Jagannath's universality in the Jagannath temple in Chennai. It traces the conception and delivery of the temple and highlights the ways it maintains its distinct Odia character while appropriating local practices, thereby leading to a novel experiment in cross-cultural meaning making. The ninth chapter 'Delhiwallah Jagannath and the Odia Diaspora: Notes towards a Social History' by Gautam Choubey studies Jagannath temples at Hauz Khas and Thyagaraj Nagar of New Delhi, the defining role by these temples in transforming Odia community's socioeconomic profile and the gradual weakening of their hold on the community due to progressive diversification and concomitant fragmentation of the community. By focusing on the sociocultural ecosystem of Delhi, the chapter also explores the ways in which the place of migration determines the success of diasporic enterprises. The tenth chapter 'Jagannath in Tripura: Disappearance and Dissemination' by Samik Malla weaves together three related arcs of the waxing narrative of Jagannath in the contemporary discourse of Tripura: first, the confounding question of his 'disappearance' in the experiential reality of the devotees of the Jagannath Temple in Agartala; second, its symbolic consequences in our understanding of embodiment, *darshan* and 'bhakti'; and third, the emergence of Jagannath from the sacred to the secular space. The eleventh chapter 'A Scholarly Community around the Lord: The Orissa Research Projects' by Uwe Skoda explores the formation of a 'scholarly community' evolving around Lord Jagannath. Drawing from two major ORPs around the early 1970s and early 2000s and sharing many characteristics with other 'communities of practice', the chapter starts by looking at the joint goals and common approaches before turning to the mutual engagement and interaction within and beyond this community and finally shifting to the resources and repertoires created by it that outlived the project periods.

Notes

1. Culturalism—a term popularised by Richard Johnson (1979)—challenges the idea of culture as a set of traditional values required for social cohesion and order. Though not a coherent theoretical template, culturalism as an approach was more inclusive and democratic by assigning agency to the working class. E.P. Thompson (1978), who was Johnson's colleague in the Birmingham Centre for Contemporary Cultural Studies, had questioned structuralism for ignoring history and politics and instead focusing only on abstract theorisation. The present anthology moves away from textual and institutional approaches and a move towards a popular/vernacular conception that is not oblivious of multiple layers of meaning making. The usage of 'culturalism' or 'culturalist' in this book differs significantly from other understandings according to which individuals and their actions are simply determined by their 'culture' as encompassing and inescapable wholes.
2. Praxis as different from 'theoria' and 'poiesis' in Greek philosophy referred to an action-oriented approach to knowledge. Here, we are more concerned with the process and operationalisation of knowledge, that is

to say, how ideas associated with Jagannath are materialised. This focus takes us to Jagannath not merely as a symbol of bhakti but as a multi-faceted site of social relations.

3. Following John Storey's seminal work (2001), popular culture whether contrasted with folk culture, dominant culture, etc. always implies otherness, presence as well as absence. Often linked uncritically to 'mass' culture, such a quantification may refer to the production, circulation or consumption side. Stressing a politically sensitive approach, Arjun Appadurai and Carol Breckenridge (1995: 5) prefer the more recent term public culture in order to express a dynamic 'zone of cultural debate, [...] contestation and mutual cannibalization, in which national, mass, and folk culture provide both mill and grist for one another'—characteristic for modernity in India.
4. The term 'dividual' coined by McKim Marriott (1990) in his study of Indian subjectivity highlights the transmission of what Marriott called substance-codes (such as blood, food or even knowledge) from one body to another or from one caste to another. The dividual is a person who absorbs these substances who in turn constitute the person. Unlike the individual who is indivisible and distinct from others, dividuals have porous selves and are constantly circulated and transformed.

References

Appadurai, Arjun. 1990. 'Topographies of the Self: Praise and Emotion in Hindu India'. In *Language and the Politics of Emotion*, edited by Catherine A. Lutz and Lila Abu-Lughod, 92–112. Cambridge: Cambridge University Press.

Appadurai, Arjun and Carol A. Breckenridge. 1995. 'Public Modernity in India'. In *Consuming Modernity: Public Culture in a South Asian World*, edited by Carol A. Breckenridge, 1–22. Minneapolis: University of Minnesota Press.

Babb, Lawrence A. 1981. 'Glancing: Visual Interaction in Hinduism'. *Journal of Anthropological Research*, 37(4): 387–401.

Banerjee-Dube, Ishita. 2018. 'Myths, Metaphors, Meanings: Kalapahar in Bengal and Orissa'. In *On Modern Indian Sensibilities: Culture, Politics, History*, edited by Ishita Banerjee-Dube and Sarvani Gooptu, 60–77. Abingdon: Routledge.

Behera, Subhakanta. 1999. 'Oriya Literature and the Jagannath Cult, 1866–1936: Quest for Identity'. Unpublished Ph.D Thesis, University of Oxford, Hilary.

Bhattacharya, K.C. 2001. 'The Concept of Rasa'. In *Indian Philosophy in English: From Renaissance to Independence*, edited by Nalini Bhushan and Jay L. Garfield, 193–206. New York: Oxford University Press.

Brubaker, Roger. 2005. 'The "diaspora" diaspora'. *Ethnic and Racial Studies*, 28(1): 1–19.

Cohen, Robin. 2008. *Global Diasporas*. London: Routledge.

Das, Hemant Kumar. 2006. 'The Origin of Oriya Jatra'. *Indian Literature*, 50(1): 166–171.

Dash, G.N. 1986. 'Jagannatha and Oriya Nationalism'. In *The Cult of Jagannath and the Regional Tradition of Orissa*, edited by Anncharlott Eschmann, Hermann Kulke and Gaya Charan Tripathi, 359–374. New Delhi: Manohar.

Eck, Diana. 2017. *Darsan: Seeing the Divine Image in India*. New Delhi: Motilal Banarasidas.

Eschmann, Anncharlott, Hermann Kulke and G.C. Tripathi, eds. 1986. *The Cult of Jagannath and the Regional Tradition of Orissa*. New Delhi: Manohar.

Ghosh, Ujaan. 2018. 'Chariots of the Gods: Histories of Jagannath, "Juggernaut," and the Rathayatra in the Nineteenth Century'. *History of Religions*, 58(1): 64–88.

Greig, Michael J. 2002. 'The End of Geography?: Globalization, Communications, and Culture in the International System'. *The Journal of Conflict Resolution*, 46(2): 225–243.

Gupta, Ravi M. ed. 2016. *Caitanya Vaisnava Philosophy: Tradition, Reason and Devotion*. London: Routledge.

Hirschi, Travis. 1969. *Causes of Delinquency*. Berkeley: University of California Press.

Johnson, Richard. 1979. 'Three Problematics'. In *Working Class Culture: Studies in History and Theory*, edited by J. Clarke and C. Chritcher, 201–237. London: Hutchinson.

Kulke, Hermann. 1986. '"Juggernaut" under British Supremacy and the Resurgence of the Khurda-Rajas of Puri'. In *The Cult of Jagannath and the Regional Tradition of Orissa*, edited by A. Eschmann, H. Kulke and G.C. Tripathi, 345–358. New Delhi: Manohar.

Kulke, H. and G. Berkemer, eds. 2011. *Centres out There? Facets of Subregional Identities*. Delhi: Manohar.

Kulke, H. and Burkhard Schnepel. 2001. *Jagannath Revisited: Studying Society, Religion, and the State in Orissa*. New Delhi: Manohar.

Malinar, A., ed. 2007. *Identities in Time: Perspectives on the Regional Traditions of Orissa*. Delhi: Manohar.

Marriott, McKim, ed. 1990. *India Through Hindu Categories*. New Delhi: SAGE.

Mazzarella, William. 2009. 'Affect: What is it Good for?' In *Enchantments of Modernity: Empire, Nation, Globalization*, edited by Saurabh Dube, 291–309. New Delhi: Routledge.

Mohanty, Satya P. 2008. 'Alternative Modernities and Medieval Indian Literature: The Oriya "Lakshmi Purana" as Radical Pedagogy'. *Diacritics*, 38(3): 3–21.

Mohapatra, Bishnu N. 1996. 'Ways of "Belonging": The Kanchi Kaveri Legend and the Construction of Oriya Identity'. *Studies in History*, 12(2): 203–221.

Narayanan, Vasudha. 2006. 'Hinduism in Pittsburgh'. In *The Life of Hinduism*, edited by John S. Hawley and Vasudha Narayan, 231–248. Berkeley: University of California Press.

Paranjpe, Anand C. 2002. *Self and Identity in Modern Psychology and Indian Thought*. New York: Kluwer Academic Publishers.

Pati, George. 2011. 'Temple and Human Bodies: Representing Hinduism'. *International Journalof Hindu Studies*, 15(2): 191–207.

Pattanayak, D.B. 1992. 'Sant Literature in India'. *Indian Literature*, 30(3): 115–120.

Pfeffer, G. ed. 2007. *Periphery and Centre: Groups, Categories and Values*. Delhi: Manohar.

Pinney, Christopher. 2004. *Photos of the Gods: The Printed Image and Political Struggle in India*. London: Reaktion Books.

Pua Mora Kala Thakura. 1988. Film directed by Raju Mishra. Eastern Media Limited: Bhubaneswar.

Routray, Sailen. 2008. 'Refocusing on Regions in South Asia'. *Contemporary Perspectives*, 2(2): 360–371.

Safran, William. 2005. 'The Jewish Diaspora in a Comparative and Theoretical Perspective'. *Israel Studies*, 10(1): 36–60.

Sahney, Puja. 2016. '*Darsan*, Decoration, and Transnational Hindu Homes in the United States'. *Asian Ethnology*, (75)2: 279–302.

Saroglou, Vassalis. 2011. 'Believing, Bonding, Behaving, and Belonging: The Big Four Religious Dimensions and Cultural Variation'. *Journal of Cross-Cultural Psychology*, 42(8): 1320–1340.

Schweig, Graham M. 2002. 'Humility and Passion: A Caitanyite Vaishnava Ethics of Devotion'. *The Journal of Religious Ethics*, 30(3): 421–444.

Storey, John. 2001. *Cultural Theory and Popular Culture*. London: Pearson.

Thompson, E.P. 1978. *The Poverty of Theory and Other Essays*. London: Merlin Press.

Tripathi, G.C. 1986. 'The Daily Puja Ceremony of the Jagannatha Temple and its Special Features'. In *The Cult of Jagannath and the Regional Tradition of Orissa*, edited by Anncharlott Eschmann, Hermann Kulke and Gaya Charan Tripathi, 285–307. New Delhi: Manohar.

Vertovec, Steven. 2000. *The Hindu Diaspora: Comparative Patterns*. London: Routledge.

Waghorne, Joanne Punzo. 2004. *Diaspora of the Gods: Modern Hindu Temples in an Urban Middle-Class World*. New York: Oxford University Press.

Section I

Mediating Jagannath

1

IN THE EYES OF GOD: JAGANNATH ICONOGRAPHY IN POPULAR CULTURES

Shaswat Panda

Introduction

In an eighteenth-century Odia text known as *Dardhyata Bhakti* (Das n.d.), lies the incredible tale of a lower caste devotee of Jagannath, namely Dasia Bauri, who in one of those moments of spiritual awakening sees the eye of Jagannath in the rice and *sag* that is served to him. He feels ecstatic at the sight of God on his plate and refuses to partake of the meal until his wife and villagers convince him that it is just food and not the Lord's eye that he has to eat.

For Dasia, just the mere illusion of the Lord's eye invigorated his spiritual ecstasy but three centuries later the government of India was unhappy with the image of Jagannath which not only had the eyes but fully formed limbs. The government was planning to release commemorative coins on the occasion of Navakalevar 2015[1] which would carry images of Jagannath. Unhappy with the design which showed Jagannath having hands and feet, the secretary in the Department of Revenue (an Odia himself) wrote to the Ministry of Culture that 'the design hardly looks like Lord Jagannath'. The Odia writer and scholar, J.P. Das, a member of the committee appointed by the Ministry of Culture to intervene in the matter clarified that there were *besas*[2] of Jagannath in which limbs are fitted to the body of Jagannath. The matter was eventually put to rest and the coins were officially released in 2018. The coins released did carry an image of a fully formed Jagannath.

While this issue was still being debated, Puri was witnessing a host of controversies over (a) the selection of divinely ordained trees from which the images of Jagannath, Balabhadra and Subhadra were to be carved out, (b) transfer of Brahma or the divine substance from the older bodies to the newer ones and (c) the imposition of a new rule which prevented devotees from touching the images. To this day, the controversies originating at the local level refuse to die. But it would be interesting to note that the servitors who were being looked at with suspicion not only kept on repeating that there was no foul play involved in the Navakalevar ritual but that the new deity was visibly mighty; someone who had the potential to punish the wrongdoers. Even as the devotees were being prevented from touching the deities, the images of Jagannath were witnessing unprecedented proliferation across media and spaces. Across these seemingly sporadic events—from Dasia Bauri's personal experience to the secretary's attempts to look for a standardised image of Jagannath, to local controversies and global circulation lies the rich and complex history of the symbol that is Jagannath.

In other words, the image of Jagannath is characterised not only by omnipresence but also by intimacy. The images being polymorphous and multivalent are not easily taken to rigid standardisation and as they gain wider circulation across the globe the regional character continues to assert itself. Lest it should suggest something of spiritual abstraction, the elusive symbolism of Jagannath must be studied by underlining 'the spiritual economy of [Jagannath] *Bhakti*',[3] to use Kumkum Sangari's phrase (1990). The symbol draws its meanings most notably through its visibility and, therefore, in order to pare off its layers, it is important to study the iconography of Jagannath and its most conspicuous feature—the eyes.

In this chapter, I intend to study the iconography of Jagannath in popular visual cultures by emphasising two major factors which make them suitable for use and appropriation. The first factor, I argue are ideas of benediction, protection and watchfulness associated with the eyes in the absence of any history or legend linked to retribution. The second factor includes routine change of appearance and attire and repetition of life-cycle. The event occurs periodically between 8 and 19 years though recent history reveals it has taken place mostly after a gap of nineteen years. Called Navakalevar (literally meaning the new body), the ritual is characterised by the creation of a new body which is indispensable to the very being of Jagannath even as the divine substance or the Brahma remains the same and is transferred from one body to another.

I must, however, add here that the events and rituals I have just mentioned previously apply to Jagannath's siblings also—his elder brother Balabhadra and their younger sister Subhadra. The three siblings (Figure 1.2) are the presiding deities of the temple that is largely identified with Jagannath. But what makes the image of Jagannath distinct from his siblings and most other deities depicted in Odishan iconography is the pair of round eyes (Figure 1.1). The eyes of Jagannath are all pervasive not just in a spiritual sense (as illustrated in the Dasia story). A look at any three-dimensional image of Jagannath will persuasively demonstrate that one of the pair of round eyes seem to follow the onlooker even when s/he moves to the left or right side of the image. Some of the two-dimensional representations also show the two eyes looking in opposite directions giving the impression that no matter how far the devotee moves away s/he is always under God's protective gaze.

Figure 1.1 The eyes of Jagannath
Source: Picture taken by the author with the permission of the proprietor of Sadgranth Niketan, Manorama Puspalak.

Figure 1.2 A picture of the deities with their arms raised upwards
Source: Picture taken by the author with the permission of Manorama Puspalak, the proprietor of Sadgranth Niketan.

To the dynamism of the eyes, one could also add the distinct black colour of the face. In fact, the colour of the face itself has become the defining characteristic of some of his other popular names such as *kalia suna* (black gold), *kala srimukha* (the beautiful black face), *kala thakura* (the black God) or simply *kalia* (the black one). The name *kalia* is uttered with much fondness and many are nicknamed after the complexion of God. The significance of the black colour is not merely coterminous with the dark complexion of Krishna; it goes way beyond that. Devotees fondly embrace the image whenever they get the opportunity and smear black colour of the god's face on the bodies. Interestingly, when this became a contentious issue and the devotees were not allowed to touch the deities, one servitor defended the practice citing a very popular devotional song *kalia, mo dehe boli de, to deha kala* (O Kalia, smear your black colour on my body) (translation mine). The hope for and the possibility of having marks of the lord on the body increases the proximity and breaks the barriers between the sacred and the profane for the devotees. Physical proximity leading to spiritual intimacy is a well-known idea of the bhakti movement. The famous bhajan *rang de chunariya* (colour my garment…) by Mirabai is a classic example. But in the case of Jagannath, the desire for physical contact is often materialised and, therefore, the corporeal aspect of devotion becomes very important.[4] Through numerous examples provided further, it will become clear that the proximity of god to the devotee which is an integral part of the identity of Jagannath facilitates the spread and sale of Jagannath images.

The adaptability of the Jagannath image to various forms and on different platforms while retaining a strong emphasis on the original shape of the eyes intact suggests that despite the various experimentations with the image, the idea of a basic blueprint has not entirely been jettisoned. This implies that the eyes are the site of bonding between the Lord and the devotees and that *darshan* (dynamic process involving reciprocatory gaze from the god) is the quintessential process of spiritual awareness. But more importantly, as we shall see, the eyes also become metonymic for the Jagannath culture itself that despite its gradual global spread this culture remains hinged to regional traditions. I shall further delve into the questions of the local and the global by looking at the trade and circulation of Jagannath images.

In the sections that follow, I discuss how the benign image of God and and the periodic recreation of his images have helped in commercial reproduction of the images in various forms. Since the genealogy of the deities has been widely discussed and debated for years and a considerable portion of these arguments are centred on the iconography, I shall only briefly touch upon these issues and to the effect that they pave way for the major concerns of this chapter.

Similarly, instead of devoting much time to the traditional art forms such as *patachitra*,[5] I shall explore mass-produced images like printed photographs, posters, logos, etc. by focusing particularly on their production and circulation especially in the 1990s and after. The period in consideration is important to my work because of the significant surge in mass production of images (first in print and then on the digital platform) and the interesting transformations the images have undergone.

The Creation of a Kind God: The Eyes of Jagannath and Questions of Iconography

In this section, I emphasise three points to understand the popularity of Jagannath iconography: (a) the projection of benign attributes of God, (b) the formation of state cult around Jagannath and his representation as a watchful god and (c) the Navakalevar ritual and legitimisation of mass production of images of gods.

The origin of Jagannath is still a matter of debates and speculation and the same applies to his iconography. The fact that Jagannath is identified with many other deities from Vairav to Narasingha to Dakshinakali to Jina and Buddha and that now there is even a temple called the Sai Jagannath temple goes on to show how easily he has been appropriated by other cults.

There are many reasons why the eyes of Jagannath are important (certainly for the purpose of my chapter) but the fact that the overwhelmingly large and round eyes are sometimes used as indicators to trace the origins of the gods also speaks for their historical significance.[6]

Since it is not the purpose of this chapter to trace a detailed history of the iconography, I shall dwell on the issue as long as it helps in understanding how attributes like kindness and watchfulness might have been attached to the eyes of Jagannath.

As has been argued by several scholars before, the origins of Jagannath are difficult to trace. There are several links that scholars have painstakingly shown. But in terms of iconographical similarities, Narasingha remained and remains an important figure because of certain facial resemblances. In an essay titled 'The Vaisnava Typology of Hinduization and the Origin of Jagannatha', Anncharlott Eschmann (1986) attributes the uncanny iconography of Jagannath to a gradual process of 'Hinduization'. Eschamann maintains

> The peculiar shape of the Jagannath figures is a result of their tribal origin … but not because such figures are typical of tribal religion but because such figures are typical products of the process of Hinduization. (Eschmann 1986: 100)

Eschmann reasons that the uniconic form of Jagannath and the peculiar shape of the eyes, the head and the mouth bear resemblance with those of Narasingha. A close observation of the two images when placed side by side would help one understand Eschmann's idea better. The importance of Narasingha to the tradition of Jagannath has been established beyond doubt.[7] However, despite the similarities, the important question that remains is how come the nature of Jagannath differs so starkly from Narasingha. As compared to Narasingha, there is hardly any history of aggression or fury related to Jagannath. The twin aspects associated with Narasingha are fury and eroticism. But neither of these aspects find resonance in popular culture connected with Jagannath. There is little textual evidence to suggest the same. The lasting image of Jagannath, as I have pointed out in the beginning, has always been benign. If we were to go by the myth of Indradyumna, it is Yajna Narasingha who serves as the inspiration for the creation of the deities and not Ugra Narasingha. In Puri, there is a temple dedicated to Narasingha where the deity has two faces—Shanta Narasingha when viewed from outside and Ugra

Narasingha when viewed from inside the temple. The images are believed to be of the eighth century. Irrespective of having two faces, the one which is calm is visible to the outside world. This suggests that the *ugra* or aggressive aspect was not meant to be projected. The temple of Narasingha is not the only instance where the aggressive side of the deity is suppressed to promote the gentler one. Two other female deities Dakshinakali[8] and Vimala[9] who are associated with Jagannath do have aggressive sides to them but such aspects are very rarely invoked.

But the larger point we gather from the examples of Dakshinakali, Vimala and even Narasingha is that the *ugra* aspects of Jagannath's character are kept suppressed if not entirely gotten rid of and are selectively invoked on a few occasions.

H.V. Stietencorn (1986) has argued that with the coming of the Vaishnavites from the south and subsequently under their influence the amorous character was suppressed to project the asexual aspects of a God who would rather reside with his siblings than his wife. Could the same Vaishnavism or its succeeding avatars account for the representation as well? It is a tempting speculation but with scanty evidence to support it.

Along with these developments, there was also another important evolution taking place which was the state patronage of Lord Jagannath and formation of a state cult around him[10] which might be responsible for the projection of a watchful god.

The rise of this state cult got attached to Jagannath's image as a protecting lord, a custodian under whose gaze the kings had to operate. This goes well with the iconography of Jagannath where the open eyes indicate a protective gaze. As for the role of the Lord as an all-seeing god, there is the story of Purusottama who in one of his inscriptions mentions Jagannath as a witness to his just actions (Kulke 1986: 206–207). Although in the two instances mentioned previously there are no direct references to the eyes, however, there is a clear invocation of the roles which have become defining attributes of the eyes.

Irrespective of his status as a protecting Lord, Jagannath and his siblings were subject to physical vulnerabilities and to that one might add political vulnerabilities also. The images being carved out of wooden logs are anyways vulnerable to ravages of time. Besides the images had been moved out on quite a few occasions when the Jagannath temple faced external aggression. G.C. Tripathi states that during the 'turbulent period of political insecurity' Navakalevar became a routine affair (Tripathi 1986a: 229). The psychological impact of Navakalevar, according to Tripathi, was greater because 'the images of Jagannatha etc. are by their very nature, a transitory and perishable object' (1986a: 229). While the (hypo)thesis of periodic change of body might have served as a major source of consolation and relief centuries ago, for the purpose of this chapter it is important to note how this very ritual facilitates re-creation, reproduction and circulation of Jagannath images.

The next part of the chapter offers a study of the re-creation of the Jagannath image within the religious domain and outside it.

Temple and Trade: From Within to Without

This section throws light on the popularity of Jagannath images by arguing how such proliferation, selling and circulation was made possible from traditions of trade that began from within the temple and were subsequently aided by and adaptable to technological innovations.

If we were to look for the earliest instances of circulation of Jagannath images we need look no further than the premises of the temple itself. Apart from being an integral part of the temple rituals especially during the period of convalescence, the *pata* paintings were also up for sale within the temple premises. As Anna Schmid observes, in the mid-nineteenth century, a daily fair was organised to sell the *pata* paintings (Schmid 2010: 311). The sale of paintings was legitimised and facilitated by a widely held belief that 'pilgrimage to Puri was incomplete unless the pilgrim took back with him five *patas* of Jagannatha, five beads, five cane sticks and *nirmalya* (dried rice from the temple kitchen)' (Das 1982: 61).

Pata paintings have come to be identified as emblematic of Odishan art. But despite their rich history and legacy, the *pata* paintings are conventional in terms of their colours, motifs and basic iconography. For instance, the arms of Jagannath and Balabhadra are shown as raised upwards. For the longest time, this was a common blueprint for the pictures that were worshipped in common household. This very position of the hands also remained the blueprint for the pictures that were sold in the 1980s. There were additions made to this basic model in terms of colour, as can be seen in the picture with a deeply saturated red background. The picture appears strikingly similar to the mass-printed versions of Tanjore paintings, especially with regard to the depiction of gold ornaments (Figure 1.2). According to Harekrushna Pushpalak, this picture had been printed at Sivakasi. However, the pictures that were available later did not show the arms raised. They bore a close resemblance with the arms of the deities in the temple. The transition from these traditional images to the ones that came in vogue in the 1990s make for an interesting story.

K. Dharma Rao of Puri who has been in the business for more than fifteen years and now practically rules the roost, told me how in the 1980s artists from Madras (now Chennai) would come to Puri and sell Jagannath stickers which were portable and available at cheap prices. He was not sure if these came from the famous Sivakasi but they found many takers. The image of Jagannath's face with the big prominent eyes could be pasted anywhere from bands of wrist watches to walls or on the cover of notebooks and sometimes on cupboards or the more familiar almirah. The trade route of Jagannath images between Puri and Chennai became a two-way one. The *pata* paintings model of the images was fairly old and new models were always welcome. Besides the popularity of the images that the so-called Madras artists brought with them compelled their counterparts in Puri to think anew. There were other reasons as well. The late 1980s and increasingly the 1990s were the age of television. These were the times when a lot of sensational content was available particularly linked to Hindu gods but the Jagannath temple was not so friendly to the camera and there was little scope to show the deities let alone show any miracle. On the face of this change, the need to produce new images was felt. Besides with a change in the larger economic policies, the social ethos was slowly undergoing a change. At a time when television could show everything from live action on the battlefield to hair raising acts of daredevilry, paintings with conventional motifs would not have sufficed. It was the wisdom a man named Damodar Pushpalak which worked wonders.

Born into a family of servitors, Pushpalak served the cause of Jagannath in the commercial domain, rather well. He seemed to understand the demands of his times well and judiciously brought paint and print together. Although his enterprise itself requires a different discussion but suffice here to say that this man who ran his shanty in the temple premises selling books and souvenirs, got the painting of Jagannath, Balabhadra and Subhadra made in Puri and got them mass printed at Sivakasi. This was, perhaps, the first and certainly one of the pioneering efforts at getting a realistic painting of Jagannath printed. I call it realistic because it is strikingly similar to the original Badasinghara *besa* in which the deities appear decked in flowers (Figure 1.3). It must be noted that in the picture, the arms are not raised upwards (which was a major departure from the traditional *pata* painting). This chromolithographic reproduction of the painting capitalised on its fame by being available in all sizes. There was not only the poster or the framed picture but also miniatures, paperweights and pendants.

Figure 1.3 The iconic Badasinghara *Besa* mass printed at Sivakasi
Source: Picture taken by the author with the permission of Manorama Puspalak, the proprietor of Sadgranth Niketan.

However, the popularity of this image escalated and its profits multiplied once it was available in laminated frames. Characterised by their unnoticeable thin, black borders and their hard ply base, the laminated photo frames made images appear overwhelming to the eyes simply because of the space they occupied. The picture would merge into the borders without making the frame visible. Unlike the wooden frames which would carry the traditional engravings on them, the laminated frame was neat and trimmed. Therefore, the frame would offer minimum distraction and enhance what Christopher Pinney has defined as the 'corposthetic' experience—'a desire to fuse the image and the beholder' (Pinney 2004: 194).

The laminated Badasinghara photo added to the experience because of the dark backdrop and the invisible black borders which make the three deities overwhelmingly conspicuous. The picture creates an illusion of the gods being projected from some mysteriously unfathomable space. The Badasinghara image marked the beginning of a trend. This was a desire to see the real deity from close proximity. The picture became popular in no time and the profits made from selling them were not disappointing either. The temple administration bought the picture from Pushpalak and sold them at the information counter which is located right outside the temple. But if we were to go by the account of Manorama Pushpalak (the wife of Damodar Pushpalak) the mass printed pictures for which her husband had undertaken considerable hardship got 'copied' and sold in other shops outside and away from the temple. The easy and wide availability of the picture at other (rival) counters did not augur well for Pushpalak's business. They suffered indirect loss through competition and there is not a single copy of the picture available at their shop. The irony of the situation lies in the fact that the same technology which had aided Pushpalak's venture boomeranged on him. The painting which had been mass produced exclusively at Pushpalak's behest got copied and could be sold by anybody who did not have locational privilege like Pushpalak or a direct collaboration with the temple administration. In fact, most of the images that are now sold by the temple administration are bought from people like Dharma Rao who took advantage of the digital medium which was making its presence felt in the early 2000s. The case of Damodar

Pushpalak points to larger trends and tendencies. Photos of gods were available prior to his pioneering intervention. But it was inevitable that his success would not last long simply because around the time of Navakalevar 1996, the camera was keen to capture the newly formed images of the deities, there was television and newer technologies were making inroads. Pushpalak gave the devotees what they had always wanted but in the wake of the Navakalevar, the real images of gods were preferred to artistic recreations. How real could these pictures get, we shall see.

Like the Badasinghara *besa*, the *Suna besa* (Figure 1.4) or the golden attire of Jagannath on the chariot scripted another success story in the market of laminated images. Supposedly taken by a member of the Daitapati community, much of its fame drew from the access and proximity of its photographer to the god. The significance of the proximity in the minds of devotees cannot be dismissed easily. The reverence for Daitapatis among devotees (mainly Bengalis) is owing to their ancestral ties to Jagannath. There is clearly a performative aspect to this proximity not only at the level of rituals but in terms of appearance. More often than not the Daitapatis standing close to the deities can themselves be seen adorning heavy jewellery. The importance of this appearance is also marked by the fact that the gods, particularly Jagannath appear complete in terms of physical manifestation. A fully formed body decked with gold

Figure 1.4 Jagannath adorned with gold ornaments during *Suna besa*, seen here with Daitapatis
Source: Shyam Sundar Mahapatra, used with the permission of the photographer.

brings together affluence and physical prowess and added to that is the reminiscence of its proximity to human beings, of which no other picture bore any trace. If pictures of Gods bring elements of liveliness with them, the lingering memory of human activity around the gods would only add to such liveliness. The *Suna besa* image is important for yet another reason. The image went well with a burgeoning aspiring middle class. But the photograph of the gods in their golden attire appealed to middle-class aspirations for acquisition. More than the puja rooms, these images would be seen often in middle-class drawing rooms. It is important to remember that the puja rooms usually either have wooden images or printed images which are characterised for not being realistic. These images show the gods in a reified environment that is mostly in a colourful background and studded with glittery particles. The pictures in puja rooms are supposed to present an aura around the gods and, therefore, the choice of such pictures.

However, realistic images like the *Suna besa* image spelt good luck for people like Dharma Rao for a different set of reasons. Rao says that his frequent journeys to Calcutta brought him in contact with people who 'were doing new things with photos'. In short, he was referring to Photoshop, the instrument of instant gratification when it came to pictorial miracles. For Rao, who clearly had a wider clientele in mind, it was not just enough to get a glimpse of Jagannath but also to constantly remind his customers that Jagannath came from Puri. The pictures would, therefore, carry the temple and sometimes the sea in the backdrop. This was the middle-class Bengali's pilgrimage and vacation rolled and packaged in one image. Even to this day, Rao targets the lower middle class and the poor, who he believes, propagate the cult through its domestication in distant places. The frequency of Bengalis' visits to Puri and production of new Jagannath images are unlikely to be inversely proportional.

A study of Rao's experiment would show how far has one come from the traditional J.B. Khanna images that scholars and devotees are familiar with. Rao's recent offering which came out in 2016 is a mixed-media art showing the eyes and mouth of Jagannath superimposed on the image of the temple with soft edges and the entire image is set against a black backdrop (Figure 1.5). The picture is set within a plain-black plyboard frame. Rao calls it 'modern art'. For Rao, it is modern because of the use of digital media and also perhaps because of its minimalist features. Yet, the image in this so-called modern art is a collage of conventional images and is available for ₹80.

Figure 1.5 A mixed-media image of Jagannath, which the proprietor K. Dharma Rao calls 'modern art'
Source: Picture clicked by the author with the permission of the proprietor.

From Wood to Gold

I have argued before in this chapter that the ritual Navakalevar has facilitated the recreation of Jagannath images not only in the main temple but elsewhere as well. Historically speaking, the *pata* paintings or as we have seen the production of what came to be called the laminated pictures gained popularity, particularly during the Navakalevar years. The last Navakalevar which took place in 2015 also saw the proliferation of Jagannath represented on new platforms adoring new bodies and new forms. The major change that took place between the Navakalevar of 1996 and 2015 was the unprecedented popularity of the Internet and subsequently of social media and e-commerce. During these years, we have seen websites being devoted to Jagannath. In fact, one was created by the Jagannath Temple Administration itself. The forms of visual representation had not only undergone changes but their means of circulation too. Among the new forms, two examples are the gold plated Jagannath images and the all-black Jagannath images.

The new venture in question was started around 2015 just when the Navakalevar was about to take place. Images of Jagannath (and not the trinity) of five inches height are sold in two forms. One is a twenty-four-carat gold plated image (Figure 1.6) and the other is black (Figure 1.7) with a matte finish. In either of the images, the entire body is of a singular colour except for the eyes, the mouth and the u-shaped tilak mark on the forehead which is attributed to the impact of *Ramanuja Vaishnavism*. There is no deviation from the temple images in terms of shape and colour of the three most identifiable features mentioned previously. Just as the uniform colour, equally striking is the minimalist artwork or design. The conch and the *chakra* are embossed on either arm. The black version has diamond jewellery surrounding the torso. In the black image, the conch and the *chakra* stand out distinctly of their starkly contrasting golden colour. Equally striking is the fact that the image is of black and no other colour.

Figure 1.6 The gold-plated image of Jagannath sold by Goldtree
Source: Picture downloaded from www.goldtree.co.in by the author, with the permission of the proprietor of Goldtree, Sanjeeb Daitapati.

Figure 1.7 The all-black image of Jagannath sold by Goldtree
Source: Picture downloaded from www.goldtree.co.in by the author, with the permission of the proprietor of Goldtree, Sanjeeb Daitapati.

I spoke with Sanjeev Daitapati, the co-owner of Goldtree, the company which produces these images. It is run by two brothers Sanjeev and Raj Kumar Daitapati, they belong to the same Daitapati community which claims its ancestry to Jagannath and performs major functions during the period from Snana Purnima to *Niladri Vijaya* (the day when the trinity returns to the temple after the rath yatra). Upon being asked about the idea behind the images, Daitapati remarked that it drew from the *Suna besa* or the famous golden attire which the gods adorn on five occasions in a year though the appearance during the rath yatra is most famous.

Daitapati says that a few years before they ventured into this business, he had clicked a picture of the Sri Payar or the holy golden feet of Lord Jagannath and circulated it online after which it became popular. Being a servitor who gets to be around the images for a long time, Daitapati must have had better access to click pictures of the god from vicinity—something not easily available and more often than not denied to others. The choice of feet over the iconic eyes might have seemed strange but given that the golden feet are not regular features and are added on a few occasions makes them special. Besides, the *Suna besa* on the chariots is an event which draws maximum crowds to Puri. So the importance could not have been missed by someone who understands the event all too well; the time for launching the products could not have been more propitious either. But along with time, it was necessary to map the territories it wanted to reach out to. Daipati emphatically mentioned that with the improvement in communication the idea was to expand the business and propagate the cult as far as possible. The clientele, Daitapati tells me, ranges from Calcutta to the Middle East and even sometimes Europe. He also adds that they have witnessed good sales in Odisha too. But from his remarks, it seems these images have struck a chord with NROs and NRIs. He says, '*murti* means sentiments'. He adds that the farther one is the greater is the desire to have some souvenir of the lord. More than a conventional sense of devotion, it is nostalgia which draws them towards the images. I asked him a few questions on the materials and the choice of an all-black colour of images. To the first, he answered that the deities are made up of marble-dust instead of the conventional neem wood. He said it is because of the inextricable link of the deities with the neem wood or wood in general that people feel compelled to follow the rituals in details. As opposed to that, Daitapati mentions that stone images do not carry the burden of tradition and can be simply used as artefacts. We have reasons to believe in Daitapati's statement because the images have been made in the past using various materials from thermocol (polystyrene) to filigree to paper. These objects are kept in homes and offices alike but mostly not subject to ritualistic worship whereas it is commonplace to burn incense before wooden images. As for the significance of neem wood, Jugal Maharana, a veteran artist who now occasionally paints the images and owns a shop told me about the two-fold significance of neem wood. The conventional wooden images which are sold for mass consumption are available in broadly two varieties: images carved out of neem wood and images carved out of the wood of mango tree. Quality aside, the neem tree is also significant for its symbolic association with the god himself. Regarding the all-black images, he said it is a way of invoking the significance of the black face of the God which is often be held in affection. He categorically mentioned that the fondness for blackface is a subversion of the widely prevalent biases against the dark skin in our society. Promoting an all-black image is a good way of promoting racial harmony. About the eyes, he says that the basic features have not been modified; certainly not the eyes because they evoke strong emotions in people.

The marketing and promotional strategies that the Daitapati brothers have adapted are perfectly in sync with their times. The images are promoted and sold online through their website Shreejagannath.com. The logo of the website itself carries the face of Jagannath cast within a greater white circle, there are patterns drawn in golden colour both within and outside the circle. The website sells these products, displays pictures of Jagannath in various attires and these pictures have been taken from 'across the globe' including Puri. This is in consonance with the philosophy of the company which is to bring the local and the international together, but paying special attention nevertheless to an international clientele. The website has links which provide information on various topics related to Jagannath. One of the links is called 'global Jagannath' which provides information on rath yatra across the globe. The website also runs a blog and allows people to post their queries. As we have seen this is not the first digital platform devoted to Jagannath but the website is important for its interactive nature and also for the unique nature of the images which are sold here. It may be mentioned that apart from the images Goldtree sells silver and gold plated pendants of Jagannath, a gold plated pendant of the Neelachakra and sterling silver coins. The cheapest item (the Neelachakra pendant) comes for ₹1,800 while the 'masterpiece' Jagannath image is available at ₹55,000. From the price range of the products, it is fairly clear that the primary target is not the usual lower middle-class. Daitapati admits that inspiration comes from the popularity of Ganapati products (images, stickers, websites, etc.). He told me (without furnishing any statistical details) that the highest selling religious merchandise in India is that of Ganesh followed by Balaji of Tirupati. Even though a platform like the Internet has helped Goldtree to reach out to a great many people but its widening reach is only in terms of area and it does not seem to cut across economic boundaries.

I believe this has been the general trend with e-commerce insofar as Jagannath is concerned. The idea has been to reach out to people who have the means to afford expensive items and whose desire to buy has been driven by nostalgia.

Conclusion

The Daitapati brothers are by no means, the only ones to repackage the image of Jagannath. There are scores of websites and blogs which have added a so-called postmodern touch to Jagannath. An online shopping website sells t-shirts called *Being Odia* which bear the eyes of Jagannath, the benevolent eye of Jagannath now finds itself on the logo of a start-up initiative taken up by the government of Odisha. What might be more interesting is, an artist named Rajul Dhaimade, has actually brought Jagannath and Kali together in a heady combination of postmodern parody. But how effective has the impact of these images been? Attempts at widening the clientele for buying Jagannath products have been increasing. But the widening as we have observed in the two examples cited previously has been in the direction of the upper classes and other cultural elites. Irrespective of the changes we have witnessed in the images, over the years, they tend to hinge on a central idea of a quintessential Jagannath that would translate to the presence of the sacred not only in the secular but also in the ordinary. As we have seen in case of most of the images discussed, technology and innovation were always welcome as long as they retained a quintessential idea of the Jagannath symbol, which is expressed most notably through the eyes.

Acknowledgements

I would like to thank to the following for their valuable help and contribution at various stages of writing and editing of this chapter: J.P. Das, Jyotirmaya Tripathy, Jatindra Kumar Nayak, Animesh Mohapatra, Surendranath Mishra, Manorama and Harekrushna Pushpalak, Padmanava Panda, Swagat Panda, Shikha Vats and Ankit Ashirbad.

Notes

1. Navakalebar is a ritual involving the carving out of new images of the principal deities of the Jagannath temple at Puri—Jagannath, his sister Subhadra and his brother Balabhadra. It occurs within a gap that could vary from eight to nineteen years, the determining factor being the occurence of two consecutive months of Asadh in the Hindu lunar calendar.

2. Besas are the various adornments of the deities, which are routinely changed and customised for specific rituals and festivals.
3. My use of the expression draws on the essay by Kumkum Sangari entitled, 'Mirabai and the Spiritual Economy of Bhakti' wherein 'transcendent value [is] grounded in the dailiness of a material life within the reach of all' (Sangari 1990: 1464).
4. Not only are offerings made to Jagannath easily available to devotees, sometimes parts of his costume and shreds of his garment are available too.
5. Pata Chitra is a traditional art form from Odisha. The paintings are made on cloth piece mostly using natural dyes and colours. The themes of these paintings are mainly religious.
6. According to Mahimohan Tripathy (who bases his study on the findings of Rai Charan Das and Julian Jaynes), the greater the eye index (that is the proportion between the size of the head and that of the eyes) the older is the image. He specifies that gods with a higher index could date back to at least 500 BC. In case of Jagannath whose eye index is close to 28, it is a point worth considering given that there is no certainty regarding the origins and that the eyes could serve as decisive factors even though the claim is open to contestations (Tripathy 2012: 46).
7. As Tripathi, Kulke and Eschmann show, Narasingha is the guardian deity of the temple, during the transfer of divine substance from the old body to the new as a part of the Navakalevar rituals, the mantras that are chanted are originally meant for Narasingha; it is Narasingha who serves as the representative of Jagannath during his period of convalescence, the statue of Narasingha in the premises of the Jagannath temple is certainly one of the tallest and most conspicuous.
8. *The Mahanirvana Tantra* states that Jagannath is Dakshinakali herself (Devi 2009: 84).
9. During the Sola puja, Vimala acts as the representative of Jagannath in the temple.
10. Herman Kulke notably among others has demonstrated the rise in the status of Jagannath from being the state deity to being the divine ruler. Beginning with King Anangabhima of the thirteenth century, the king became but a 'deputy of the lord of Puri' and more importantly a representative of the 'king of the Orissan empire' (Kulke 1978: 154). This move not only cemented the position of the king but also led to the 'formation of a state cult' (Kulke 1978: 200).

References

Chaka Aakhi sabu Dekhuchi [The Eyes Bear Witness]. Directed by Raju Mishra. Cuttack: Eastern Media, 1987.

Das, J.P. 1982. *Puri Paintings: The Chitrakara and His Work.* New Jersey: Humanities Press.

Das, Ram. n.d. *Dardhyata Bhakti.* Cuttack: Dharmagrantha Store.

Devi, Parama Karuna and Rahul Acharya, eds. 2009. 'The Tantric Jagannath'. In *Puri: The Home of Lord Jagannatha.* Piteipur: Jagannatha Vallaba Research Centre.

Eschmann, Anncharlott. 1986. 'The Vaisnava Typology of Hinduization and the Origin of Jagannatha'. In *The Cult of Jagannath and the Regional Tradition of Orissa*, edited by Anncharlott Eschmann, Herman Kulke and Gaya Charan Tripathi. New Delhi: Manohar Publications.

Eschmann, Anncharlott, H. Kulke and G.C. Tripathi. 1986. 'The Making of the Jagannatha Triad'. In *The Cult of Jagannath and the Regional Tradition of Orissa*, edited by Anncharlott Eschmann, Herman Kulke and Gaya Charan Tripathi. New Delhi: Manohar Publications.

Kulke, H. 1986. 'Jagannatha as the State deity under the Gajapatis in Orissa'. In *The Cult of Jagannath and the Regional Tradition of Orissa*, edited by Anncharlott Eschmann, Herman Kulke and Gaya Charan Tripathi. New Delhi: Manohar Publications.

Mishra, Kanhu Charan. 1984. 'Jagannatha in Tradition'. In *The Cult of Jagannatha.* Calcutta: Firma KLM Pvt Ltd.

Pinney, Christopher. 2004. 'What Pictures Want Now'. In *Photos of the God: The Printed Image and Political Struggle in India.* London: Reaktion Books.

Sangari, Kumkum. 1990. 'Mirabai and the Spiritual Economy of Bhakti', *Economic and Political Weekly*, 25(27).

Stietencorn, H. Von. 1986. 'The Advent of Visnuism in Orissa: An Outline of its History according to Archaeological and Epigraphical Sources from the Gupta Period up to 1135 AD'. In *The Cult of Jagannath and the Regional Tradition of Orissa*, edited by Anncharlott Eschmann, Herman Kulke and Gaya Charan Tripathi. New Delhi: Manohar Publications.

Tripathi, Gaya Charan. 1986a. 'On the Concept of Purusottama in the Agamas'. In *The Cult of Jagannath and the Regional Tradition of Orissa*, edited by Anncharlott Eschmann, Herman Kulke and Gaya Charan Tripathi. New Delhi: Manohar Publications.

Tripathy, Mahimohan. 2012. 'Sri Jagannath Tatwa' [Theories around Jagannath] in *Sri Jagannath.* Bhubaneswar: Ama Odisha.

2

WORLDLINESS OF THE OTHERWORLDLY: DISSEMINATION OF DEVOTION FROM EARLY MODERN TO CASSETTE ERA

Animesh Mohapatra

Janana is an immensely popular form of devotional song in Odisha and its neighbouring regions. The term is used almost exclusively for songs addressed to Lord Jagannath—undoubtedly the most loved deity in Odisha and contiguous areas. But what distinguishes *janana* from bhajan, another widely used genre of devotional music? How have *jananas* been disseminated over the centuries, especially after the introduction of new technologies such as print and recording and have still managed to retain their popularity? What happened to the status of the genre when the literary public began privileging 'modern' genres? This chapter addresses these questions by tracing the journey of *jananas* through several discrete but overlapping forms of circulation: palm-leaf manuscripts and orality, print and finally, recorded reproduction of orality.

Jagannath, Janana and Ali

Janana (literally the act of apprising) is a specific form of devotional song where a devotee addresses the Lord in an intimate manner and expresses without inhibition a range of emotions such as complaint, demand, love, ecstasy or even anger. However, using a distinctive tonal character the devotee/singer/song-writer strategically hides her/his supplication through a peculiarly playful combination of lament and complaint (known in Odia as *ali*) and often threatens the Lord with the consequence of being denied the devotee's friendship and love. The word *ali* is generally used in Odia to describe the unrelenting demands that powerless children make of their parents.

In *jananas*, the *ali* is almost always about the devotee's desire to come closer to the Lord (the unification between the *atman* and Brahman at a spiritual level) and rarely, if ever about any mundane, material benefits. An example would make this point clearer:

> O Jagannath dear!
> I do not seek from you any boon,
> Neither wealth, nor men!
> I beg from you
> Only a handful of dust
> From the Sands of Love.
> My eyes do not wish to have any other sight
> Except a glimpse of your pretty countenance;
> My ears wish to hear no other sound,
> Than the sweet melodies of
> Hymns sung in your praise. (152) (Subas Pani's translation 2004)

Written by the eighteenth-century poet Banamali Das, this is among the most popular *jananas* ever written. The devotee in this poem is not interested in any material object but only longs to come closer to the object of his devotion. He uses a familiar metonymic expression—Sharadha Bali, or sands of love or affection, the wide-open ground in front of the Gundicha temple to its south—in order to voice his plea.

It is now imperative to distinguish *janana* from another form of devotional poetry called bhajan that is found in many other Indian languages. Bhajans are hymns or songs of praise addressed to a certain deity. The celebrated Odia novelist, Kalindi Charan Panigrahi, defines the genre thus: 'Bhajans are songs written in simple language. The word means meditation on God. Ordinarily with the help of symbolism Bhajans explain the yogic system and the philosophy of the Vedanta' (1947: 115). However, Debi Prasanna Pattanayak disagrees with Panigrahi and asserts that bhajans are not necessarily always philosophical. Bhajans, Pattanayak explains, rather reflect the simplicity of people's faith in the deity (1958: 59). Bhajans sing the glory of the deity by using numerous epithets and by rehearsing Her/His many past miracles but these lack the passionate intimacy of a Jagannath *janana*. It has already been mentioned that the term *janana* is used almost exclusively to refer to songs addressed to Jagannath, but whether this exclusivity is merely for an alliterative effect or a result of the compassionate nature of Jagannath is anybody's guess.

It cannot be denied that there is a lot of overlap between bhajans and *jananas* but the latter allows the poet to point out the Lord's shortcomings. Accusations in a *janana* are possible for Jagannath has usually been perceived as an extremely compassionate god. The usual epithets used for him by people of Odisha are Krupasindhu (ocean of mercy), Dinabandhu (friend of the destitute), Artatrana (remover of pain) and Patitapavan (rescuer of the fallen).[1] One can cite numerous instances where the poet berates Jagannath for being indifferent but the most extreme and one of the most well-known is Baladev Ratha's (1789–1845) *Sarpajanana.* And I cite below two stanzas from the poem in Subas Pani's (2004) translation:

> If you feel hurt, do grant me pardon,
> Or else ignore me for an instant
> O one who in love play does Rama entertain
> O Jagannath, I shall berate you as I feel
> Till my heart has had its fill.
> O Treasure House of Grace!
>
> Cowering in fear and apprehension,
> The learned do call you by the appellation
> Of the Ocean of Compassion!
> You are indeed the deadly serpent, full of poison,
> That does devour the life's breath of every person.
> O Treasure House of Grace. (166–167)

Though the poet uses a disclaimer in the first stanza, and in fact is trying to praise the Lord under the pretext of berating Him, such an extreme form of verbal irony is perhaps never used in the bhajan form. In other words, the element of *ali* which is absent in bhajans occupies a central place in *jananas.*

Devotional poems addressed to Jagannath have a long tradition in Odisha. It starts with the *adikavi* (or the first poet) Sarala Das (*c.* fifteenth century) and continues to be written in the twenty-first century. Sarala Das in the Odia *Mahabharata* invokes Jagannath several times for inspiration, and more importantly, equates him with

Krishna. This proved to be immensely useful for later poets (especially Vaishnavites) who referred to the familiar miracles of Krishna and Vishnu as performed by Jagannath. Later, the seventeenth-century poet Dibakar Das popularised the idea that Jagannath is an *avatari* (one who appears in different incarnations) and Krishna, His 'avatar'.[2] The first major poet who expressed his angst at Jagannath's apparent indifference towards his devotion is certainly the early sixteenth-century poet Balaram Das. In his *Bhava Samudra* (Ocean of Emotions) he equates Jagannath to Rama and chides him in the following manner:

> That you Jagannath, let your wife go to Ravana,
> Is very like you;
> Not able to maintain your own wife
> Why did you blame another for doing it?
> And she, tired of suffering so much with you,
> Went rightly to a man who would make her comfortable!
> And are you indeed worthy of that beauteous daughter of King Janaka?
> Believe me, My Lord, You look like no more
> Than a servant beside her!

After a series of such disparaging outbursts, the poet's emotion of grief and anger subsides and he sings,

> You made me a prisoner in the hands of the King,
> But I have made you a prisoner in the secrecy of my heart!
> Tell me, My Lord, that you are my Prisoner,
> And that gives me blessed happiness. (92–93)
> (Mayadhar Mansinha's translation 1962)

Apart from the two poets mentioned earlier, almost all major Odia poets wrote such devotional songs addressed to Jagannath, alongside writing *kavyas*. Several writers like the early seventeenth-century poet Salabeg are known only for their *jananas*; and several other songwriters like Saria Bhika (seventeenth century) and the Gajapati king Bira Keshari (1737–1793) became immortal only for a few of their Jagannath *jananas*. Most of these writers set to tune their compositions or followed existing melodic modes. Even when some devotees wrote their *jananas* on palm leaves using an iron stylus, the songs were primarily circulated orally.

Change in Taste and the New Arbiters of Odia Literature

At this point, it may be mentioned that much of Odia literature before the late nineteenth century was primarily religious, mythological or devotional in orientation. It is another matter that the gods and goddesses portrayed in most of those texts were distinctly anthropomorphic, which allowed the poets to effortlessly weave ordinary human experiences into their narratives. In other words, there was a lot of overlap between what we now conceive of as the sacred and the secular and the distinction between the two categories was not quite obvious. When Monmohan Chakravarti published the first narrative history of Odia literature, he classified the Odia literary repository not so much into periods but genres. The broad generic categories he used are 'songs' and 'religious poems'. He uses the umbrella term 'songs' to encompass diverse poetic forms such as *chautishas*, *chhandas*, *chapois* and different melodic modes (*banis* and *bruttas*) such as *Chakrakeli*, *Abakasha*, *Bhagabata*. He further adds that the content of 'songs' is primarily derived from one or several of the episodes of the religious texts and deals chiefly with episodes from the lives of Radha or Krishna, though on rare occasions feelings and experiences of human lovers are also conveyed (1898: 336). Chakravarty's narrative clearly highlights the preponderance of devotional literature in pre-colonial Odisha and later historians, as we shall soon see, have not disagreed with him on this account.

In the last quarter of the nineteenth century, the Odia literary field underwent a radical transformation as modern readers experienced a profound change in literary taste (*ruchi parivartan*). A crucial catalyst for this transformation, as has been well documented, is the printing press. Publication of books and periodicals, along with the availability of more advanced means of communication and transport, significantly altered the fundamental nature of the circulation and dissemination of texts, and consequently, the relationship between the author and the audience. In pre-colonial Odisha, production of palm-leaf manuscripts was an expensive undertaking and only a few wealthy and enthusiastic people could afford to hire scribes to make copies of texts.[3] As a result, 'even the literate reader had to depend upon the professional group specialized in the oral transmission of texts' (Das 1991: 34). Thus, texts were composed in such a manner that they could be sung aloud and aid oral circulation through retention and live reproduction (whether professional or amateur).

The printed text, on the other hand, encouraged private and silent reading and led to distinctly different forms of writing such as blank verse or prose. In this context, one may quote at some length Mayadhar Mansinha's observations on the early modern literary landscape in Odisha, which Sisir Kumar Das thinks are 'true of the whole of Indian literature' (35):

> the old Oriya literature served its purpose in a unique manner as the expression of the mass mind of the Oriyas …. It had filled Orissa's 50,000 villages with music, recitation, street plays, poetic contests, literary discussions. In a word, it had made the whole of Orissan people, women not excluded, literature conscious. It is no compliment to the modern system of education or to the new patterns of literature adopted in imitation of European models, nor to the new writers, that with the printing press and the postal services at their disposal, they have so far failed to make as deep an impression on the masses, as did the old Oriya literature written laboriously on palm-leaves with an iron stylus, and having very limited means of publicity. (Mansinha 1962: 63–64)

The quote mentioned is important for us for a number of reasons. Not only does it present us with an overview of the transmission of pre-print literature, it also offers key insights into understanding the lack of popularity of modern literature. For, a major cause of concern for early writers of modern Odia literature and editors of periodicals is the lack of readership. In the pre-colonial period, even knowledge-texts were written in the form of songs.[4] As the print industry widened its network, we see a shift in the status of the consumer of literature from that of a 'listener' to a 'reader'. While writers who wrote for listeners paid more attention to the figures of sound (alliteration, anaphora, epistrophe, rhyme, etc.), reader-centric writers leant more on *amitrakshar* (an indigenous variation of the blank verse) and prose and employed realism as a technique to give expression to their creative energy.

However, this should not lead us to believe that the shift from one literary convention to another was a sudden one or without any continuity. If we look at the early works of the foremost modern poet Radhanath Ray such as *Nandikeshwari* or *Usha*, then we clearly see that the poet follows existing melodic modes to compose his poems. However, for his magnum opus *Mahayatra*, he chose the *amitrakshar chhanda* and perhaps anticipating a backlash against this work, got a rather defensive foreword written by his acolyte, the poet Madhusudan Rao. Even while Rao argues that the greatness of a poem does not lie in rhyme or the lack of it but in its ability to evoke the intended feelings (*bhava*), he goes on to add that often end-rhyme is employed to conceal the lack of *bhava* in a poem (Rao [1896]1962: 167–168). In other words, the content of the poem began to be seen as more important than its form. In the early twentieth century, most modern poets eschewed the idea of making their poems 'singable' and the subject of literature was also desacralised with increasing focus on realism. Moreover, prose gradually began to overtake poetry as the most privileged medium of literary expression.

Devotional songs, however, continued to be composed. Madhusudan Rao, a major poet of late nineteenth-century Odisha was accorded the honorific epithet 'Bhaktakavi' (or the devotee-poet). However, the devotional poems he authored were addressed to the largely unfamiliar and formless Brahmo god. Thus, even when his poetry was appreciated by the English-educated reader or the Brahmo intelligentsia, they failed to garner mass appeal. Nevertheless, there were several other writers who adhered to the conventional 'aural' style before and after Rao. In fact, if we look at the list of poets in one of the most comprehensive anthologies of devotional songs on Lord Jagannath—that is, *Kabikanthe Srijagannath*[5] compiled by Murarimohan Jena ([1979]2015)—we clearly see an increase in the number of poets with the passage of each century (barring one exception). The anthology begins with two poets from the fifteenth century (Sarala Das and Madhabi Dasi) and comprises songs of 76 poets from the twentieth century; in between the book contains the works of five poets from the sixteenth century, eight from the seventeenth century, thirty from the eighteenth century and twenty-six from the nineteenth century.

Not surprisingly, the only century that witnessed a decline in the composition of devotional poems on Jagannath (that is if we follow Jena's list) is the nineteenth century when print-literature gained prominence in Odisha.[6] Moreover, there are barely any devotional poets in the anthology who wrote in the last quarter of the nineteenth century. It is also a matter of great amazement that, while the first half of the nineteenth century witnessed the composition of devotional poetry by major writers such as Abhimanyu Samantasinghara, Baladev Ratha and Gopalkrushna Patnaik, we do not see the continuation of this poetic tradition in the last quarter of the same century.[7] Those days, in the print domain, two kinds of writings were promoted: (a) texts written in the modern style, largely following the current trends in Bengali literature; (b) some popular, pre-colonial texts, for their market value and also in order to lend tangibility to the Odia literary heritage. Publication of new texts written in the conventional style was not encouraged. It is not surprising then that we do not come across a single history of Odia literature that accommodates writers of devotional literature during this period.

Natabara Samantaray in an insightful archival study of modern Odia literature convincingly establishes how a new aesthetic sensibility was consciously and successfully propagated by major modern Odia writers. He writes,

> Moreover, writers of Radhanath [Ray] and Madhusudan [Rao]'s calibre engaged themselves in writing textbooks. They imported certain features of Bengali literature uncritically into Odia literature. Without caring much for *traditional aesthetic conventions and practices*, they allowed themselves to be inspired by trends and conventions from the West and created a new literary sensibility. (Umasankar Patra's translation, Samantaray 2017: 62; my emphasis)

He further adds that using their position as administrators in the Education Department, they took recourse to the preparation of textbooks and conduct of examinations in order to promote this new aesthetic sensibility among the public. However, one needs to keep in mind that the 'public' that Samantaray mentions here is the school-educated public which then was numerically insignificant. Thus, it was nearly impossible to find a group of readers who would purchase a copy of the book and thereby help sustain the publishing industry. Eminent littérateur, J.P. Das points out that often writers themselves had to bear the expenditure of publication. A few influential writers could seek and obtain royal patronage to meet the expenses but perhaps the only profitable business for the publishers was the printing of textbooks. Das cites a letter written by Fakir Mohan Senapati to Vishwanath Kar (dated 21 October 1915) where Senapati informs Kar ruefully how he had to drop a few chapters from his novel *Mamu* and, thus, could not develop a few characters in order to keep the printing expenses within manageable limits (Das 2017: 150).

In spite of such insurmountable constraints, the print-public in the late nineteenth and early twentieth centuries continued to promote modern literature. Official records show that the literacy rate in Odisha had not reached even 16 per cent by 1951. Thus, the new literature that was published then in the print domain could only find an extremely limited number of readers. This observation regarding the struggle of modern literature to find a wider readership is echoed in the latter half of the twentieth century as well. Pre-eminent historian Krushna Chandra Panigrahi (1909–1987) gives a list of reasons for the continuing popularity of pre-colonial texts in the post-Independence period and among the most important of them is the inextricable association of literature with music:

> The second reason why the literature of [Upendra] Bhanja era remains widely popular is because it was composed in conformity with the well-known *ragas* (melodic modes). They are more than mere written texts; they were also enjoyed as songs. Traditionally in Odisha music and literature have been inseparably linked to each other. Thus, when a poem is composed, the poet's primary task was to set it to music so that it can be sung. True, the poets of this age displayed a great fondness for rhetoric and their poetry was filled with eroticism but it must be admitted that literature and music together fulfilled deeply felt needs of the Odia readers and listeners. (1972: 280; Ujaan Ghosh's translation)

Panigrahi further adds that in spite of the linguistic complexity of the works written by Upendra Bhanja and his contemporaries, the familiar content of the texts which generally drew on ancient Indian epics, made them accessible to Odias. Moreover, he points out, 'literature of this era is also read as religious texts' (280). Panigrahi, thus, very perceptively identifies two notable qualities of pre-colonial Odia literature—aural effect and religious content—for which they continued to remain popular, even in the print domain. But these features were overlooked by modern writers and a literary convention that was so predominant in the cultural life of Odisha almost suddenly went out of favour. Poets, perhaps, did not stop writing bhajans and *jananas* but they no longer enjoyed the hallowed status granted to their predecessors.

As I have pointed out earlier, the conventional form of literature which was meant to be sung was not print-conducive and required a different medium for its continuance and meanwhile, modern literature alienated itself from the masses and struggled to find an extensive readership. Thus, there emerged an unconscious segregation of the 'intellectuals' and the 'masses'. In *The Intellectuals and the Masses*, John Carey (2005: 4) compellingly argues that 'modernist literature can be seen as a hostile reaction to the unprecedentedly large reading public created by late nineteenth-century educational reforms'. While we cannot equate the context of modernist literature in England with that of modern literature in Odisha, we can certainly draw some useful parallels. If in England the division was a result of mass literacy, in Odisha it was the result of the introduction of a new form of education that was accessible to only a small minority. However, this English-educated minority, much like the small group of modernist writers in England, was influential in the public sphere and gradually came to form the middle class in Odisha. One can cite numerous instances where members of this newly educated class rejected the conventional forms of writing that depended primarily on orality for their transmission. As early as 1874, Pyarimohan Acharya, an educationist and the first indigenous author of the history of Odisha, expressed strong disapproval of the *kavyas* of celebrated writers such as Upendra Bhanja, Brahma Das and Abhimanyu Samntasinghara and affirmed that they could not be prescribed for schoolchildren (*Utkalaputra*:

3 June 1874). The reasons for which Acharya disapproves of existing literature include among other things their religious content and ornate wordplay. The first poet whose *kavyas* Acharya dismissed is Upendra Bhanja, popularly known as the Kavisamrat (or emperor among poets). Bhanja is among the most difficult of Odia poets, yet he was immensely popular.[8] It was over Bhanja's poetry that a major controversy raged in the 1890s and two periodicals—*indradhanu* (rainbow) and *bijuli* (lightning)—were published to give voice to the opinions of the defenders of the *prachin* (ancient) poets and the promoters of *adhunik* (modern) poetry. However, amidst all this, as Acharya had foreseen, the newly-educated reading public went through a change in literary taste and most of them could no longer appreciate traditional Odia literature. Moreover, the system of patronage had also undergone a radical transformation and the centre of creative expression had shifted from temples and royal courts to printing presses and publishing houses. And even if a few writers continued to compose in the traditional vein, their work did not get the same attention as that of the new arbiters of literature.

Though new literature written in the conventional style was not promoted in the print domain, already existing texts could not be entirely ignored. Since the late nineteenth and early twentieth centuries were the time of linguistic nationalism in Odisha, it also became necessary for the print-public to preserve their cultural heritage. Thus, we can see several attempts during this period to not only transfer texts from numerous palm-leaf manuscripts to the book form but also to record in print the narratives and songs that were being circulated only orally. And sometimes there was resistance to such attempts as well. I shall conclude this section by citing one such instance for it presents us with a first-hand account of an important agent of transmitting devotional songs and the apprehensions people initially had for printed texts. Shyamsundar Nanda, the teacher of the Raja of Narasinghpur, narrates the ethical challenge he had to face while collecting the poems:

> An elderly person begs by singing the verse of Bhakta Arakshita Das, in this area. There is no one to take care of him and those songs are his only means of receiving some alms. I often tried to

> collect the verses as they were melodious and didactic, but the old mendicant, fearing that once these were written down, he would be deprived of his sole source of income, was reluctant to allow circulation through writing or print. (translation mine; Nanda 1903: 199–200)

Mendicants played a key role in the circulation of orature. The mendicant in this instance is neither the author nor does he ever claim authorship of the text. His attachment to the text is established through the labour of retention and its live aural reproduction. With the prospect of the text getting printed, he feared, his role as a disseminator of the text would be marginalised or dispensed with, resulting in economic deprivation. Interestingly, Arakshita Das, a sixteenth-century devotee of Jagannath, whose *jananas* had become a source of livelihood for the early twentieth-century mendicant, had himself turned to begging after going through a series of misfortunes (Nayak and Nayak 2010: 68). Shaymsundar Nanda further informs us that he had to wait until the demise of the mendicant to publish the volume of Arakshita's songs.

Banikantha, His Song-offerings and Emergence of the Singer-Devotee

If the anonymous singer mentioned earlier was reluctant to get 'his' songs transferred to a new form of technology, so was one of the earliest Odia singers whose songs were first recorded in a studio. However, unlike in the previous era, when singers almost always performed in anonymity, we have the name of the singer whose renditions have the distinction of being among the earliest recorded songs in Odisha. I have deliberately kept the second part of the last sentence in the passive form as this singer also happened to be visually challenged and legend has it that his songs were recorded without his approval. Apanna Panigrahi (1893–1936), also known as 'Andha [blind] Apanna', was a legendary singer and music teacher from Paralakhemundi, a princely state in the south of Odisha. Sometime in the early 1930s, the king of Paralekhemundi Srikrushnachandra Gajapati requested him to have some of his renditions recorded. He is believed to have refused by saying that he already was devoid of vision and if his voice was transferred to the *kalagauna* (or machine singer) then his life would not be worth living.

However, the king, unlike Shyamsundar Nanda who merely wanted to print the songs of Arakshita Das, could not have waited till Panigrahi's demise to have his songs recorded. Legend has it that the king took him to Kolkata and asked him to sing. Everything had been pre-arranged and two songs in Panigrahi's voice were recorded without his knowledge. He was furious when he learnt the trick of the king but the king managed to persuade him to record another six songs of Banamali Das, Abhimanyu Samantasinghra and other poets in his voice (Acharya 2018: 96-97). When the record was finally released by the Hindustan Record Company, the singer was invited to hear his own rendition. Legend has it that upon hearing the record player reproducing his own voice, Panigrahi was distraught and said that since his voice had been taken away from him, god would also take him away. And, not long after, he passed away.[9]

Such apprehensions about losing one's voice if it got recorded, however, did not persist and one soon witnessed the arrival of the first major celebrity-singer in Odisha. Nimai Charan Harichandan (1901–1983), recorded his first song 'Bitalaku Alingana', an excerpt from Upendra Bhanja's *Baidehisha Bilasa*, for HMV in Calcutta in 1933. The record became an instant success and he was invited to perform at AIR, Kolkata the following year. His high-pitched voice with a unique resonance proved suitable for singing *jananas*. In a career spanning almost half a century he went on to record scores of songs. Though he sang songs belonging to different genres such as folk, Odissi, *champu*, *chhanda*, it is for his rendition of devotional songs addressed to Jagannath that people in Odisha chiefly remember him.

Harichandan, awarded the Padmashree in 1976, not just sang devotional songs, he also lived the life of a devotee. He started living in Puri from 1971 and sang ten prayers before Lord Jagannath everyday, till he breathed his last in 1983. In an e-mail correspondence (dated 14 October 2018) the distinguished linguist, B.N. Patnaik, shared with me his first-hand account of Harichandan's performance before the Lord inside the temple at Puri. Patnaik wrote,

> While singing his *jananas* in front of Jagannath, Nimai Babu unwaveringly looked at Him—his eyes would not turn this way or that. He was totally oblivious to the presence of other listeners around him. He sang to him; he sang for Him. And through his songs, it seemed to me, he made an offering to Him. (like people offering *tulsi*/flower garlands)

This image of a celebrated artist as the devotee is significant as this may be seen as a revival of a long-established tradition that dates back to the sixteenth-century poet Balaram Das. The seventeenth-century poet Salabeg (or Bhakta Salabeg as he is popularly known) occupies a central place in this tradition.

Of course, there have been devotees who became famous for writing only one or two *jananas* such as Saria Bhika or Chandan Hajuri and others who achieved legendary status primarily for their exemplary devotion such as Dasia Bauri or Bandhu Mohanty. But what sets Harichandan apart is that he is the first celebrated singer-devotee. Though Odisha has had a long tradition of music and singing, no one became famous only for her/his singing before the twentieth century. One can think of numerous poets who have been accorded reverential epithets and more often than not people would use solely those epithets to refer to those poets. 'Atibadi' can refer only to Jagannath Das and none other than Upendra Bhanja can be called the 'Kavisamrat'. But in the recorded past of Odisha no singer, prior to the twentieth century, was ever addressed through an epithet. That is understandable for there were many singers and they could only reach a limited audience. But with technological reproduction of songs, the distinctiveness of individual singers became more pronounced and the singer (not the poet) took centerstage. After the arrival of recording technology, songs increasingly began to be associated with the singer of the most famous rendition, rather than the author, and epithets began to be bestowed on singers.

'Banikantha' is perhaps the first famous epithet given to a singer in Odisha. Songs recorded in Harichandan's voice continue to be extremely popular even now in Odisha. Since his songs, recorded on 78 rpm records, were not easily available by the late 1980s and early

1990s, Dukhishyam Tripathy tried to recreate his aura by imitating his *dandi*[10] style of vocalisation. This is also a new phenomenon where new singers are so devoted to their icons that they completely surrender their individuality and try their best to present the renditions as Harichandan's, a phenomenon reminiscent of a pre-print era literary practice when writers cutting their teeth would use the name of a famous predecessor in the signature line in order to gauge the listener's reception. Thus, some features of a primarily oral culture are reproduced in the record industry era but the focus of attention here has shifted from the writer to the singer.

Modernisation of Jananas and 'Songs from People's Soul'

While Harichandan was undoubtedly the most celebrated singer in the early phase of song-recording in Odisha, the contribution of other prominent music teachers and performers cannot be ignored. Kalicharan Patnaik (1897–1978; popularly known as 'Kavichandra' or the moon among the poets) revived the tradition of writing devotional songs in Odisha. Singhari Shyam Sundar Kar (1908–1975) trained a generation of singers in the Odissi style who carried forward his legacy. They both wrote theoretical books on the Odissi style of music and it is through the efforts of such inspiring teachers and practitioners that Odissi achieved wider recognition. The noted Odissi singer, Shyamamani Patnaik (b. 1938) in a personal interview (4 July 2018) distinguished between the way traditional songs were sung in villages and those performed by trained singers. She sang the opening stanza of the eighteenth-century poet Bhakta Charan Das's 'Manabodha Chautisha' in two distinct styles to explain how a conscious attempt was made in the Odissi style to add feeling to each expression in the song through variations of pitch and intonation and by prolonging certain vowel sounds. Thus, in a song, a word should not merely mean but independently evoke a sentiment. She mentioned the names of Singhari Shyama Sundar Kar and Balakrushna Das (1928–1993) among others who brought about this significant change in the music tradition of Odisha. However, one also needs to keep in mind that, before the arrival of EP or Extended Play (c. 1968) and LP or Long Play (c. 1974) records, the maximum time an artist could get to sing a song was three and a half minutes and perhaps there was not much room for singers who recorded till then to experiment with the tune of songs.

In spite of the availability of several gramophone records and their important role in re-popularising devotional songs in Odisha, it must be admitted that radio was the chief mode of disseminating devotional songs. Record players were expensive and records were not easily available. Bibhuti Bhushan Acharya, who in the mid-1960s started the business of playing music at festivals, special occasions such as marriage and funeral ceremonies and public gatherings using tannoys or funnel-shaped loudspeakers (erroneously called mike [mic] in villages), told me in a personal interview (30 June 2018) that very few households possessed record players as most people could not afford these. There was no recording studio in Odisha until the mid-1980s, which compelled artists to travel to Kolkata to record their songs. Moreover, only up to seven minutes of recording was possible on an SP or standard play (78 rpm) record that substantially limited the quantity of music production.

Radio changed all this. Even before the establishment of an AIR centre at Cuttack on 28 January 1948, broadcasting in Odia had already started from the Kolkata Centre in 1939. The slot for Odia was at 5:30 PM for half an hour and the programme usually comprised the announcement of government messages and war-related radio plays. After the establishment of the AIR Cuttack centre, an effort was made to popularise the music tradition of the land. Analysing the nature of radio programmes in Odisha, Jayanta Kumar Das mentions that programmes related to music occupied 43.63 per cent of the total airtime in comparison to the national average of 38.1 per cent (1987: 30). Though it is difficult to determine whether the unique popularity of music in Odisha led to more airtime to music or vice versa, radio nevertheless created far more opportunities for artists than was earlier imaginable.

The year 1976 is a landmark year in the history of recorded music in Odisha. In early March that year two EP records 'Bhajans of Salabeg' (7 songs, 20 minutes) and 'Bhajans of Bhima Bhoi' (5 songs,

15 minutes) were released by HMV; these two were soon followed by an LP titled 'Songs from People's Soul' (10 songs, 41 minutes). Two of the albums were devoted exclusively to Jagannath *jananas*. What is of crucial importance for us here is that the then chief minister of Odisha, Nandini Satpathy took active interest in the project and wrote the following message on the back jacket of the last-mentioned record.

> For Oriyas, Jagannath is religion, history and a way of life. The peculiarly intense attachment between a people and its God is difficult to explain except by the range of Sri Jagannath's appeal. Differences in caste and creed are dissolved in the ecstatic devotion Sri Jagannath inspires. The quality of this devotion is typical in that it establishes a highly informal and personal relationship between the devotee and the Lord, and encourages spontaneity and freedom in expression of thoughts and sentiments.
>
> Some of the popular Bhajans are reproduced in this L.P. record. The unaffected tone and the patent sincerity of these poems have given them their timelessness, their poignancy, their unmistakable power to stir a whole community as only few poems, in any language, can.

An Odia version of the chief minister's message was also given alongside the one in English, and the album details were also provided in both languages. The intention perhaps was to project this to the world outside as the best specimens of Odia music. The translation of the title which is 'Jagannath *Janana*' in Odia to 'Songs from a People's Soul' in English is not without significance; it succinctly highlights the sincere and unaffected quality of the songs. Such enthusiasm from the chief minister of the state would no doubt have inspired the artists. And the album had the best of them—some who had already made a mark and were revered and others who were to dominate the music industry for the next couple of decades.

Balakrushna Das scored the music for all three albums that included singers like Das himself, Raghunath Panigrahi, Bhikari Bal, Pranab Kishore Patnaik, Akshaya Mohanty, Prafulla Kar and Sikandar Alam. Of these singers, Akshaya Mohanty went on to become the most prominent singer and composer of *adhunik* Odia songs and

Bhikari Bal, of devotional songs. Most of these singers had earned a reputation as AIR artistes. Every effort was made to maintain an excellent production quality and eminent artist Dinanath Pathy was involved in designing the covers of the albums. The numbers in these albums are sung in a style clearly distinct from the *dandi* style of Harichandan. One can clearly discern this change if one compares Harichandan's rendition of '*thaka mana chala jiba*' with that of Balakrushna Das. While Harichandan's version (in 2 minutes and 58 seconds) is performed in his signature high-pitched and monotonal *dandi* style, Das's rendition (in 3 minutes and 49 seconds), through precise tonal variations, effectively evokes the sentiments of a tired pilgrim on the last leg of his journey.

From Kavisamrat to Bhajansamrat

Till then most Odia records had been released by HMV. However, the company suffered a major fire accident in 1977 and incurred huge losses. This created conditions for other entrepreneurs and a few Kolkata-based companies such as Gathani and INRECO became more active in producing Odia records. Two major singers, Akshaya Mohanty and Bhikari Bal, became exclusive artists for Gathani and INRECO respectively, and started releasing solo albums. But another important change took place in 1982 when Satyanarayan Agrawalla (1932–2008), an Odia entrepreneur from Puri, set up the JE Cassette Company in Cuttack. Four years earlier, he had set up Jagannath Electronics, a shop that sold and repaired transistors and records.

As a child Agrawalla had immersed himself in the cultural life of Puri and later became an important organiser of cultural events in different parts of Odisha. His interest in music, like that of many of his contemporaries, grew from his association with local theatre groups. Such local theatre groups (or *jatra*/*nacha* parties as those are called) deeply impacted the cultural ethos of twentieth-century Odisha. JE Cassette Company along with Samrat Cassettes revolutionised the music industry (for that is what it had become by the late 1980s) in Odisha. One cannot underestimate the importance of cassette technology in this context. Portable, less expensive, and having greater run-time than even LPs, cassette became extremely popular by the late 1980s and early 1990s. Moreover, cassette players were significantly less expensive and way more convenient to use than record players. Given his keen interest in and intense familiarity with the cultural life of Odisha, his company went on to release many albums on the traditional and folk music, apart from many modern albums.

I have already mentioned the crucial role that mendicants played in disseminating devotional songs. It is not without any significance that the most famous singer of Odia devotional songs in the last quarter of the twentieth century happens to bear the name Bhikari Bal (1929–2010). Bhikari in Odia (and in several other Indian languages) means mendicant or beggar and is not an unusual proper name in Odisha. For a long time, when the infant mortality rate was extremely high, parents and grandparents would deliberately give their children apparently undesirable names so that the children do not attract the attention of Yama, the god of death. But the name Bhikari also suggests devotion, as the child would always remain a beggar before Lord Jagannath.

Agrawalla (2006: 47), who produced several of Bal's albums, remembers in an essay how in the mid-1970s he had invited Bal to give the inaugural performance at a *bhajan samaroha* (an all-night event for the performance of devotional songs) in Puri, organised by Shrikshetra Kala Prakashika. Before recording his solo albums in the 1970s Bal had earned considerable reputation as an AIR artist. He also had sung the maximum number of songs in the path-breaking album 'Songs from People's Soul'. Agrawalla mentions that two of his early solo LP records 'Sharadha Bali' and 'Bhakti Puspanjali' created a sensation in the music world in Odisha. Bal also started singing devotional songs written by his contemporaries. After Nimai Harichandan, Bal became the most revered and sought-after singer of devotional songs in Odisha, and like his illustrious predecessor, lived the life of a devotee. The title '*Bhajansamrat*' (or the emperor among the singers of bhajan) was bestowed on him by the Gajapati Divyasingh Dev and he is popularly known by this name.

It has been mentioned earlier that there was a strong tradition of referring to poets by popular epithets. However, we do not know of a single Odia singer prior to the twentieth century who is known by such an appellation. But in the twentieth century, a reversal of the phenomenon took place. Moreover, songs (especially devotional ones) began to be ascribed to the performer and not to the writer. Very few people would associate the name of Kshirod Chandra Pothala with the song 'Kotha Bhoga Khia'; people generally receive it as Bhikari Bal's song. So, in the era of technological reproduction, the singer could not be separated from the song. Since there was a great demand for *jananas*, more devotional songs came to be composed but they were almost never published in book form. Even if a few published their devotional songs in book form, they did not attract much attention. Moreover, writers of both devotional and *adhunik* songs did not achieve much recognition in the literary sphere. Thus, the separation that had begun to take shape in the late nineteenth century between orature and literature seemed to have reached a point of no return.

While Bal continued to perform well into the twenty-first century, greater demand for devotional songs witnessed the arrival of several other stars (though none as revered as Harichandan or Bal). Sitaram Agrawalla, Director of Sarthak Entertainment Pvt. Ltd., asserted in a personal interview (4 July 2018) that nowhere in India has he seen a greater market for devotional songs than in Odisha and that the phenomenal success of 'Keri Keri Suna Duba' sung by Anuradha Paudwal released by T-Series in the 1990s almost compelled him to invest more in the production of devotional songs. The cassette industry also witnessed another significant change in the 1990s; from almost an exclusive focus on Jagannath, one now sees songs and albums devoted to other goddesses and gods such as Durga, Tarini, Santoshi, Gojabayani, Mangala, Biraja, Shiva and Hanuman. In this context, one cannot forget the tremendous success of *Lakshmi Purana* sung by Namita Agrawalla and released by Sarthak Music in 1999. Sold in a set of two cassettes (with a run-time of almost one hour and forty-seven minutes), '*Lakshmi Purana*' reproduced the text composed by the early sixteenth-century poet Balaram Das. Since the reading of Das's text is part of a ritual performance on all Thursdays of the month of Maragasira (November–December), the cassettes began to be played in almost all villages and towns of Odisha. However, this was not the first cassette version of the text; in 1990 Pabitra Entertainment had released 'Lakshmi Purana Bahi Gita', rendered by Shantilata Barik. The release of several audio-versions of the same text clearly hints at the uninterrupted demand for traditional Odia texts.

Conclusion

Almost as a reversal of the *adhunik–prachin* literary controversy of the 1890s, a movement was started against the 'vulgarisation' of devotional songs in 1990s. Bhikari Bal, among others, threatened to go on a strike which led the Government of Odisha to promise the constitution of a separate censor board to regulate and streamline the release of private albums (Mishra 2006). Perhaps this loss of trust in the new performers saw a decline in the consumers' demand for devotional music around the end of the twentieth century, which almost coincided with the end of the cassette era. But the arrival of several Odia YouTube channels in the second decade of the new millennium has revived the interest of Odia people in traditional Odia music. Sitaram Agrawalla claims that all YouTube channels of Sidharth TV combined get around 6 million hits on a peak day. This figure appears even more astounding given the fact that his company set up its first channel on YouTube in 2016. He further adds that despite the change in medium, the act of listening to devotional songs, continues to be as important in Odia life as having breakfast, lunch and dinner. To substantiate his point, he analysed the graph on his YouTube page to conclude that most people watch/listen to devotional songs on his channel between 5.30 AM and 8.30 AM. The success of the YouTube channels of his company and that of several others, he says, is indicative of the resumption of the journey.

In this chapter, we have seen the circulation and dissemination of the *janana* form of devotional literature through the ages and through different technologies. We saw how, with the introduction of print technology, this form was relegated to the domain of the non-literary, and later, with the popularisation of the recording technology, the form was reinvented, but never acquired its former status. Thus, it carved a separate space for itself in the larger cultural domain and coexisted with print-literature as the growing gulf between the intellectuals and the masses that began to appear in the late nineteenth century widened further in the latter half of the twentieth century.

Acknowledgements

I am grateful to J.P. Das, Anant Mahapatra, Sudarsana Acharya Shyamamani Patnaik, B.N. Patnaik, Sumanyu Satpathy, Jatindra Kumar Nayak, Dhirendra Mohapatra, Sitaram Agrawalla, Surya Deo, Bigyan Ranjan Das, Ashit Mohapatra and Aruni Mahapatra for offering their help at various stages of research for this chapter.

Notes

1. For a more detailed discussion on the lack of malevolence or vindictiveness in the traditional portrayals of Jagannath, see Shaswat Panda's 'In the Eyes of God' and Jyotirmaya Tripathy's 'Becoming Jagannath in Dravidanadu' in this book.
2. The line '*E Jagannath sola kala/ethun kalae Nandabala*' (Jagannath possesses sixteen *kalas* or attributes and only one of those *kalas* make Krishna, the son of Nanda) became proverbial after Dibakar Das's *Sri Jagannath Charitamrita* (114), composed around 1690. I am grateful to Bibudhendra Narayan Patnaik for drawing my attention to this line and clarifying that the idea of Lord Jagannath being an *avatari* does not start with Sarala Das but owes much to Dibakar Das. I cannot thank Antaryami Mishra enough for helping me locate the line in the printed text and sharing the citation details.
3. For a comparison of the price of a text in palm-leaf manuscript version and in printed codex, one may look at the notification for the publication of Krushna Singh's *Mahabharata* in the October 1867 issue of *Utkal Dipika*. The prospective publishers make the following price comparison:

   > While a palm-leaf *pothi* version of the text with many impurities is available for fifty rupees, a printed version of the text containing 1500 leaves would be priced around twenty rupees if the publishers could find at least one thousand customers willing to buy the book. (quoted in Mohanty 2001: 234)

4. Sumanyu Satpathy in an unpublished manuscript titled 'Print Matters: The Early Periodical Press in Eastern India and the Making of a New Literary Culture (Odia: 1866–1919)' cites the instance of Bhaskaracharya's *Lilavati Sutra*, translated from Sanskrit into Odia by Narayan Das in the eighteenth century, that conformed to existing Odia tunes (32).
5. A literal translation of the title would be Jagannath in the Voice of Poets and such a title is significant for highlighting the voice of the poets and not their pen/stylus.

6. Jena's anthology is certainly based on the texts that survived and not necessarily on all the poems that were written during the nineteenth century or earlier. The fact that he could find more authors/texts from the eighteenth century than from the nineteenth century (chances of whose survival were certainly greater) clearly suggests that we see a decline in the composition of devotional poetry.
7. One may think of the popularity of the use of Kanchi Kaveri narrative in the modern period. However, we need to keep in mind that the version that became popular was a dramatised one.
8. Fakir Mohan Senapati in one of his public lectures mentions how many unlettered cowherds in Odisha have memorised the verses of Upendra Bhanja. Similarly, in a paean to the poet published in *Mukura*, Gopabandhu Das writes that Bhanja's *kavyas* are sung both by farmers while ploughing their fields and also dancers in palaces while performing. In the first ever Odia motion picture *Sita Vivah* (1936), directed by Mohan Sundar Deb Goswami, the boatman recites portions from *Baidehisha Bilasa*. J.P. Das (b. 1936), eminent litterateur and art-historian, shared this piece of information with me. He remembers watching the film in the mid-1940s in Banapur.
9. Surya Deo, a well-known researcher on recorded music in Odisha, narrated this anecdote to me in a personal interview (26 June 2018), who in turn had heard it in his childhood, from the legendary singer and a younger contemporary of Panigrahi, Nimai Harichandan.
10. This is a high-pitched and full-throated style of singing that the devotee is supposed perform on the *danda* (village street) while on the way to the temple. Shyamamani Patnaik mentioned that Harichandan's voice was so high-pitched that while recording a duet she sat near the microphone while he sang from the farthest point possible in the recording room (that is at the door) to be able to deliver at the same pitch as Patnaik.

References

Acharya, Sudarsana. 2018. 'Andha Apanna'. In *Samabd-Aama Odisha Sahityakosha*, edited by Dasarathi Das, Sudarsana Acharya, Debendra Kumar Dash and Gouranga Charan Das, 96–97. Bhubaneswar: Aama Odisha.

Agrawalla, Satyanarayan. 2006. 'Bhikari Bal: Kichhi Smruti, Kichhi Anubhuti'. In *Bhajan Samrat Bhikari Bala*, edited by Bijayananda Singh and Sunamani Rout. Cuttack: Cuttack Students' Store.

Carey, John. 2005. *The Intellectuals and the Masses: Pride and Prejudice Among the Literary Intelligentsia, 1880–1939*. London: Faber & Faber.

Chakravarti, Monmohan. 1898. 'Notes on the Language and Literature of Orissa, Parts III and IV'. *Journal of the Asiatic Society of Bengal*, 47(4): 332–386.

Das, Dibakar. 1927 [*c.* 1690]. *Jagannathamrita Gita va Sri Jagannath Charitamrita.* Edited by Janardan Kar. Cuttack: Madhabchandra Dan and others.

Das, Jagannath Prasad. 2017. 'Chhapakhana Loke Nihati Manda'. In *Ama Bhasa: Ama Sanskruti.* Bhubaneswar: Shiksasandhan.

Das, Jayanta Kumar. 1987. *Odia Betar Natak.* Cuttack: Kalabati Das.

Das, Sisir Kumar. 1991. *A History of Indian Literature: 1880–1910 (Western Impact: Indian Response).* New Delhi: Sahitya Akademi.

Jena, Murarimohan, ed. [1979]2015. *Kabikanthe Sri-jagannath.* Cuttack: Friends' Publishers.

Mansinha, Mayadhar. 1962. *History of Oriya Literature.* New Delhi: Sahitya Akademi.

Mishra, Badri. 2006. 'Anya Eka Bhima Bhoi'. In *Bhajansamrat Bhikari Bal,* edited by Bijayananda Singh and Sunamani Rout, 59–60. Cuttack: Cuttack Students' Store.

Mohanty, Banshidhar. 2001. *Odia Bhasha Andolana,* 2nd edition. Cuttack: Sahitya Sangraha Prakashan.

Nanda, Shyamsundar. 1903. 'Bhakta Arakshitanka Padavali'. *Utkal Sahitya,* 7(7): 199–202.

Nayak, Kshetrabasi and Labanya Nayak, eds. 2010. *Srijagannath Padyabali.* Bhubaneswar: Duduly Process and Offset.

Pani, Subas, ed. and trans. 2004. *Blue Hill: Hymns to Lord Jagannath.* New Delhi: Rupa & Co.

Panigrahi, Kalindi Charan. 1947. 'Oriya'. In *The Indian Literatures of Today: A Symposium,* edited by Bharatan Kumarappa for P.E.N. All Indian Centre. Bombay: The International Book House.

Panigrahi, Krushna Chandra. [1972] 2012. 'Adhunika Odia Sahityara Vanijya Mulya'. In *Krushna Chandra Panigrahi Granthabali.* Cuttack: Cuttack Students' Store.

Pattanayak, Debi Prasanna. 1958. 'Odia Bhajan Sahityara Bhumika'. In *Konark.* Bhubaneshwar: Odisha Sahitya Academy.

Rao, Madhusudan. [1896]1962. 'Mukhabandha'. In *Radhanath Granthabali.* Cuttack: Cuttack Trading Company.

Samantaray, Natabara. 2017. 'Genesis of the Modern Odia Textbook'. In *Natabara Samantaray: A Reader,* edited by Sumanyu Satpathy and Animesh Mohapatra, 17–63. New Delhi: Sahitya Akademi.

Satpathy, Sumanyu. Forthcoming. *Print Matters: The Early Periodical Press in Eastern India and the Making of a New Literary Culture (Odia: 1866–1919).*

3

SYNCRETIC JAGANNATH CULTURE AND POPULAR ODIA IMAGINATION: REPRESENTATIONS OF LORD JAGANNATH IN ODIA CINEMA

Amarjeet Nayak

Introduction

Odia film industry, also popularly known as Ollywood, a portmanteau of the words Odia and Hollywood, got the recognition as an industry in 1974 by the government of Odisha. However, history of Odia cinema dates back to 1936, when the first Odia film *Sita Bibaha* was released. Though not comparable in scale to some of the biggest film industries in India producing other language films such as Hindi, Tamil, Telugu, etc. in its more than eight-decade existence, Odia cinema has grown in both quality and quantity. Its role as a popular cultural medium among Odias cannot be overstated. Like any cinema that seeks to strike a chord with its intended audience, Odia cinema makers too have attempted to find relevant subjects. One of the predominant subjects in Odia cinema, especially in its early stages, has been Lord Jagannath, the presiding deity of Odisha whose footprint over the everyday lives of Odias is omnipresent.

This chapter looks at the ways in which Odia cinema has helped foster a bond between Lord Jagannath and the Odia community that adores Him. This aim has been pursued by looking at four dominant ways in which Odia film-makers have used Jagannath. First, it will look at how, in spite of technical inadequacies, early Odia mythological films were able to strike a chord with Odia audience. Second, it will make an analysis of how Jagannath culture has been presented as egalitarian and syncretic that exhorts the cinema-going audience to rise above socioeconomic differences and embrace universal brotherhood. Using Jagannath in Odia cinema to address issues of caste and gender, two existing fault-lines in the Odia society's quest for social justice, will be primarily addressed in this section. Third, Odia cinema's attempt at presenting the syncretic nature of Jagannath culture will be brought to the fore to show how it is different from many 'cults' whose existence is based on exclusionary practices. Lastly, the chapter will look at Odia cinema's thrust on the importance of bhakti (devotion) and *gyana* (wisdom or 'enlightenment') in a true Jagannath devotee, to bring home the point that tradition and modernity can have a happy coexistence in Jagannath culture.

Thus, the chapter tries to interrogate the ideas of equity, syncretism and modernity in Jagannath culture through an analysis of Odia cinema's representations of Lord Jagannath. It intends to capture the undertones of social justice in Odia cinema's use of Jagannath prior to 1990s. An attempt is also made to illustrate the syncretic nature of Jagannath culture that the chapter claims to be unique to it. Finally, the cinematic thrust on bhakti and *gyana* will be made in order to weave tradition and modernity in one thread. A discussion of these three ideas will be informed largely by the way Jagannath and Jagannath mythologies have been historically represented in Odia cinema.

This study focuses primarily on the Odia films produced before the 1990s. This is for two reasons. First, unlike the earlier decades, from the 1990s onwards, Odia films started losing their primacy as a major popular medium with the proliferation of Odia albums of bhajans (a form of devotional song), which became an audio-visual replacement for the experience that films had monopoly over, until then. Second, there is a paucity of Odia films solely devoted to Gods and Goddesses in the last three decades, owing in no small measure to globalisation (Westernisation). According to Chidanand Das Gupta, with the rise of the post-industrial economy, the mythological took a retreat. He further says, 'The mythological cannot deal with the multifold phenomena of modern society and becomes inadequate...' and 'cars, skyscrapers, jet planes and gun fights' endorse a new visual experience for the audience wherein the inherent awe of the extraordinary out of the world continues as a silent remnant (Das Gupta 1989: 17). So, in a way, miracles of God were replaced by technological miracles; however, when it comes to Jagannath in Odia cinema, a caveat is necessary that even in mythological films based on Jagannath, He is not shown to be performing miracles, unlike many other Gods. Instead of being seen as a God performing miracles, he is more of an intimate God, with whom a devotee can have a deeply personal relationship, almost like a family member. So, He continues to remain an important figure in Odia cinema even in the age of technological miracles as his importance in the collective Odia psyche and Odia cinema has little to do with him performing miracles.

Jagannath Mythology in Early Odia Cinema and Its Resonance with Odia Audience

Before delving further, it is pertinent to point out that the primary focus in this chapter is on Odia mythological cinema because of the supreme importance of mythology in the consciousness of a community deeply embedded in religiosity, such as the Odia community. According to Leela Rao, the lived faith of the people does not interpret mythology as a fairy tale. In India, myths are the way in which people humanise the gap visible in the world. In the passage from the known to the unknown, myth is the neutral and, therefore, stable point of transition. Symbolism is the language of mythology, where in the divine is not an entity beyond reach, but is more than human (Rao 1989). The mythological films, through their take on these myths and easy accessibility, succeed in communicating the myths (such as those regarding the origin of the Jagannath culture and Jagannath temple) or the symbolisms associated with them (such as the colour blue and its importance in Jagannath culture).

Though a significant number of mythological films have been made in India in various Indian languages based on Hindu mythologies and have been extremely popular and critically acclaimed, it is unfortunate that there is a paucity of books on critical appraisal of these films. In her extensive work in this field, Rachel Dwyer states that most books on religion and cinema are concerned with 'religious' films or with the depiction of spirituality in films, mostly drawing on Judeo-Christian tradition, wherein the focus is on the image of Christ or on theology (Dwyer 2006: 5). This is truer in terms of critical literature on Odia mythological films, which necessitates a study of the kind being attempted in this section that will hopefully add to the sparse critical material available on Odia mythological films and spur further academic enquiry into the subject.

It is important at the outset to have a brief historical overview of Odia cinema and its connection with Jagannath. From *Lalita* in 1949 to *Jagannath Dhama Puri* in 2017, Lord Jagannath continues to be all-pervasive in Odia films. Of about 650 Odia films that have been made so far, Lord Jagannath has been a pivotal figure in at least 50 of them. Of the 10 Odia films made until the end of 1950s, five were mythological films and four of those were on Jagannath mythologies. The production of Odia films saw a significant rise from the 1960s. However, the proportion of mythological films declined steadily. In the 1960S, a total of 26 films were made, out of which there were only four mythological films. Out of those, two were on Jagannath mythology and one, *Jayadeb* (1962), was based on the life of one of Jagannath's devotees. A similar trend is seen to continue in the decades that follow. However, it is pertinent to note that even though Jagannath-centric films were on the decline, Jagannath never went away from Odia cinema, which can be seen from the fact that many Odia films have either had Jagannath's name in the title or the central characters are named after him, something that will be discussed later in this chapter.

Some of these films are completely devotional in nature, wherein cinema becomes a medium for the Lord's *darshan* (act of being seen or gazed at) and the theatre-going public is expected to immerse themselves in a religious (and almost ritualistic) environment with the *mahima* (glory) of the lord being portrayed on screen, accompanied by devotional music and dance. From a purely cinematic point of view, the quality of many of these films may be questionable but the immense popularity that many, if not all of them, have had among the film-going public points at the unquestionable love and adulation that the Odia community has for Lord Jagannath, with whom their desire to bond is far too great to agonise over the occasional inadequacy of the medium.

In the mid-twentieth century when filmmakers were beginning to make Odia films, most of these films were mythological ones. Around this period, the literacy of Odisha was extremely low.[1] So, it is likely that many Odias might not have read the texts dealing with all these legends and folklores but most of them would still have been familiar with these, as they were the source of many pujas (festivals) celebrated within the Odia household such as Mahalakshmi puja, also known as Manabasa Gurubar among Odias that is celebrated within the home space or the festivals held in the public space such as 'Dola Yatra'.[2] Moreover, traditional forms of popular folk art in the Odia community such as *pala*, *daskathia*, *kirtan*, etc. used to have many such mythology-related subjects as their themes. Some of this knowledge also passed through oral tellings from generation to generation. Moreover, it is important to note here that the gaze (*darshan*) of a devotee at the Lord, when mediated by a medium such as cinema wherein actors perform God, becomes informed by their cultural beliefs.[3]

When it comes to the technical aspects of the early Indian mythological films, Dadasaheb Phalke was a pioneer in using innovative methods to connect with his target audience. One such innovation was the use of 'neo-realist' mode. P.K. Nair (1980) calls *Kaliya Mardan* (1919) the first Indian 'neo-realist' mythological film, a genre that gained popularity much later after the release of Italian film-maker Roberto Rossellini's *Rome, Open City* (1945). In *Kaliya Mardan*, Phalke improvises neorealism with myth, creating a new form. His films, therefore, use mythology in a suitably convenient way for his audience, even going to the extent of dressing his divine characters as ordinary human beings. For an Indian audience, he brought Indian Gods on screen establishing the first link between cinema and religion. In doing so, he weaved the experience of *natak* (stage acting). Indian cinema, for its mix of both tradition (mythology) and modernity (new techniques and contemporaneous treatment of the subject), has been called by Ashish Rajadhyaksha (1987) as 'neo-traditionalism' (quoted in Dwyer 2006: 1).

What Phalke achieves through *Kaliya Mardan* using a neo-realist mode, the early Odia mythological films could achieve even without taking recourse to cinematic experimentation or through innovative use of the medium of cinema. The cinematic techniques used in these early Odia films remained extremely basic, owing primarily to lack of resources (Ghosh 1984). In his Odia autobiography *Nijaswa Chitranatya: Smrutipatha* (2015), renowned Odia actor Sarat Chandra Pujari gives a first-hand account of the difficult financial condition in which the 1959 Odia film *Sri Sri Mahalakshmi Puja* was made. The production of the film took place in Calcutta city of the neighbouring state West Bengal, as there was no film studio in Odisha until 1982 when Kalinga Studio was established in Bhubaneswar. He recounts how the actors and technicians had to spend almost six months in extremely congested rooms with barely any basic facility.[4] Yet, they could still succeed in making their films resonate with the theatre-going Odia public. It is true that the early Odia film-makers presented the Lord in the traditional way, in terms of the way the Lord is perceived to look in the appropriate costumes, ornaments, etc. However, the very fact that the Odia community considers Jagannath not just as a God, but as someone whose rituals mimic the behaviour of a normal human being such as the ritual of falling ill, of taking bath, of having food, etc. make him almost human-like and, in fact, He is seen by the larger Odia community as almost a family member.[5]

A close-reading of an important scene from the film *Bandhu Mohanty* (1977) may provide an answer as to how early Odia cinema dealing with Jagannath myths and legends resonated with the Odia audience, mostly constituting of unlettered Odias at the time. In the said scene from the film, we find that Lord Jagannath gives *darshan* to his devotee Bandhu Mohanty in the form of a shepherd boy. However, it is not the learned Mohanty but his not-so-learned wife who alerts him to the possibility that the simple shepherd boy could be the Lord himself in human form. She may be said to represent an average unlettered Odia cinema-going audience whose easy and uncomplicated understanding of Jagannath mythology comes as a significant advantage for the makers of early Odia Jagannath-centric films. This prior understanding of the subject and the love and connect with it, become important factors in the mythological films having resonance with their audience. So, in a way, it was not necessary for the Odia film-makers to use advanced cinematic techniques to make their mythological films accessible to the largely unlettered, but well-informed audience.

Use of Jagannath-centric Legends and Folklores in Odia Cinema to Address Social Issues

In Indian culture, mythology has traditionally been used to communicate a set of prescriptive roles like those based on class, caste and gender. A popular modern medium such as cinema can play a vital role in disseminating mythology to address social issues. Odia film-makers have successfully done that by using cinema to communicate and re-emphasise the sociocultural messages of Jagannath mythology among Odia cinema-going audience. Stating that culture is a 'subsystem within a larger social system' (399), Usha Reddi emphasises that communication plays a key role in integration, legitimisation and socialisation. While in ancient and medieval India, apart from interpersonal communication, dance, drama and songs were also a medium for communication, in modern India, mass communication platforms (films, primarily) have been a catalyst to this 'integration, legitimization and socialization' (Reddi 1989: 401).

Odia cinema has played an instrumental role in communicating the egalitarian ideas of social justice and equality. The discourse of Jagannath, as presented through Odia cinema with its many legends, folklores, scriptures, hymns, songs and literary works, has often tackled the ills of the society that come in the way of bonding between Man and the Lord. The division of society on the lines of caste and gender are two such obstacles that Odia films on Jagannath have not shied away from, but tackled upfront.

One of the earliest Odia mythological films to deal with caste discrimination is *Sri Sri Mahalakshmi Puja* (1959). This is a cinematic rendition of the popular legend of Manabasa Gurubar based on the ancient scripture *Lakshmi Purana*, penned by sixteenth-century devotee-poet Balaram Das. It tells the story of Sri Jagannath's wife Lakshmi teaching a lesson on equality to her husband and brother-in-law Balabhadra for succumbing to the evils of the caste system.

This story known in almost every household in Odisha is a lesson in the equality of human beings, where there is no caste-based discrimination. In the film, Lord Jagannath, like Ram, Krishna or other avatars (incarnations) of the Lord, is seen to be behaving not as the all-knowing God, but as the one who, like every human being (and unlike the concept of God being perfection personified), makes mistakes that a common man may be prone to. Compelled by the conventions of a society increasingly divided on the basis of caste, this *leela* (event as planned by God) tries to imbibe the importance of treating everyone equally. Such *leela*s of various avatars of the Lord in their human forms, unlike the strict guidelines of scriptures in many religions, attempt to teach the humanity lessons of morality, duty, and in this particular case, that of equality in a non-coercive, yet effective manner.

This film, based on an event that takes place during the puja (worship) of Goddess Mahalakshmi, shows the importance of accepting one's mistake and rectifying it—in the process addressing the crucial issue of a social evil such as caste-based discrimination in the Hindu society. In this case, the mistake is committed by Lord Jagannath and his elder brother Balabhadra, who ostracise *Maa* (Mother) Lakshmi and stop her from entering into the temple because Lakshmi, the Goddess of wealth visits Sriya, a devotee of hers who is from a 'lower' caste (Chandaluni) on the day of Lakshmi's worship (Manabasa Gurubar) and bestows blessings on her. When Balabhadra provokes Jagannath against Lakshmi for her disregarding the caste hierarchy, Jagannath feels compelled to deny Lakshmi entry into their house (temple). This apparent injustice angers Lakshmi who ensures that the brothers suffer by taking away all their wealth, including basic necessities such as food. Jagannath and Balabhadra are finally made to realise their mistake of looking at humanity from the prism of caste hierarchy and it is only then that Lakshmi comes back to the temple.

The film *Sri Sri Mahalakshmi Puja* based on Balaram Das's *Lakshmi Purana* uses the popularity of the sacral text among the Odia community. The considerable success that the film got, points out the role of a popular medium of entertainment such as cinema in making such a legend associated with Jagannath, easily accessible to a large section of the Odia community who may have been familiar with the legend, but would not have read Das's text. In disseminating the legend and the social message associated with it, the film also helps underscore the inherent humaneness of the Jagannath faith. The hugely popular Odia bhajans sung by the Odia Muslim singer Sikandar Alam known as the 'Salabeg of modern Odisha' (Panda 2010) in Odia cinema, are a further testimony to the unequivocal acceptance of all into the fold of the Jagannath universe.

Like caste, Jagannath-centric Odia films have dealt with issues of gender as well. They have projected strong female characters who have assimilated both tradition and modernity. It is interesting to note that *Lalita*, the first Odia film to deal exclusively with Sri Jagannath and his devotees, is not titled after Nila Madhav ('blue lord', another name for Jagannath) or his three male devotees—King Indradyumna, the tribal king Visvabasu or Vidyapati, the Brahmin emissary of King Indradyumna. The folklore has traditionally focused on the Lord (Nila Madhav), the two kings—one mythical and the other tribal—and a Brahmin devotee. Lalita too has an important role to play in the folklore but she is in no way a more important character than the other four, the Lord and three men. Though faithful to the original folklore in content and spirit, the film-makers have brought the female character Lalita to the forefront by naming the film after her. By doing so, the film attempts to resonate with the Odia women folk, a major constituent of Odia cinema-going audience, wherein they could see the very important role that Lalita plays in the Lord transforming himself from Nila Madhav to Darubrahma (Lord in wooden form), the current state of Lord Jagannath in the Puri temple.

Like the titular character in *Lalita*, we come across many important female characters in Odia films centring around Jagannath mythology or folklores. Sriya in *Sri Sri Mahalakshmi Puja*, Lakshmi in *Bandhu Mohanty* are two examples of women who are portrayed as strong characters. Their religiosity does not come in the way of their independence and strength of character, undermining the notion that modernity and tradition are antithetical. This also falsifies the claim that it is only in the contemporary Indian films that the common man and woman have become central figures. Critic Maithili Rao, while assessing the public sentiment of the 1990s India, argues that the common man or common woman in contemporary

Indian film narrative has occupied consumer and aesthetic space. In an interview, identifying the reasons for success and growth of Viacom18 Media, producer of women centric films like *Tanu Weds Manu* (2011), *Kahaani* (2012) and *Queen* (2014), CEO, Sudhanshu Vats claims that the new hero of the Hindi cinema is story, heroine and the common man (Singh 2016). If the Indian film critics had not been largely oblivious to the Indian mythological films in Hindi and other regional languages, they would have come across strong female characters in those films as in *Sri Sri Mahalkshmi Puja*, *Bandhu Mohanty* and even female-centric mythological films such as *Lalita*. It is through such Odia mythological films that an idea of a strong Odia woman, steeped in tradition is formed and fostered. These films also show that modernity and religiosity need not be seen as opposites and in fact can happily coexist in an individual.

Syncretic Jagannath Culture and Odia Cinema

The Jagannath culture encourages inclusion and acceptance of all belief systems, and Odia films, both mythological and social drama, reflect the same. In the film *Bandhu Mohanty*, even though Lakshmi is the daughter of a devotee of Lord Jagannath, she is seen to be a devout follower of Goddess Biraja, the presiding deity of Jajpur, Odisha. It is through the character of Lakshmi and the still popular devotional song '*Maa go Mamatamayi Mata*' which she sings in the village Biraja temple, that we find the Goddess Biraja getting a prominent part in a film which is primarily about a celebrated devotee of Lord Jagannath. So, unlike some other religious cults that thrive on the exclusion of others, the Jagannath culture is actually all encompassing that embraces all sects of Hinduism—Vaishnavism, Shaivism and Shaktism. Lord Jagannath is seen as a form of Vishnu, but in almost all of his temples, his idol is flanked by those of his brother (Balabhadra) and sister (Subhadra), who represent Shaivism and Shaktism, respectively. Guruprasad Mohapatra and Swati Samantaray point out how this symbolic coexistence of the three sects has been acknowledged by many historians: 'Some historians argue that while the triad was formed, the state was dominated by three important sects. Those were Saivism, Saktism and Vaishnavism. Hence the three idols of Subhadra, Balabhadra and Jagannath represented the three sects' (173). As discussed earlier, films like *Bandhu Mohanty* reaffirm this aspect of Jagannath culture.

Even in later Odia films which are not about Jagannath but have made use of the Lord's name either in the title or named the film's hero after Jagannath, we see the invocation of Jagannath culture to spread the message of universal brotherhood. For instance, in the 1991 film *Kotie Manisha Gotie Jaga*, we find the central character named as 'Jaga' that is also a shortened form for Jagannath, a name many of the Lord's devotees affectionately call him by. The film is a social drama where the hero wages a lone battle against injustice suffered by common people in the hands of powerful and corrupt politicians. The climax of the film takes place in an open field in front of a gigantic Jagannath idol seated on the dais. Interestingly, the Lord is not flanked by his brother and sister, as is often the case that mimics our titular hero's situation who is also fighting his battle alone. The hero's final speech before dying in front of Lord Jagannath and a congregation of common people exhorts the people to rise above caste, creed and religion and fight together. He says that if people continue to remain divided on these lines, then 'why me, Jagannath himself would not be able to save you.' In many Odia films such as this one which are ostensibly about issues of social justice, the message of social equality is packaged with religious sentiments, so that religion becomes a conduit for social reform. The Odia film-makers have thoroughly understood the pulse of Odias who would be more willing to accept progressive ideas of modernity, when those are not divorced from religion.

Not just the plot or dialogues in Odia cinema, but the use of bhajans too has played a major role in disseminating the syncretic and egalitarian ideas of Jagannath's philosophy. We find one such example in the film *Sri Jagannath* (1950) which is about Jagannath's location at *Nila Parbat* (blue mountain) in the form of Nila Madhav (blue God). The film depicts the tribal origin of Lord Jagannath whose bond with the tribal community—a community perceived to be marginalised in the modern world—is a significant part of him being seen as the Lord of all and not just of the privileged. The fact that tribal and non-tribal symbolism and rites exist and influence each other within the Jagannath culture is truly reflective of its syncretism. The colour blue is extremely significant in the discourse of Jagannath and one can consider this colour to represent the *sabara* (tribal) culture that the Brahmanical symbolism has imbibed. The film *Sri Jagannath* takes recourse to a beautiful song '*Nila Sindhu Teere*' (On the shores of the blue sea) sung by *Banikantha* (one with the divine voice) Nimai Harichandan, to highlight this aspect of Jagannath culture. At this point it is instructive to point out that with *Banikantha*, there was the emergence of the 'singer-devotee' tradition in Odisha.[6]

Many Odia film-makers, especially those producing mythological films in Odisha, revolving around Lord Jagannath used Harichandan's voice in bhajans to promote their films. That way, they successfully connected with the Odia audience who looked upon such singers with the kind of love and respect accorded to any celebrated devotee of Lord Jagannath such as Bhakta Salabeg, Dasia Bauri (another devotee from 'lower caste' whom Jagannath accepted as his dearest devotee) or Bandhu Mohanty. The Jagannath temple at Puri is also known as Nila Shaila (blue abode). There are other films such as Nila Madhav (1979) which refer to Jagannath as the 'blue' lord. The song *Nila Sindhu Teere* (lyrics by Nikunja Kishore Das) in the film describes the Jagannath temple as Nilachal (the blue abode), the sea on whose shore the temple is situated as *Nila Sindhu* (the blue sea), the wheel at the top of the Jagannath temple as *Nila Chakra* (blue wheel) and even the clouds above as *Nila Meghamala* (blue clouds).

The colour blue is of immense significance in Hinduism, as not only Lord Krishna and Lord Rama are depicted as being blue-bodied, Lord Shiva too is also called Nilakanth (the Lord with a blue throat) which is a result of him drinking poison to save humanity. Blue is the colour of nature, as sky, ocean, lakes, rivers, etc. are all blue in colour. Lord Jagannath, his temple, as well as the sea on whose shore the Puri temple is situated are all described to be blue, thus signifying the Lord being at one with Nature, in an all-pervasive manner. Through the song *Nila Sindhu Teere* in *Sri Jagannath*, the film reminds the audience of this connection with Nature, where not just everybody, but everything belongs to the Lord and the Lord belongs to all. Even though colour green is usually associated with nature, in Hindu religion, one can see color blue signifying the one-ness with nature. Spiritual leader Sadhguru Jaggi Vasudeva has the following to say about colour blue:

> Blue is the color of all-inclusiveness. You will see in the existence, anything that is vast and beyond your perception generally tends to be blue, whether it is the ocean or the sky. Anything which is larger than your perception tends to be blue because blue is the basis of all-inclusiveness. It is based on this that so many gods in India are shown as blue-skinned. Shiva has a blue skin, Krishna has a blue skin, Rama has a blue skin. It is not that their skin was blue. They were referred to as blue gods because they had a blue aura. (Vasudeva, 'Meaning of Colours', 2017, web source)

Odia Cinema's Thrust on the Importance of Bhakti and Gyana in a True Jagannath Devotee

A close look at some Odia mythological films shows a wonderful way in which spirituality and modernity can coexist, where a devotee and a progressive community can form synergies which complement and support each other for a well-rounded and fulfilling life. *Bandhu Mohanty* is one such film. One of the most pertinent issues that it explores is the way it forces the audience dwell upon the amalgamation of bhakti and *gyana* in the life of a devotee. Bhakti is often construed as an outpouring of emotions by the devotee(s) towards their chosen deity. We see an example of this bhakti infused with emotions in pilgrims thronging religious spots but more so when we witness special occasions like Kumbha Mela, Krishna Janmashtami or the Jagannath rath yatra attracting millions of devotees to Haridwar, Mathura or Puri. A large mass of people world over is steered by the belief that greater forces are at play during certain times of the year or at specific sites considered sacred. Somewhere deep down, the human race seeks redemption, relief, peace, solace and catharsis through the occasion of religion itself.

Swami Vivekananda explains the aspiration of the human race to eternal life as the very reason for religions to come into existence.[7] As he traces the history of religions in the world, he argues that at some point every religion confers the highest expression of life becoming possible, when our perception exceeds the five senses. The five senses work towards creating separations vis-à-vis another perception inspiring inclusion. Therefore, when the pilgrim sways to devotional music in Mathura or offers oblations to the deity on the banks of the Ganga, in that moment there is a bid to lose oneself. In losing oneself, the sense of separation is momentarily weakened and suddenly one feels being part of a greater whole. The lives of devotees such as Bandhu Mohanty, Dasia Bauri or Balaram Das are unconcerned of the occasion or site of devotion, since time and space are replaced by constant communion with the deity. This is what brings us to dwell upon the amalgamation of bhakti and *gyana* in the life of a devotee. The *Gita* functions as a syncretic text in weaving together ideas which could otherwise entail long stand-alone debates, like the subjects of bhakti and *gyana*. In the chapter titled 'Gyana-Vigyana Yoga', Swami Ranganathananda begins the discussion by bringing home the interdependence between these two concepts. 'Bhakti is based on emotion and it concerns with handling that emotion intelligently and in a right way with the help of *gyana*' (Ranganathananda 2015: 188). Lord Krishna tells Arjuna that with a mind intent on Him, will the devotee perceive the universe as a single consciousness. The film *Bandhu Mohanty* begins with a song by Mohanty in which he praises the Lord using the highest precepts of *gyana*: '*Nirguna aatma guna banta tora mahima*'. Mohanty's devotion has given him the realisation that the Lord who is without attributes or is *nirguna*, through his greatness has assumed *guna* or attributes. The Lord does so to make himself available to his myriad devotees who can recognise the Lord only in this form. But Bandhu Mohanty, who is the Lord's *bandhu* (friend) has learnt to see him beyond the form.

Swami Ranganathananda explains how the *vigyani*

> who is more intimately acquainted with the Brahman, realizes something more. He realizes that the steps are made of the same materials as the roof: bricks, lime, and brick dust. That which is realized intuitively as Brahman, through the eliminating process of 'not this, not this', is then found to have become the universe

> and all its living beings. The vijnani sees that the Reality which is *nirguna*, without attributes is also *saguna*, with attributes. (2015: 191)

It is through this experience that Mohanty's experience of the Lord defies space and time. However, such knowledge does not deter Mohanty from performing the required actions in his everyday life and taking strong steps. In the film, we see Mohanty unafraid of anybody. When other villagers are afraid of going to the king to inform him of their inability to pay tax owing to financial difficulties, Mohanty shows no such fear. When a villager asks him if he is not afraid of the king too, he breaks into the song, '*Mahabahu ... Tumhe thau thau kaha pada tale Lotaibi Mora Matha*' which would roughly translate to, 'Hey Lord, when you are there, why should I bow my head before somebody else?'

A possible reason for a devotee and saint like Bandhu Mohanty to have remained so fearless could lie in the religious text *Bhagabat* penned by *Atibadi* (the great one) Jagannath Das, a contemporary of poet Balaram Das. *Bandhu Mohanty* uses this seminal text at some key moments in the film to advance its theological discourse. One such key moment occurs when the king seeks Bandhu Mohanty's advice on an important matter, to which Bandhu Mohanty replies by quoting from *Bhagabat*. He quotes, '*Mana tohara nija guru, Uddhaba kete tu pacharu*', which means that one should seek answers to one's problems from deep within his heart. Thus, it is within oneself that solutions to one's problems lie. But this approach to life could sometimes be construed as asocial and individualistic. One may possibly posit a question at this point regarding the *bhakta*'s identity—does he or she have one? Society is habitual in recognising individuality within a deterministic idiom. How does one reconcile a Bandhu Mohanty and a growing section of people in the modern world whose perception of Lord Jagannath as a deity as opposed to a way of life (as for Mohanty) are two veritably different realities?

Historically seen, the lives of saints and great devotees like Bandhu Mohanty have been instrumental in bolstering faith and adulation in the deity. A life governed by love of the divine so much so that no amount of trials, insults, penury seem to deter the faith of the devotee is what marks one as different from all others. There is perhaps no identity here, but a very diffuse one, enough to carry out one's daily activities, particularly in Bandhu Mohanty's story. The Odia community's identity surrounding the Lord, on the other hand is significant, since it inspires the Odia people to embrace a humanism inspired by Lord Jagannath's universal spirit. Guruprasad Mohapatra and Swati Samantaray espouse:

> The cult of Lord Jagannath is the rendezvous of religion with philosophy. Jagat (cosmos) is the Flux. Jagannath (Jagat + nath) is revered to be the Lord of this flux inhabiting and presiding over it. Hence, He is the symbol of divine dynamism. Jagannath consciousness constitutes an eclectic stream of thoughts, assimilating and incorporating ingenious cultic influences in order to emerge itself as an exceptional convergence of diverging religiosities. (2017: 173)

The devotee's existence leans towards deeper spiritual consciousness whereas the community's identity functions to structure and support a cultural and religious movement. A survey of films in this chapter may offer a glimpse into a future when a devotee like Bandhu Mohanty and an advanced Odia community may form harmonious synergies, which complement and support each other to strive for a better way of life.

Conclusion

Though the Odia community identifies strongly with Lord Jagannath, He is referred to as *Jagat ra Nath* (Lord of the Universe). As in many folklores and literature about the Lord, Odia cinema too has addressed the issue of the Lord exhorting his devotees to rise above artificial societal identity-markers and embrace universal brotherhood and humanism. Through a close reading of select films, this chapter has tried to examine the nature of an identity formation which is not based on exclusionary practices.

Furthermore, a discussion of the said Odia films engaged with the idea of bhakti not just in terms of love and adulation, but also something that is infused with *gyana*, wherein the *gyani* (the enlightened one) understands the non-duality between him and the Lord, or understands the dichotomies of the world as tricks of the mind. Through a close reading of specific cinematic depictions, an attempt has been made to explore how the devotee negotiates with the world, especially looking at the practice of devotion by a renunciate and the householder, both framed within a single principle of bhakti. Apart from looking at the ways in which Lord Jagannath has been historically represented in Odia cinema, we have also seen in this chapter how Odia cinema has helped popularise various myths, legends and folklores regarding Lord Jagannath in interesting and easily relatable ways.

Though geographically mapped in and identified with the state of Odisha from a historical perspective, the syncretic and egalitarian Jagannath culture shines through its sacral texts and the various myths, legends and folklores that underline the inclusive nature of the Jagannath philosophy. Odia films, especially the ones dealing with Jagannath and Jagannath mythology, have played a major role in propagating the Jagannath culture among the Odia community. Through their thrust on the egalitarian ideals of a syncretic Jagannath culture, Odia films dealing with Jagannath in some way, as pointed out in this chapter, have not only helped strengthen the historic bond between Lord Jagannath and the Odia community, but have also helped foster a community identity that is both traditional and modern; it is not averse to the universal ideals of modernity, but does not elide local realities and experiences, either.

Acknowledgements

I am grateful to Prof. Jatindra Kumar Nayak, Prof. B.N. Patnaik, Dr Sagarika Chattopadhyay, Dr Animesh Mahapatra, Dr Pranay Kumar Swain and Dr Joe Varghese Yeldho for offering their help at various stages of the research for this chapter.

Notes

1. According to the Indian Census data, the literacy rate of Odisha was at 15.8 per cent in 1951 and 21.6 per cent in 1961.
2. Dola Yatra is one of many Jagannath-centric festivals celebrated in Odisha. The representative deities of Dola Govinda, Bhudevi and Sreedevi are taken in a procession to *Dola bedi*, a special dais made for the deities, located outside the outer compound of the main temple in Puri and other Jagannath temples across the state, where special rites are performed. On this day, Odia calendar gets ready and is offered to Lord Jagannath, also known as Dola Govinda.
3. For a nuanced understanding of *darshan*, and its difference from the conventional European-American understanding of gaze informed by Freud, Lacan and Kaplan, please refer to Uttara Asha Coorlawala's '*Darshan* and *Abhinaya*: An Alternative to the Male Gaze', 1996, *Dance Research Journal*, Vol. 28, No 1, pp. 19–27.
4. For a detailed account of the difficult material condition in which *Sri Sri Mahalakshmi Puja* was made, please refer to the chapter 'Tumaku Michha, Aamaku Sata' in Sarat Chandra Pujari's autobiography *Nijaswa Chitranatya: Smrutipatha*, 2015, pp. 162–174.
5. For a detailed discussion on the similarity between rituals of Jagannath temple and a normal Odia household, see Pranay Kumar Swain's 'Domestication of Jagannath Temple Rituals in Odia Households: A Sociological Understanding of the Pantheism' in this book.
6. For a detailed discussion on *Banikantha* Nimai Harichandan and the emergence of the singer-devotee tradition in Odisha, see Animesh Mohapatra's 'Worldliness of the Otherworldly' in this book.
7. Please refer to the chapter 'The Necessity of Religion' by Swami Vivekananda in the *Complete Works,* Vol. II, for a comprehensive understanding.

References

Bandhu Mohanty. 1977. Directed by Nitai Palit. Bhubaneswar: Priyadarshini Films.

Das Gupta, Chidanand. 1989. 'Seeing and Believing, Science and Mythology: Notes on the Mythological Genre'. *Film Quarterly*, 42(4): 12–18.

Dwyer, R. 2006. *Filming the Gods: Religion and Indian Cinema*. London and New York: Routledge.

Ghosh, Kartik Kumar. 1984. *Odia Chalachitrara Itihasa*. Cuttack: Odisha Bookstore.

Kaliya Mardan. 1919. Directed by Dadasaheb Phalke. Mumbai: Hindustan Cinema Films.

Kotie Manisha Gotie Jaga. 1991. Directed by Vijay Bhaskar. Cuttack: Tirumala Pictures.

Lalita. 1949. Directed by Kalyan Gupta. Calcutta: Great Eastern Movieton.

Mohapatra, Guruprasad and Swati Samantaray. 2017. 'From Inner Peace to World Peace: Jagannath Consciousness in the Literature of Odisha'. *Rupkatha Journal of Interdisciplinary Studies in Humanities*, 9(4): 169–178.

Nair, P.K. 1980. 'Silent Films in the Archive'. *Cinema Vision*, 1(1): 104–113.

Panda, Namita. 10 August 2010. 'Sur Badshah Ceases to Sing: Noted Singer Sikandar Alam Passes Away after Cardiac Arrest'. *The Telegraph*. Available at https://www.telegraphindia.com/1100810/jsp/orissa/story_12790780.jsp (accessed 15 June 2018).

Pujari, Sarat Chandra. 2015. *Nijaswa Chitranatya: Smrutipatha*. Bhubaneswar: Shiksha Sandhana.

Rajadhyaksha, Ashish, ed. 1987. *Indian Cinema*. New Delhi: Directorate of Film Festivals.

Ranganathananda, Swami. 2005. *Universal Message of the Bhagvad Gita*, Vol. 2. Kolkata: Advaita Ashram: Kolkata.

Rao, L. 1989. 'Woman in Indian Films—A Paradigm of Continuity and Change'. *Media, Culture & Society*, 11(4): 443–458.

Rao, Maithili. 1995. 'To Be a Woman'. In *Frames of Mind: Reflections on Indian Cinema*, edited by Aruna Vasudev, 241–256. New Delhi: UBS Publishers.

Reddi, U. 1989. 'Media and Culture in Indian Society: Conflict or Co-operation?' *Media, Culture & Society*, 11(4): 395–413.

Singh, V. 30 June 2016. 'We have Made the Story the New Hero'. Available at www.boxofficeindia.co.in (accessed 11 August 2018).

Sri Jagannath. 1950. Directed by Chita Ranjan Mitra. Calcutta: Rupa Bharati.

Sri Sri Mahalakshmi Puja. Directed by Biswanath Nayak. Odisha: Krushna Chandra Tripathy Sharma.

Vasudeva, Jaggi. 2017. 'Meaning of Colours and Their Role in Your Life'. Available at https://isha.sadhguru.org/in/en/wisdom/article/meaning-of-colors (accessed 30 December 2018).

Vivekananda, Swami. 1989. *The Complete Works of Swami Vivekananda*, Vol. II. Kolkata: Advaita Ashram.

4

THE *PRABACHANAS* AS PERFORMATIVES: TRACING THE MORAL GROUNDS OF SPIRITUAL DISCOURSE IN THE JAGANNATH CULTURE

Ranjan Kumar Panda

Introduction: Prabachana as a Spiritual Discourse

Prabachana is a Sanskrit term defined as *prakrusta vachana*, that is, a *bachana* (saying) which is well-cultivated or *prakrusta* (*pra+krush+ta)* before its expression. In contemporary Indian society, *prabachanas* refer to spiritual discourses given by *prabachakas* who have knowledge of some sacred texts and treatises. In a spiritual discourse, a *prabachaka* narrates many episodes while giving a *prabachana* by referring to gods and goddesses and their *leelas* (cosmic actions) and *mahimas* (greatness) that are described in Vedas, Upanishads, Puranas, the *Ramayana* and the *Mahabharata*. The *leelas* are cosmic actions, hence, they are construed as extraordinary from the perspective of ordinary everyday life. In the spiritual discourse of Jagannath, his *leelas* are narrated keeping in mind the contemporary society. The narration involves spiritual-moral knowledge which is disseminated into the *shrotas* (listeners) through the discourses. I am neither a *prabachaka* nor a participant of any such discourse. Instead, after a few sessions of repeated and attentive listening to these *prabachanas*, commentaries and speeches, this chapter seeks to examine the questions of performativity, belongingness and authenticity in the context of daily life—arguing that the act of devotion blurs the ontological distinction between the devotee and the deity, complicating the experiential relationship of communication and casting the spiritual aspect of faith with the material.

This chapter is focused on Jagannath *prabachana* and the philosophical and humanistic accounts that underlie the spiritual–moral discourses. Taking a cue from Taylor's (2013) viewpoint on the performative nature of *prabachana*, particularly with reference to *Bhagabat Prabachana* in Hindi, I have delved into *Jagannathnka Amrutabani* which is a series of recorded *prabachanas* given by *prabachaka* Charana Ram Das. References are also made to other lectures, commentaries during Jagannath's rath yatra (chariot festival) and a number of personal discussions with *prabachaka*, namely with *prabachaka* Sarada Prasanna Kar are undertaken to comprehend the essential elements of *prabachana*. Theorising upon the performative nature of *prabachana*, the chapter also highlights how spiritual discourses have both epistemic and normative grounding. However, it needs to be stated at the outset that the chapter is restrictive in its reading. One of them is that I have tried to develop this chapter by taking into account a few *Odia prabachanas* that are available on the Internet. There are also Jagannatha *prabachanas* in Hindi, but I have deliberately studied the *Odia prabachanas* because the semantics of any cultural activity and its literary history can be meaningfully traced only through its native language. Second, the chapter lacks a first-hand experience of listening to any live lectures or *prabachanas*. The availability of recorded *prabachanas* on the web has created a new genre of spiritual discourse. Particularly, the Jagannath *prabachanas* are produced in order to be consumed by the Odias who live outside the state or have no opportunity to directly participate in the discourses. The chapter, further, brings out the popularity of Jagannath and also tries to analyse the significance of materiality of religion.

The chapter is divided into three sections apart from the introduction and the conclusion. In the first section, an attempt is made to trace the historical origin of *prabachana* as a genre of practising spirituality in Jagannath culture. It was started largely by the *panchasakha*[1] with the emergence of the Puranas in Odia literature. It also brings out the act of performing a *prabachana*, with reference to Charana Ram Das's discourse on Jagannath. *Prabachana* as a performative was grounded on the normative attitude of the *prabachaka* and the *shrotas*; the addresser and the addressees. Das's narration unfolds the bonding between Jagannath and his devotees grounded on devotion. In the second section, the chapter highlights the importance of *bhakti-bhava* (devotional feeling) that creates a bond between *bhakta* and *bhagwan*—devotee and deity. Devotion creates a ground for 'belongingness' which is essential for inter-subjective understanding. Moreover, the intentionality of bhakti as an emotional force transcends the form of ordinary linguistic discourses. In this section, the intent of the listener's point of view and the changing scenario of spiritual activity referring to the presence of spiritual discourses in the form of material religion are discussed. The third section delves into the notion of authority and authenticity of *prabachana* focusing on the significance of *sabda pramana* (verbal testimony). Ramachandra Gandhi's (1974) construal of the performative is delved into by emphasising the notion of 'addressing' that 'solicits' the attention of the hearer but never to 'elicit' a response. The normativity of the act of addressing is also brought in to strengthen the intentional notion of belongingness. In conclusion, the chapter shows the mystical presence of Jagannath in the everyday life and this not only poses an epistemic challenge but also shows the unending aspirations of the people to show their 'belongingness' and to the popularisation of Jagannath culture.

Tracing the History of Prabachana and Speaking about the Deity—Lord Jagannath

Prabachanas as spiritual discourses have had a long presence in the history of Odia culture, particularly with reference to Valmiki's *Ramayana patha* prevalent in Odisha during the fourteenth century.[2] This discourse was certainly confined to a group of learned Sanskrit scholars (*panditas*)[3] who would disseminate spiritual and moral teachings of the epics and the Puranas among the masses. *Purana Panda* (a scholar with the knowledge of sacred texts) was a title given to honour someone with a mastery of the scriptures and an ability to give spiritual discourses. These scriptural discourses had moral and cultural significance. These discourses were also conducted at *Mukti Mandapa* in the premises of the Jangannatha temple at Srikshetra Puri (Malik 2007: 304).

The fifteenth century was a turning point in Odia literary history with the emergence of Sudramuni Sarala Dasa and the *panchasakha*—Balarama Dasa, Jagannatha Dasa, Achyutananda Dasa, Jasobanta Dasa and Ananta Dasa—who were also known as *Sudramunis* the saint poets and writers. All of them were deeply influenced by Lord Jagannath. And, Srikshetra Puri was already known for its religious culture and transaction as people from all other parts of India started visiting Jagannath (Das 1982: 69). Jagannath was the established deity of the Odias (Kulke 2014: 271–282) and gradually Puri gained popularity as *purusottama dhama*. The religious transaction includes the preaching of the *panchasakha*, who undermined the religious externalities and emphasised the inner voyage of life with devotion primarily to explore the inner spiritual presence of the divinity in man. Religious discussion and discourses were conducted in Odia. The vernacular medium became very popular to meet the common spiritual aspirations of the common people of Odisha.

It was during this time that 'Sarala Dasa stood against the straightjacket of the tradition of Odisha' (Das 1978: 147). Sarala's Odia *Mahabharata*, was composed approximately in the year 1475 and was one of the popular Mahabharatas of Eastern India (Satpathy and Nayak 2014: 10). It was popular not only from the perspective of aesthetic dimension but also represented 'a bold mirror of the aspirations of the contemporary society that wanted to get away from the narrow determinations of the age-long past and come to itself, come of age, come back to its own language, to its own life and enlightenment and realization' (Das 1982: 69). Sarala's vernacular intervention in the spiritual discourses of that time was a great marker of departure from the hegemony of Sanskrit and the tradition of *Purana Pandas*.

The new language was the 'language of the people' in which the *Mahabharata*, *Ramayana*, *Bhagabata* and other sacred scriptures were composed by the *panchasakha* in simple poetic forms delivering the complex content of these rich texts. This had a direct effect on *prabachana* as people were familiar with the language and the meaning was easily comprehensible. Apart from the dominance of the vernacular to meet the people's aspirations, the content of their discourses and preaching emphasised the cultivation of bhakti or devotion as the medium of relation between the *bhaktas* (the devotees) and the *bhagaban* (the deity). Thus, it opened a new vista for spiritual discourse in Odisha. It reached the common people in the villages, and gradually, the *Bhagabata* became more popular as we find the presence of *bhagabatatungis*[4] in most of the villages of Odisha (Patanaik 2009: 119). These *tungis* were the shared space for a collective engagement in spiritual discourses.

The spiritual discourse unfolds the presence of the poetic and musical elements in Odisha's literary culture which had a strong association with Jagannath. Apart from the development of bhakti literature by these saint poets, there are two other reasons which brought the impulse of musicality to the spiritual discourse. They are Jayadev's *Geeta Govindam* which used to be sung every day in the Jagannath temple. The lyrics of *Geeta Govindam* were special following which 'song and music got prominence' (Das 2009: 577) while addressing the God. And second, the *kirtan*—which literally means 'mentioning' or 'enumeration', was very popular as folk-music was used as a form of worship (Bake 1936–1937: 69). In this connection, *sankirtan*, a musical dance with devotional songs and hymns was introduced by Chaitanya, as a unique form of spiritual expression (Mukherjee 1979: 113–121). The development of poetic musicality must have positively helped not only in the development of singing bhajans and *jananas* (devotional songs) but also in the use of musical instruments during the performance which exhibits high aesthetic sensibilities.

With the expansion of the Odia language and under the influence of devotional spiritual culture there emerged bhajan and *janana* that appealed to the common people. People could relate to Jagannath for a variety of reasons and, 'He (Jagannath) appeared everything to everybody' (Das 1982: 26). This appearance is not merely symbolic, rather it shows a practical assimilation of various religious cultures[5] in the emerging waves of Jagannath culture. One could sing a bhajan or *janana* at home to capture its expressive devotional content and thereby express one's own *bhaktibahava*—devotional feelings. These bhajan and *jananas* were usually sung in the *tungis* or in a common gathering before the beginning of spiritual discourse; it opened up a new genre of practising spirituality.

Jagannath is primarily the god of Odias, but the literal interpretation of this name suggests that he is the lord of the whole cosmos that was both held by the *sabaras* and by the non-*sabaras*. As Das points out, 'Jagannath or Jaganta as the Sabaras have it in their own vocabulary meaning the "Lord of the whole universe" should with greater justification be attributed to the Sabaras who originally worshiped it, as a fetish and a symbol' (1982: 29). Jagannath represents the universal cosmic consciousness—Brahman. He is a unique God in the sense that he is fundamentally different from the gods who are present in *tridhamas*—Badrinath, Dwarikanath and Rameswar. Purusottamakshetra or Srikshetra being another *dhama* regarded at par with the spiritual significance of other *dhamas*. The uniqueness of *Purusottamadhama* is traced not only in its history and culture, but also in the dissemination of meaning of consciousness of Brahman.

Charana Ram Das begins his discourse invoking the Lord Jagannath as *sachidanandaswarupa* an embodiment of existence, consciousness and bliss. He further describes him as *anandakanda*—the abode of bliss. Invocation is an essential part of *prabachana* and it signifies an attitude of obedience offered in the form of prayer. Almighty is addressed through prayer and blessing and is thereby 'solicited'. Gradually, Ram Das 'invites' the audience to participate in the spiritual discourse. The cardinal features of this spiritual engagement commence with the uttering of *Harinama*. *Harinama sankirtan*, for Ram Das, is a simple means of expressing devotion to God in *Kaliyug*. Chanting *Harinama* is a performative act, because only a living person can chant this for attaining spiritual well-being. A devotional chanting has the power of immersing the person in spirituality. Using an idiom, Ram Das simplifies saying: 'Do not worry, make merry and repeat Hari.' The 'chanting' is not a repetitive mechanical exercise of uttering a name, rather it refers to the process of meditative thinking, devotedly undertaken in order to realise its 'transformative power'.

According to Charana Ram Das, it is essential to realise the significance of the transformative power of spiritual discourses as they aim at explaining the significance of values like love, trust, happiness, friendship, etc. in society. He narrates two episodes referring to this relationship between the devotee and the deity. They are, Dasia's offering of *sriphala* (coconut) to Jagannath, and

Jagannath's own inclination to eat *panasha* (jackfruit) along with the poet Balarama Dasa. In both the episodes the deity Jagannath has shown immense evidence of sharing 'love' and 'trust' with his devotees. In these episodes, Ram Das recounts that a devotee must have integrity and devotion in life. The narrative style of *prabachana* is such that it highlights various other episodes from the Puranas, the *Ramayana* and the *Mahabharata*, such as Krishna-Sudama, Gaja-Kumbhira, Ratnakara-Valmiki, etc. and relate them interestingly to various aspects of real life situations.

The *prabachaka* finds that many social problems have arisen due to loss of morals in the society. While explaining the deterioration of morals, Charana Ram Das interestingly furthers the discourse stating that 'the whole culture has emerged from war—"*amara sanskruti jyudhyaru srusti*"'. The source of this conflict is *ahamkara* (ego). The egoistic attitude has been destroying social peace and harmony. Sometimes in family life we fail to overcome ego and act irresponsibly. This capricious behaviour results in the overlooking of certain basic commitments and obligation of life which consequently destroys peace and harmony in the family. Hence, he urges us to overcome ego which will help in loosening the grip of conflicts and differences and it could be transformative if love and affection prevail in us. Therefore, Charana Ram Das's another *mantra* is 'Help ever; Hurt Never'.

To love (*prema*) is a virtue that helps in sustaining a relation. In this regard, Ram Das says, *patnyat trayate ja sa patni*—that is 'wife is a person who saves her husband from a moral failure'. Loving relations create life. The other meaning of *patni* refers to *pratisruti*—a person to whom the husband is committed. Commitment, obligation, care, love and affection if nurtured in a family then transform it into a home of noble values—*baikunta sama se ghara*; *paraspara sneha bhava thaenirantara*—a home becomes heaven if its people live together with love and affection. In this connection, he urges us to lead a life following *dharma*—which signifies the normativity of life. This chapter is not interested in discussing the notion of *dharma*, rather I would like to draw your attention to the notion of *bhava* and then return to reflect on the notion of *dharma* in the concluding section.

Being in Devotion: The Presence of Shrotas during Prabachana

Devotion is bhakti which refers to a form of emotional feeling called *bhava.* Being in devotion is about experiencing the deepest feeling—the *bhakti-bhava.* Tracing its presence in philosophical religious tradition of India, Krishna Sharma elucidates,

> In Indian Philosophy, *Bhakti* or devotion has an important place. It is the emotional relationship of man with God. In Indian theology Bhakti is self-sufficient for leading man to Salvation. Like all the other philosophical systems and religious thoughts in India the root of Bhakti is also placed in Vedas. The Upasanakandas of Vedas are the origin of the Bhakti marga. (1987: 28)

To live in the path of bhakti underlines the normative condition in which the self is passionately involved in search of god. This is a loving non-dual involvement where the devotee does not recognise himself or herself in dissociation with god. This aspiration unfolds two significant aspects of bhakti; one shows the experience of feeling or the *bhava,* whereas the other corresponds to the realm of the higher values of life—mukti.

In a performative framework of communication, particularly in the spiritual discourses, it is solicited that the *shrotas* (the devoted listeners) will be able to taste the *bhakti-rasa.* As far as the affective content of this 'feeling' is concerned it could be characterised as *bhakti-rasa* which is one of the kinds of *rasa.* As Daya Krishna explicates this *bhava*, 'Man seeks something beyond what he is, something more than just feeling or emotion, and the creation, and the creation of art itself is an evidence of this, just as are his enterprises in other fields such as knowledge and action' (2011: 90). Daya brings out the creative element of the *rasa* in the artistic creation of life. The *bhakti-rasa* has the power of elevating life to the higher realm of consciousness. It is thereby no less powerful in comparison to knowledge (*jňana*) and action (*karma*). In fact, there is a convergence of knowledge, action and devotion that yields 'self-knowledge' (Sharma 1987: 65). Nevertheless, devotion (bhakti) is spiritually more powerful because it immerses the devotee (*bhakta*) in the free flowing stream of bhava in order to grasp the spiritual (Sharma 1987: 48). Thus, it is important to expedite how the *prabachana* as a communicative art invokes this spiritual devotional feeling in the heart of the devotee—the *shrotas*.

The *prabachaka's* invocation and narration are an effort to induce *bhakti-bhava* by highlighting, as mentioned in the earlier section, various popular episodes depicted in Puranas (sacred scriptures). As *bhavas* are located in the body, *prabachana* as a genre of the performative refers to various modes of speaking where the facial expression, modulation and tenor of speech change (Austin 1962). Unless *prabachana* creates a devotional atmosphere in which *prabachaka* and *shrotas* are spiritually engaged, the merit of the *prabachana* is doubtful. One can doubt the sincerity and honesty of the *prabachaka* and challenge his intention and feelings because these all are based on first-person authority (Heal 2002). The normative condition of a performative expression tries to overcome this limitation which is discussed in the subsequent section of the chapter. Rather, the main contention is how *prabachana* as performativity could be discussed as a meaningful source of experience that yields a bond between the devotee and deity.

According to Ram Das, the sharing of *bhakti-bhava* creates devotional communicative relationship that develops through love and affection, trust and obligation, commitment and simplicity, compassion and submission in life. While dwelling in this emotional communicative 'field' of devotion one can renounce the power of ego/self which is otherwise hard to give up. Hence, the *prabachaka* appeals to the listeners to reflect upon the normative content of sharing. In devotion, 'sharing' maintains no hierarchy between the deity and devotee; it is nurtured with the content of 'caring'. In this regard, the episode of Dasia Bauri reveals how the Brahman (the priest) rushed back home with an intention to learn the secret mantra from Dasia, so that he can be like Dasia. At that moment, Brahman realises that 'to be' is to be like Dasia.

The Brahman's aspiration to become someone like Dasia shows a 'transformative moment' of life which makes him believe that a 'meaningful existence' could be above the realm of mantra and tantra. And such existence can be purely conceived in the state of *bhakti-bhava.* God in this context is, therefore, known as *bhava binodiaya.* Exchange of *bhava* in *binoda* is something that takes away the veil of ignorance. The Brahman realises this when he encounters Dasia's wife. He learns how a family ought to live, share and care for each other. And such mode of sharing deconstructs the social structure of learning. In Ram Das' interpretation, Brahman had no inhibitions in learning from the wife of Dasia. Thus, the *prabachaka* establishes the contemporary significance of equality not only in terms of caste but also in terms of gender.

Following the ethos of *panchasakha's bhakti-bhava*, *prabachaka*, Sarada Prasanna Kar during one discussion mentioned that *prabachakas* try to uphold the culture of bhakti tradition. Referring to the language and *bhava*, A.K. Ramanujan writes,

> Feelings are more important than learning, status, and privilege. In fact, status, punditry, even maleness and the pride that goes with such things are seen as obstacles to a true experience of god. Once such a position is taken, anyone at all qualified to experience god. To be human is to be qualified. (1992: 54)

A *bhakta* is known by the *bhava*—the true intent of devotion. Social status and qualifications are insignificant. Dasia's devotion qualified because of his true 'feeling' for Jagannatha. Dasia's feeling for seeking god's grace transcended all kinds of language, of *mantra* or *tantra* by the pundits. Dasia had no desire to 'become' powerful or wealthy; on the contrary, he 'solicited' the blessings of Jagannath who responded in an extraordinary manner.

This extraordinary reciprocity that lies between a *bhakta* and *bhagwan* is not just symbolic, but has the power of melting down the ontological division between the human and the god. Devotional engagement creates an 'intentional bond' between the deity and the devotee to live together. Illustrating this bond, Ramanujan points out that, 'The god is as human as he is divine' (Ramanujan 1992: 53). A new form of identity thus emerges from this devotional bonding. The *prabachaka* tries to translate and simplify the dense content of the devotional bonding.

In a *prabachana* many types of people assemble to listen to the *prabachaka*. They can be categorised in terms of their intent of engagement in the spiritual discourses, clarifies *prabachaka*, Sarada Prasanna Kar. Some *shrotas* are deeply immersed in the devotional content of the scriptures and the *prabachana* does help them to grasp its content. They belong to the first category. There are a few who ask questions and their concern is confined to rational interpretation of the scriptures. They are argumentative and their approach can be categorised as rational information centric. And, the last category of *shrotas* is the one that comes for amusement—they come to listen to music and to 'gaze' at the lady singers or the beautiful lady *shrotas* present at the gatherings. The erotic perception of the *shrotas* cannot be ruled out in such a gathering. Hence, Kar prudently mentions that it is always a challenge to be attentively narrating the contents to all these kinds of *shrotas*.

Laghukathas or idioms are basically used during *prabachanas* to attract the attention of the *shrotas*, simply to delight the audience and thereby succeeding in also simplifying some of the complex concepts. For example, during the *prabachana*, Ram Das starts by saying, '*Kaliara nahi jati lo Rangabati*'. *Rangabati* is a very popular folk song in Odisha. In the song the terms refers to a beautiful lady. Kalia Jagannath as he is popularly addressed is a great lover of beauty and hence for him there is no discrimination of any kind. He loves everybody. The term, *rangabati*, beauty, love, etc., when put in colloquial terms ignite a different *bhava* in the audience. Lady listeners feel shy whereas the *shrotas* who have gone there merely for enjoyment find it amusing.

In the contemporary society when there are *Pravashi Odias* (Odias who are living outside the state of Odisha) it is rare to participate in the live *prabachanas* but it is easy to watch and listen to the recorded versions. The virtual participation in such spiritual discourses has many nuances which are *bhava* centric. Hence, the aesthetic prominence of *prabachakas'* style of presentation, accompanied by female singers and the musicians, beautification of the stage, cannot be ignored. In a real life scenario, sometimes female accompanying singers do attract young audiences and these viewers of the *prabachanas* do admire the beautiful voices, their looks and smiles, clarifies *prabachaka* Sarada Prasanna Kar. Similarly, in the virtual world, 'visibility and visual subjects are sharing a complex relationship which is shaped by modes of perception' (Heidbrink and Miczek 2010: 3). These modes of perception whether in real or in the virtual life engagement are what Michel Foucault calls 'seeing through desire'—people take pleasure in whatever they intend to see (Rajchman 1988: 105). Hence, it is important to note that being engaged in a devoted fashion and watching religious programmes is not merely about spiritual imagination or the use of reason. Instead, the sensual dimension of religious practices cannot be ignored, because that constitutes the *material religion* which refers to the virtual presence of religion on the Internet (Heidbrink and Miczek 2010: 3). In religion and religious engagement, particularly when this kind of materiality is accessed, it shows active sensuous involvement. In this connection, the religious engagements put emphasis on 'the body and the space it inhabits' (Heidbrink and Miczek 2010: 4). Thus, the modes of perception of the *shrotas* are very important as far as their participation in the spiritual discourses is concerned.

However, modes of perception of the *shrotas* don't entirely wash away the spiritual content of the discourse. The *prabachaka* rather aims at retaining the spiritual ethos of the *prabachana* by using bhajans (devotional poems) and *laghukathas* (parables) intermittently, and addressing the *shrotas* as *sadhujana* (ascetic people) or *bidagdha shrota mandali* (devotionally immersed fellow listeners) which could prompt them to return to the main theme of the discourse. As a *prabachaka* he not only tries to relate to the audience, but also intends to relate to the divine. *Prabachana* is an important mode to establish co-identity with the divine, remarks McComas Taylor (2013: 274). Even if the *prabachaka* uses idioms and colloquial terms to amuse the fellow audience, still this effort could be construed as a form of 'localising god'. For Ramanujan, the use of 'mother tongue' while expressing your devotion shows how 'god is localised and worshiped in local forms' (1992: 54). This in fact, was initiated by the *panchasaka* and continues to prevail. But how does this linguistic form of communication forge co-identity? To understand this Charana Ram Das explains the semantic significance of the *bhakti-rasa*—the aesthetic element of devotion.

The aesthetic element of bhakti, as we have mentioned, is ultimately grounded in intentional 'felt experience' and hence sometimes during the spiritual discourse, the *prabachaka* transcends the conventional structural boundaries and the genre of poetic expression. The *prabachaka* gets so deeply immersed in thought that referring to this intentional mode of engagement, Sitakanta Mohapatra says, 'The spatial and the theological depths are given up but there emerges a new realm of co-presence where the mind, its objects, other minds and the base of both minds and things are simultaneously present' (1971: 32). Thus, being in the state of devotion during *prabachana* defines its own language that suitably fits the *shrotas*. This fitness is necessary to unfold the 'feeling' of belongingness which is an epistemic relation that shows the absence of duality and, thus, succeeds in melting down the hierarchy.

Bhakta-bhagwan relation is not a master-slave relation, instead it forges an identity—that is, for Ram Das, an evidence of asserting 'sharing is caring'. In this connection, he brings out an interesting conversation between Balarama Das and Jagannath and their co-presence in sharing the jackfruit and being meted out punishment by the security guards of the Gajapati. In such poetic conversations, the language of 'felt experience' becomes unique in asserting the 'authenticity' of meaning. The *prabachaka* tries to induce authenticity repeatedly to attract the attention of the listeners. However, the auspiciousness of participation is not ignored. Rather, authenticity receives its due when the *prabachaka* succeeds in convincing the listener by citing evidences. In such cases the authenticity is an enchanting experience that facilitates showing 'objectivity' involved in 'felt experience' (Mohapatra 1971: 29).

Authority and Authenticity of Prabachana: The Normative Significance of Testimony and Addressing

The notion of authority is central to the performative discourses. The power of authority is not only derived from the person's sense of belonging to an institution but also from how one has internalised the normativity of one's being. Institution as a source of power is discussed by John Searle while theorising the nature of performative expressions. A person's intentional performative attitude is governed by the regulative rules (Searle 1969) and Gandhi (1974) critiques Searle's theorisation. In fact, Gandhi (1976) relies more on Vedantic notion of *sabda pramana*—verbal testimony (Saksena 1951). In the Indian philosophical tradition, testimony has normative significance and is considered as an independent valid source of knowledge. With reference to spiritual discourses, the notion of authority is recognised on the basis of some normative conditions, such as truthfulness, reliability and rationality. The speaker must be generally regarded as a truthful, virtuous and rational person (Saksena 1951: 48).

One can conceptualise Jagannath as an institution; his *seba* (service) and the activities of his *sebakas* (who provide seba) are devotedly carried out as not only the order of the institution but also with devotion. Unless a *prabachaka* truly acts in this order, that is, as a *sebaka* and his *prabachana* as his *seba*—(Das 1978) he would lack the authority to disseminate spiritual moral knowledge, states *prabachaka* Sarada Prasana Kar. That is to say, it is not the *panditya* and the oratory skill which enable a *prabachaka* to be engaged in spiritual discourses; rather devotion is how spiritual moral values are internalised and conceived as the guiding force of everyday life that constitutes the integral part of *prabachaka's* authority.

As an authority of scriptures and as narrator of the spiritual discourses, his prime duty is to invoke a spiritual atmosphere through the lecture. If he himself does not believe in devotion and devotional engagements, then his speech would totally misfire. Hence, in order to immerse 'others' in the devotional discourse, he has to immerse himself. He must, therefore,'believe' in whatever he says to the *bhaktas*—the devoted listeners. In this connection, *sabda pramana* emphasises three basic principles of inculcating knowledge.

They are *sravana* (listening), *manana* (being thoughtfully engaged) and *nididhyasana* (assimilation and reflection). In other words, as seeker of knowledge one not only has to listen mindfully but also assimilate those ideas through critical reflection. Therefore, uncritical examination of testimony is unacceptable (Saksena 1951: 42).

While giving testimony on the content of a discourse on 'offering', Charana Ram Das mentions that a truly heartfelt 'offering' is always accepted by god. Referring to the incident during a *prabachana* one devotee mentions that she has a plantain tree and she has 'offered' those beautiful leaves to the God. And she is curious to know whether God will accept her offering. In response to her curiosity, Charana Ram Das says, 'Of course, God will come and accept your offering as you have devotedly offered them.' Meanwhile, two days pass by and the lady keeps asking Ram Das when Jagannath will come and take those leaves. On the third day, their servant comes rushing when Ram Das is having lunch along with other devotees and mentions that one big black bull has put its front legs on the boundary walls and is stretching its mouth and eating those leaves. Hearing this news, Charana Ram Das goes running out to that bull and does *sastanga pranipata* (completely lying down on the ground with folded hands) to express his gratitude. Clarifying further, the content of this event, he addresses the lady 'Maa! If you had offered food, then Govinda, the God, would have come in human form to eat; you have offered leaves, hence Govinda arrived in animal form to eat those leaves.'

This justification sounds reasonable so far as *sabda pramana* is concerned, because what he could 'see' through this evidence is the significant element of the testimony. An ordinary person may fail to conceive of it meaningfully. As *sruti* demands confirmation through *anubhava*, similarly Ram Das as seeker of spiritual knowledge provides a competent evidence to prove that he is an *apta*—trustworthy person (Rambachan 1987: 362). *Anubhava* is one of the criteria of truth that *sabda pramana* admits to. While making a reliable claim Ram Das narrates that in order to *realise* the grace of the deity, one has to touch the feet of his beloved devotee—'*Govindaku paibaku hele Govindara bhaktara pada ku sparsha karibaku heba*'. Referring to the Puranic episode he rationalises his act of expressing gratitude to the bull—the divine. He mentions that this is what was performed by the *kumbhira* when he pulled the *gaja* into the deep water and the queens of Krishna did to Sudama in Dwarika. Thus, the *prabachaka* while delivering spiritual discourse exhibits his commitment and integrity to the tradition of *prabachana* as the genre of seeking truth. In this sense, *prabachana* has pragmatic intent to disseminate moral knowledge to devoted listeners.

The intent of *prabachana* goes beyond its pragmatic concern because like the devoted *shrotas*, the *prabachaka* is also a seeker of truth; while *addressing* the *shrotas* intermittently as *bidaddha shrota mandali* during *prabachana*, he nurtures the basic idea that how we can truly *address* Jagannath—the *Purusottama*, in our day-to-day life. The *prabachaka* through his *prabachana* not only tries to evoke the sense of devotion, but also intends to show how each one of us could cultivate a sense of reflective and devotional attitude in everyday life. Devotees like Dasia, Bandhu Mohanty, Balarama Dasa and many others, have lived an ordinary life but have been fortunate in 'receiving' the glimpse of the gracious presence of Jagannath in their act of 'addressing' and have remained in communion with Jagannath in their devotional engagement.

'Addressing', according to Gandhi, not only initiates an act of communication, but also shows an act of 'acknowledging' (1976: 27). He writes,

> Addressing comes off as a full-fledged act when my act of addressing you solicits your communicative attention, as it was your readiness to enter into a communicative relationship with me. It is this coming forth of you which is the basis of my thought of you as a 'you'. All referential, predicative, thinking falls away when you respond with communicative attention for my act of addressing you. I cannot even say I am confronted by you. The situation of communicative arousal is such that I cannot point towards you in communicatively arousing you. I cannot indicate to you or to myself the presence before me of any sort of substance ... yet I acknowledge you as you, prompt you to attend me communicatively. (1976: 33)

So when 'you' are being 'addressed' by me then 'you' and 'me' enter into a communicative relationship in which your response is solicited, that is, you are being invited to be a part of communicative attention in a personal experiential form of referring to one another. By mentioning the conceptual significance of the act of 'addressing' and 'soliciting', Gandhi critiques the Western theorisation of performatives by Austin and Searle. In a communicative mode of engagement, both the concepts have normative as well as cognitive significance. The devotee addresses the god and solicits his blessing; addressing and soliciting not only offers autonomy to the addressee but also shows how the addressee is being placed in the intentional-experiential realm of communication.

In the experiential relationship of communication 'I' experience 'you' neither as a substance nor as any other creature but rather as a caring soul who 'acknowledges' the presence of the other. While explaining further the attentive experiential form of 'addressing', Gandhi writes,

> Our experience of soul is wider when I cast another person, you, in the role of an audience ('you' arise for me in this way), I regard you as a soul—as yourself and not, or not merely, as a certain sort of creature .... The thought I am called and the thought you are full experience of soul. They are realizations of (a) the fact that I am being regarded as soul, and (b) the fact that I am regarding you as a soul. Indeed I cannot think the thought 'you' unless it amounts to my regarding you as a soul. One can say that the thought 'I' is a visualization, the thought 'you' is a realization. (1976: 30)

Here, in the context of *prabachana* when the *prabachaka* addresses the devotees as *bidagdha shrota mandali*—the learned listeners; he imaginatively 'visualises' them as aspiring 'souls' who have 'cared' to listen to him and joined him in the discourse as 'seekers' of knowledge to 'realise' the divine. This realisation enables the *prabachaka* to enter into an authentic discourse of 'seeking truth' or the presence of divine grace. Thus communicative attentions constitute a normatively driven intentional field of experience where there is mutual aspiration of 'knowing' and 'acknowledging' that results in 'intersubjective understanding' (Grossberg 1982).

As far as the mutual aspiration for 'knowing' is concerned in the context of spiritual discourse, both the *prabachakas* and *shrotas* in their act of addressing intend to have communion with God. The extraordinary absorbing gaze of Jagannath is a symbolic act of 'inviting' the devotee to be engaged in the communicative attention with him. It is a matter of 'realisation' that his benign 'soul' reciprocates to 'you' as a seeking 'soul'. This reciprocity is the meeting of the two 'souls'—the *atma* meets *paramatma* in their communion with each other. In prayer or while chanting, the *nama* initiates the communicative act. Gandhi seems to be quite persuasive to show how the seeker enters into the realm of the divine while seeking to have communion with the presence of the divine. While being initiated one might fail sometimes to experience the extraordinary that is a part of the ordinary everyday life. But for Gandhi, this experience would certainly help in 'discovering' ourselves—that is how we 'realise' ourselves. This discovery of the self is necessary to understand the presence of the divine because you 'feel' that you are being 'acknowledged'.

Conclusion: The Mystical Presence of Jagannath

To conclude, it may be stated that it is always a challenge to comprehend the mystical presence of the divine. The divine presence of Jagannath projects an ordinary form of life to people and conceals the extraordinary. Hence, the devotees as seekers need to 'discover' the extraordinary hidden in the ordinary. As Stanley Cavell mentions, 'a seeker may keep discovering' (1997: 26). While seeking spiritual knowledge the depth of understanding life is widened and a true seeker remains 'communicatively engaged' with the divine. This reciprocity of an engaged divine communion projects the divine, as Gandhi suggests, 'communicative being' (1976: 41). Largely the devotees believe that Sri Jagannath listens to the devotees and their proof comes from their personal experiences. Charana Ram Das' episode on 'the bull's eating of the banana leaves', may appear merely symbolic, but the content is true from the perspective of spirituality. For a sceptic, there is no argument to prove anything because such truths cannot be demonstrated.

Responding to the sceptics, Cavell argues that, 'We need to discover our incapacities in human knowing, but sometimes an insufficiency in acknowledging the other might result in a failure to understand oneself. This is a consequence of truth of scepticism that philosophers have largely nurtured' (1997: 26). To have an understanding of Jagannath as the incredible legend of Odisha we need to believe how Jagannath symbolises the mystic backbone of Odia culture and unless we care to 'see' divinity present in the 'ordinary'; we would fail to recognise his divine presence. It does not require any advertisement, rather demands the will to cultivate 'divine' knowledge to interpret the facts of life. His presence can only be 'felt' if we give up the attitude of egoism and scepticism altogether and cultivate the spirit of 'self-knowledge'.

Keeping the mystical presence of Jagannath and the performative nature of spiritual discourse may be construed from the perspective of primacy of the ethical; no doubt, it casts an undoubted 'faith' on God, as maintained by Emanuel Levinas (Avram 1996). The divine here is symbol of *dharma* which prevails as the binding force of making this 'living' sustainable and ever evolving. The bonding with Jagannath is grounded in bhakti and *jňana*. The *prabachakas* belong to the tradition of bhakti but their ability to interpret the scriptures highlighting their contemporary relevance shows their adherence to knowledge. For them, the culmination of knowledge and bhakti results in showing the 'transformative power' that forges an identity between devotee and deity. The transformative power of devotion and devotional engagement shows the devotee's commitment, obligation and trust in the deity. Jagannath as source of *dharma* has created this normative bond to hold his devotees together. This bonding of Jagannath is sacred and secular. Human existence is not just societal; it is normative and thereby cosmic. The normativity of spiritual discourse contains the spirit of epistemic and metaphysical inquiry, that is, *Brahma jijnasa* (aspiration to know Brahman). Jagannath being *purusottama*—cosmic universal consciousness or the Brahman has manifested in several forms; namely, Darubrahma, Annabrahma, Sabda brahma, Sangitabrahma, claims Charana Ram Das.

The notion of *Brahma jijnasa* can be traced in the intent of the ordinary expressions and actions. Charana Ram Das observes that our society is troubled by misfire, rhetoric, false propaganda and egoism that are causing violence and social unrest. Practising spirituality by means of listening to spiritual discourse may have a therapeutic value; over and above, it might kindle the spirit of Brahma *jijnasa*. Though, for some, *prabachana* is form of entertainment, still at least the presence of those who are thoughtful and devoted their effort to comprehend reality beyond its material presence cannot be neglected.

Spiritual discourses viewed through YouTube videos or television serials represent 'material religion'. The space it occupies in present social condition is largely sensuous; but one could go beyond the form to its presence and experience a new form of practising spirituality. Since society is driven by materialism and consumerism, it becomes difficult to 'see' beyond the senses. Nevertheless, spirituality demands a moment of transcendence.

In contemporary times, many people are benefited by the electronic media through which they learn and listen to all these *prabachanas* and speeches while living faraway from Odisha. The live transmission of rath yatra and its commentaries by learned *prabachakas* and scholars are spiritually engaging and are also an occasion of enchantment of the spiritual ethos of Jagannath culture. The material religion in this sense has pragmatic value. It recreates a new form of bonding that *localises* the person with its own culture. Though Charana Ram Das believes that violence is the source of the beginning of our culture, still the intent of this violence becomes the source of peace and prosperity. This connection, the birth of Jagannath, could be traced from an episode of violence where Jarasabara kills Krishna; evidently this killing transforms him into an emissary of 'seeking' peace through his devoted service to the deity. Jarawas, a seeker of divinity and 'bliss', never knew that those relics one day would give birth to a new culture—a popular and flourishing Jagannath culture.

Acknowledgements

I express my gratitude to *Prabachaka* Sarada Prasanna Kar with whom I had three sessions of discussion, and I also thank Professor Sudha Shastri for reading the chapter and suggesting necessary corrections and providing valuable comments.

Notes

1. *Panchasakha* refers to five saint poets of Odisha in the sixteenth century. They were, Achutananda Das, Ananta Das, Jasovanta Das, Jagannatha Das and Balarama Das. Their writings are spiritual and mystical. *Panchasakha* were great devotees of Lord Jagannath.

2. Ramayana was read out in the fourteenth-century and there are references by scholars like Paula Richman and others. See https://commons.wikimedia.org/wiki/File:14thcentury_Adhyatma_Ramayana_manuscript,_Sanskrit,_Oriya_script.jpg (accessed 9 January 2019).
3. It was believed that Atibadi Jagannath Dasa's father had earned the titled of *Purana Panda* and was well-versed in Sanskrit Ramayana. And, Jagannath Dasa also used to chant and give discourses. Available at: http://puriwaves.nirmalya.in/saints/atibadi-jagannath-das (accessed 3 December 2018).
4. Tungi is hut type house commonly built at the centre of the villages and used for reading religious texts, singing bhajanas and *jananas*, and engaging in discussions of moral and spiritual ideas. Since the *Bhagabatas* was popularly read in this place, it got the name *bhagabatatungi*, see Patnaik (2009).
5. The Buddhists', the Jains' and the Tantrikas' mode of worship is symbolic of this assimilation. Along with this, many sadhus and the pioneers of Bhakti movement, such as Nanak, Tulsidas, Sri Chaitanya and many others have come and experienced the spiritual presence of the Lord. Available at https://ipfs.io/ipfs/QmXoypizjW3WknFiJnKLwHCnL72vedxjQkDDP1mXWo6uco/wiki/Jagannath.html (accessed 10 December 2018).

References

Austin, J.L. 1962. *How to Do Things with Words*. Oxford: Clarendron Press.

Avram, W. 1996. 'On the Priority of "Ethics" in the Work of Levinas'. *The Journal of Religious Ethics*, 24(2): 261–284.

Bake, A. 1936–1937. 'Indian Folk-Music'. *Proceedings of Musical Association*, 63: 65–77.

Cavell, S. 1997. 'Something Out of the Ordinary'. *Proceedings and Address of the American Philosophical Association*, 71(2): 23–37.

Das, C. 1982. *A Glimpse of Oriya Literature*. Bhubaneswar: Orissa Sahitya Akademi.

Das, M. 1978. 'Experiments in Modern Writing,' *Indian Literature*, 21(2): 147–153.

Das, M. 'Legends of Sri Jagannath'. A Talk by Prof. Manoj Das. Available at https://www.youtube.com/watch?v=QLV7DHSk_BQ (accessed 3 September 2018).

Das, Ram C. *Jagannathnka Amrutabani*. Available at http://www.likemusic.info/file/shree-jagannathanka-amrutabani-full-by-charana-ram-dasp-hd-musica- (accessed 2 September 2018).

Gandhi, R. 1974. *Presuppositions of Human Communication*. New Delhi: Oxford University Press.

Gandhi, R. 1976. *The Availability of Religious Ideas*. London: The Macmillan Press.

Grossberg, L. 1982. 'Intersubjectivity and the Conceptualization of Communication'. *Human Studies*, 5(3): 213–235.

Heal, J. 2002. 'On First-Person Authority'. *Proceedings of Aristotelian Society*, 102: 1–9.

Heidbrink, S. and N. Miczek. 2010. 'Introduction to the Special Issue—Religions on the Internet: Aesthetic and the Dimensions of the Senses'. *Online—Heidelberg Journal of Religions on Internet*, (4)1: 1–11.

Krishna, D. 2011. 'Rasa: The Bane of Indian Aesthetics'. In *Contrary Thinking: Selected Essays of Daya Krishna*, edited by Nalini Bhushan, Jay L. Grarfield and Daniel Rave. New York: Oxford University Press.

Kulke H. 2014. 'Jagannatha as the State Deity under the Gjapati of Orissa'. In *The Cult of Jagannath and the Regional Tradition of Orissa*, edited by Anncharlott Eschmann, Hermann Kulke and Gaya CharanTripathy, 271–282. New Delhi: Manohar (Revised edition).

Malik, B.K. 2007. 'Emergence of the Sudra to Subaltern Consciousness in Medieval Orissa (AD 1450–1600)', *Proceedings of the Indian History Congress*, 68: 303–312.

Mohapatra, S. 1971. 'Tension between Felt Experience of Formal Structuring'. *Indian Literature*, 14(1): 29–46.

Mukherjee, P. 1979. 'Sri Chaitanya in Oriya Literature'. *Indian Literature*, 22(1): 113–121.

Patnaik, T. 2009. 'Buddha and Jagannath: A Study of the Impact of Buddhism on the Orissan Bhakti Movement'. In *Perspectives on Orissa: Cultural-Intellectual Contributions*, Vol. VI, Part 7 in series of *History of Science, Philosophy and Culture in Indian Civilization*, edited by P.K. Mohapatra and R.C. Pradhan, general editor D.P. Chattopadhyaya. New Delhi: Centre for Studies in Civilizations.

Rajchman, J. 1988. 'Foucault's Art of Seeing'. *October*, 44: 88–117.

Ramanujan, A.K. 1992. 'Talking to God in the Mother Tongue'. *India International Centre Quarterly*, 19(4): 53–64.

Rambachan, A. 1987. 'Where the Words Fail: The Limits of Scriptural Authority in the Hermeneutics of a Contemporary Advaitin'. *Philosophy East and West*, 37(4): 361–371.

Saksena, S.K. 1951 'Authority in Indian Philosophy'. *Philosophy East and West*, 1(3): 38–49.

Satpathy, S. and J.K. Nayak. 2014. 'Sarala Mahabharata: Introduction'. *Indian Literature*, 58(3): 7–14.

Searle, J.R. 1969. *Speech Acts: An Essay in Philosophy of Language*. Cambridge: Cambridge University Press.

Sharma, K. 1987. *Bhakti and Bhakti Movement: A New Perspective, A Study in the History of Ideas*. New Delhi: Munshiram Manoharlal Publishers.

Taylor, Mc. 2013. 'Stories of God: Contemporary Oral Performance of *Bhagavatakatha*'. *International Journal of Hindu Studies*, 17(3): 261–268.

Section II
Practising Jagannath

5

EATING WITH EYES: THE FOOD ECONOMY OF JAGANNATH CULTURE

Umasankar Patra

Introduction

A familiar scene appears in Nandakishore Bala's novel *Kanakalata* (1927) where the women of the Harichandan and Paikaray family exchange vows to get their children married. The vow, which is made by having the *mahaprasad*, bestows this earthly alliance a heavenly sanction. Similarly, in Fakir Mohan Senapati's (2014) short story 'Madha Mohantynka Kanyasuna' a character becomes the *dharam maa* (foster mother) of the protagonist by offering her the *mahaprasad*. From Fakir Mohan to Mohapatra Nilamani Sahoo, one would find numerous such examples in Odia literature where unbreakable bonds and relationships are forged over the *mahaprasad*. In Odia society many people have become relatives, friends and foster mothers, fathers, daughters and sons over the *mahaprasad*. It is through and in the *mahaprasad* that the bond is secured and sustained. *Mahaprasad* becomes the witness as well as the mediator of that bond. It is the lord's approval of the vows made by the humans; a blessing and also a promise that the lord is watching and watching over the fates of those involved in the consumption of the *mahaprasad*. The word that is used for such kind of relation is *dharam*, colloquial term for *dharma*, suggesting a sacred (and) sanctioned bond.

Moreover, the *mahaprasad*'s crucial role in forging social bonds that are outside the conventional familial and caste association is at the centre of the Jagannath culture. Jakob Roesel attributes Jagannath's popularisation to the consumption of the *mahaprasad* that takes place across caste hierarchies (Roesel 1983). At Puri, the Brahmin and the untouchable are supposed to eat from each other's plate and drink from the same containers (Roesel 1983: 46–47). The *mahaprasad*, thus, achieved a democratisation of the Jagannath culture that endeared the lord to those outside the caste and community privileges. However, a unique phenomenon has been witnessed in the last couple of decades in urban Odisha. The *mahaprasad* of Jagannath which once was locally cooked and available for consumption in Puri,[1] is now prepared and sold in several temples across urban Odisha in the form of *prasad*.[2] Though this *prasad* draws its religious and sacred value from the *mahaprasad*, it is not identical either in terms of production or consumption. *Prasad* is now cooked and sold not only in Jagannath temples across Odisha, but also in the temples of other gods and goddesses such as Shiva, Manasa, Tarini, etc. as a sacred vegetarian meal.

This is unique as these temples never had such elaborate food preparations as part of their traditional rituals. *Prasad* prepared in all these temples has become their foremost source of revenue, thanks to its blending of religiosity and competitive pricing. Thus, unlike the *mahaprasad*, which was localised in Puri, the *prasad* has made Jagannath available to every Odia in the last couple of decades. The devotee does not have to come to Puri; instead, the lord has reached out to their households. In the process, the culture has also opened itself to non-devotees in the form of a sumptuous and inexpensive vegetarian meal. However, unlike the *mahaprasad* which is the 'real', *prasad* is mostly thought of as an imitation that is made available to satiate the demands of the customer. Yet, *prasad*'s deterritorialised, secular, democratised and economised nature has unveiled a new discourse on sacrality and thereby, on Jagannath culture. However, the rich body of scholarship on the Jagannath culture has not yet engaged with the *prasad* culture. Moreover, available scholarship on the food culture of Jagannath has restricted itself only to the *mahaprasad* that is prepared at the Puri temple.[3] *Prasad* that has become the metonymy of Jagannath's presence across Odisha by reaching households, has mostly remained out of scholarly scrutiny till now.

This chapter seeks to provide a supplement and focuses its attention on the *prasad* culture witnessed outside Puri, in the urban parts of Odisha. It argues that this *prasad* culture, governed by an amalgamation of the effect of devotion and commercialisation, has led to a significant expansion of the culture without devaluing the sacred. I also argue that this new avatar unveils a multi-territorial movement undertaken in multiple commercial idioms of the local temples that is similar and yet different from the earlier moment of democratisation as elaborated by Hermann Kulke.[4] Unlike the former, this movement is not occasioned by immediate sociopolitical concerns but more by the interrelated triad of commodification,[5] modern lifestyle and religiosity. But both moments of democratisation are similar as they are movements driven by the 'periphery' to subvert the centralisation of authority symbolised in the Puri temple. With the help of empirical data from Jagannath, Shiva, Tarini, Kali, and Hanuman temples in Balasore, Cuttack and Bhubaneswar,[6] I study the multiple vocabularies in which Jagannath's presence is experienced in Odisha via *prasad*.

This chapter operates on two major planks: the first dealing with the material aspect of the *prasad* culture wherein I detail the production and consumption of the *prasad* and its intertwined affiliation with the larger spiritual economy, by coordinating the spatial and social relations it participates in and partakes of. The second examines the governing node of the affective: the devotee establishing a kinship with god through the religious victual within the framework of commodity culture. In the process, it has ensured revenues for the temples as well as vegetarian food for the devotees and non-devotees, forming a symbiotic relationship between the religious and the commercial. Needless to say, they are closely related and the following sections of the chapter—the materiality of the *prasad*, understanding the affective bond, laying out the interrelated spatial and social associations—demonstrate this symbiosis amply. The questions, therefore, that this chapter asks are: What happens at the site of production and consumption? Has commercialisation changed the nature of divinity or is divinity governing the rules of commodification? And how this phenomenon has altered the nature of *prasad* and that in turn has impacted the temple structure, specifically its spatial arrangement. My attempt would be to analyse the welter of signification offered by the amalgamation of religiosity, materiality and commodity taking a cue from Arjun Appadurai who notes, 'commoditization lies at the complex intersection of temporal, cultural, and social factors' (1987: 15).

Prasad Culture

Hermann Kulke observes that the democratisation of the Jagannath culture was only possible after the downfall of the central dynasty of Odisha. He argues that the 'Kings of the Ganga and Suryavamsa dynasties seem to have "monopolized" the Jagannath cult in their religious and political centres, that is Puri and Cuttack' (1993: 87). In the wake of the defeat of the central dynasty after 1568, Kulke notes, the new provincial kingdoms started asserting their independence and it was symbolised in the establishment of numerous Jagannath temples across Odisha. This was a remarkable change as under the Ganga and Suryavamsa the cult had grown into a 'symbol of Hindu kingship and royal authority in Orissa' (1993: 87). Therefore, the construction of these Jagannath temples meant 'a symbolic declaration of Independence' (1993: 87).

Kulke's perceptive observation draws our attention to the nexus of Jagannath culture with the socio-politico-religious world of Odisha and the culture's central role in shaping it. The democratisation of the culture enabled Jagannath to be more pervasive, sometimes at the cost of the local deities who in the contemporary scenario did not play a very important role in facilitating political autonomy. With the establishment of Jagannath temples across the newly independent kingdoms, manifold social changes also occurred. The adoption of the royal symbols by local chieftains and import of Hindu rituals into tribal regions meant both the expansion of the Brahmanical authority as well as the inclusion of tribals into the Hindu caste system. Kulke aptly terms this phenomenon 'Sanskritization from both below and above' (1993: 90). So the change from a concentration of political and religious power in Puri and Cuttack to a dissolution of political power only strengthened the religious authority of Jagannath as he entered new domains and became more pervasive. H.V. Stietencron (1986) and Kedarnath Mahapatra (1977) carry forward the tenor of Kulke and catalogue the existing Jagannath temples, not only in Odisha, but also in Vishakhapatnam, Bankura, Ranchi, Dhaka and Imphal.

Moreover, circa the sixteenth century, around the time of the fall of the central dynasty, the *Ananda bazaar* (literally meaning the market of bliss, spatially refers to the place inside the temple where *mahaprasad* is sold) was established in Puri facilitating the consumption of the *mahaprasad* by everyone across caste boundaries (Roesel 1983: 46). Kulke and Roesel's observations alert us to a significant moment in Odisha's social history that led to the popularisation of the lord. Kulke diagnoses what I call the first moment of democratisation of the culture which was born out of the political upheaval and engendered a new social system in Odisha. However, Roesel provides us an important part of the shift as he argues that following the establishment of the *Ananda bazaar* the *mahaprasad* enabled Jagannath to travel farther (both geographically and in terms of traversing caste affiliation). It resulted in eating of the food of the lord becoming 'more important than seeing him' (Roesel 1983: 46). As can be seen in the incidents noted from the literary works, by nineteenth century, Jagannath had started travelling metonymically through the *mahaprasad* (specifically the *nirmalya*[7]) into various parts of Odisha. Thus, the lord was present literally in the local Jagannath temples and symbolically in the form of *mahaprasad*.

Now, the *prasad* (the local variant of the *mahaprasad*) is prepared in almost all the major temples of the urban centres in Odisha. However, the *prasad* that is prepared in these temples is different on many counts. A typical *prasad* consists of *kanika* (sweet rice), *anna* (plain rice), *dali* (lentils), *mahura* and *besara* (versions of mixed veg curries), *khata* (a dish mostly made out of dates and/or tomato, mango) and *kheeri* (kheer). The last two items are optional. Along with it, many special curries like *aloo-potala, vada kofta, sola-potala*, fruit salad, *matar paneer*, etc.[8] are also part of the menu (Figure 5.1). But the qualitative difference of the *prasad* from the *mahaprasad* does not seem to affect the sale of the *prasad*. A normal *prasad* may cost between ₹ 40 and ₹ 60 depending on the place and the assortment that is offered. The model is so lucrative that now it is not only the Jagannath temples that are selling the *prasad* but temples of all other gods and goddesses (Kali, Shiva, Hanuman, etc.) have also started distributing *prasad*.

Figure 5.1 Advertisement inside Dakshinakali temple, Baramunda, Bhubaneswar, detailing the kind of *prasad* that is sold
Source: Author.

Following Kulke, I argue that this democratisation, secularisation and economisation of the *mahaprasad* is much like the earlier moment in history when Jagannath temples were established in various parts of Odisha. The 'independence' of curating and commercialising the *prasad* is a furtherance of the symbolic independence that has been outlined previously (Kulke 1993: 87). In short, we are witnessing a new avatar of the Jagannath culture which has aligned itself with the modern consumerist society and delimited its precincts. This is, hence, the second moment of democratisation shaping the Odia society. The following section outlines the materiality of this democratisation by elaborating the process of preparation and sanctification of the *prasad*.

Nativisation of the Foreign

One of the primary distinctive features of *mahaprasad* is the use of 'native' vegetables and the indigenous cooking style. Vegetables such as potato, tomato, various kinds of gourd, cauliflower, etc. that are considered 'foreign' are prohibited (Mishra 1984: 197). However, the temples that are preparing *prasad* do not seem to abide by such rigid rules. Many of these prohibited vegetables and new curries are making their way into the menu of the *prasad*. One common binding assumption of the temples' is that they are cooking a vegetarian meal which is sumptuous and affordable, and retains the *satvik* aura. So the person consuming the *prasad* is not coming to a restaurant but is enjoying the blessings of the god. Out of the 87 people I talked to in the course of my fieldwork, 64 primarily viewed the *prasad* as a vegetarian meal which is inexpensive and one can eat to his/her full. Compared to the restaurants where there is a restriction on how much one can eat, the temples are generous. This is one of the primary attractions of *prasad*.

However, the religiosity associated with the *prasad* cannot be undervalued. Many from those 64 when prodded whether they have it as an inexpensive meal or for its sacred quotient, were unable to point out their preference. Even though they had earlier mentioned that their interest stemmed from the pricing and quantity of the food offered, there was hardly any denial that part of the attraction of the *prasad* lied in the idea that it is the lord's blessing. In other words, the consumerability and religiosity are deeply entwined and reinvigorate, replenish and sustain each other. Drawing the distinction between consuming *prasad* vis-à-vis food at a restaurant, the priest at ISKCON Bhubaneswar commented that *prasad* is not consumed to satisfy one's carnal desire of hunger but to fulfil one's spiritual angst. Hence, it is *satvik* as the aim is of purification of the self.

What is important to note is that these temples are harping on the idea of a vegetarian meal which is religiously sanctified. So one does not only eat but also earns *punya* (goodwill). Through this meal he/she is earning god's blessings. The sight of touching *prasad* to the forehead before eating is a common sight. However, such a sight is not confined only to the *prasad*. One can touch their regular meal on their forehead as a paean to the almighty, underscoring the relationship of the sacred with the food. Moreover, this gesture underlines *prasad*'s liminal status both as a regular meal and a sacred one. Nevertheless, the temples here seem to turn the debate away from the idea of the use of 'indigenous' to the overall objective of achieving *punya*. Hence, the attention veers away from the mode of production to the ends consumption which is to let the devotee earn the god's blessing. In other words, it is not the means but the ends that matter for the temples.

The economic here is reasoned via the affective. Though the *prasad* does not adhere to the Puri norms still it is the 'lord's *prasad*'; hence, the reason for touching the food to the forehead. The devotional valence is what sells the *prasad* as it arouses the affect of experiencing a kinship with the lord by consuming his leftover. Affect as characterised by cultural theorists, does not rest on the idea of rationality or consciousness (Connolly 2011; Figlerowicz 2012; Leys 2011). Therefore, once the affective is invoked, discussions about the native/foreign, *satvik/tamasik* become redundant. Constructing the emotional bond with the lord seems to be the underlying rationale of the temples. The food economy is reliant on this bond and the temples and the consumers both harp on this affective framework to bestow legitimacy to the *prasad*.

Authenticity and Consumerism

The importance of forging this affective bond becomes clear if we sample two examples where temples claim to retain the 'authentic' aura of the Puri *mahaprasad*. Banthia Jagannath temple's (in Balasore) claim of authenticity is based on the premise that their *prasad* is offered to both Jagannath and Bimala, imitating the Puri temple ritual. In other Jagannath temples, it is only a fake *prasad* as there are no Bimala deities in those temples. Therefore, their *prasad* can claim to be 'authentic' and that in the others (such as Dakshinakali at Baramunda, Shani temple at Vani Vihar and Rameswara temple in Balasore) are fake. Chandni Chowk Jagannath temple in Cuttack based its authenticity on the use of 'indigenous' vegetables in line with the Puri temple. Similarly, the temple at CDA, Cuttack, claims to have a Puri *panda* (Brahmin servitors of the Puri temple) who is in charge of the preparation of the *prasad* retaining the 'original' cooking style, flavour and aroma (Figure 5.2). However, upon enquiry, the claims were found to be untrue. The *panda* was also not a *suara*—servitors in charge of cooking at the Puri temple.

Figure 5.2
Advertisement on the wall of the Jagannath temple, CDA, Cuttack, highlighting the method of preparation of *mahaprasad*
Source: Author.

All these examples seem to stress on the authenticity of their *prasad* in different things: the first on the mode of sanctification and the second and third on the mode of preparation. This is distinct from the earlier examples where the temples emphasised on neither of these two but on the *satvik* value—the goodwill one reaps after eating the *prasad*. Thus, the affective economy of the *prasad* is dependent on various stages of the *mahaprasad* ritual: (a) mode of preparation, (b) the process of sanctification and (c) the *satvik* value. The competitive marketplace has ensured that temples draw the consumers by satisfying these requirements. However, the first—the mode of preparation—is a difficult one to emulate as it is impossible for these smaller temples to cook according to the temple rituals practised at Puri.[9] The last, *satvik* value, seems to be the easiest to attain as it does not require mammoth efforts from the temples in terms of infrastructure (adhering to strict rules of cooking) but on the sanctification of *prasad*.

Therefore, authenticity is claimed not in the process of cooking but in the process of sanctification. These temples seem to locate the uniqueness and religiosity not in the process (the choice of the vegetables or the process of cooking) but in it being the product (the *prasad*). In Puri, as mentioned earlier, the *mahaprasad* is sacred owing to both its process of production and the fact that the lord eats it (mode of sanctification). Here, the process of production is no more the guarantor of sacrality. So what is left is the process of sanctification which relatedly would ensure the *satvik* quality of the food. Therefore, accounting for the process of sanctification becomes important as the entire reasoning is located on the idea that it is the 'lord's *prasad*'. Since the affective is the underlined basis of the entire economy, it is crucial to understand the foundation on which this bonding between the lord and the modern consumer is based.

Kotha Bhoga: Experimenting with the Tradition

The *mahaprasad* in Puri is sanctified through the ritual of *kotha bhoga.* The entire meal consisting of 56 delicacies are not placed before the lord but bits and pieces of the meal are offered to him which is known as *kotha bhoga.* The lord eats this *bhoga* through his eyes and after that basil leaves are put in it. Then, it is offered to goddess Bimala, after which it assumes the status of *mahaprasad.* Some of the temples such as the one at Chandni Chowk, Cuttack and the Laxminarayan temple in Balasore offer the *kanika*, *dali* and *mahura* and *besara*—items that are cooked according to the Puri convention—to the lord as the *kotha bhoga* and the rest of the items such as kofta, paneer, kheer, etc. are not offered as part of the *bhoga.*

Another way of using the *kotha bhoga* is practised in the Banthia Jagannath temple in Balasore. Parts of the cooked food—*kanika, anna, mahura, besara*—are not offered as *kotha bhoga*. But they offer *khichdi*, *dalma* (lentils with vegetables) and sprouts that are bereft of any 'foreign' element as *kotha bhoga*. The *kotha bhoga* is prepared separately and then offered to the lord. After basil leaves are put in the *kotha bhoga*, it is sprinkled on the entire cooked food intended to be sold. Thus, by extension, the cooked food sanctified with the sprinkling of the *kotha bhoga* and basil leaves becomes *prasad*; fit to be sold and consumed. Many temples, including those of Kali, Shiva, Shani and Hanuman use this method to sanctify their *prasad*.

The lord accepts the offering and basil leaves are put in this *kotha bhoga* as a symbol of his acceptance and blessing. Unless the basil leaf is put in the cooked food, it cannot be *prasad* even though it is prepared in the temple. And it can be put only after Jagannath or Krishna (or any avatar of Vishnu) accepts the offering. The Dakshinkali temple at Baramunda, Bhubaneswar, is a case in point.

Once the new bus stand was built in Baramunda, it opened up the demand for a place to eat. Around the same time, a Radha-Krishna temple was built in the premises of the Kali shrine, paving the way for the preparation of the *prasad*. Other temples such as the Rameswara temple and the Shani temple have also instituted either Jagannath or Krishna in the premises so that the cooked food can be attributed the status of *prasad*.

So, the sanctification process is heavily dependent on the presence of Jagannath or Krishna which has ensured the prevalence of Jagannath culture at a literal level. Thus, one sees Jagannath in every temple. This in turn, facilitates the affective kinship and an argument towards authenticity, distinguishing itself from other kinds of vegetarian food it seems to be competing with: food from eateries and home-cooked vegetarian food. Hence, the basil leaves, a proof of the touch of the lord, have become a passport for the affective bond to be forged. Thus, the traditional *mahaprasad* is allowed the space of experimentation while retaining the same traditional methods to sanctify the same experimentation. Therefore, limited desacralisation of the *mahaprasad* becomes possible as the process of cooking (use of 'native' ingredients as well as the process of cooking practised in Puri) is bypassed, but the mode of sanctification (sprinkling of basil leaves) is retained. However, as was evident, except for certain temples, the absence of Bimala makes it a limited sanctifying process.

Here, tradition and experiment weave an equation of interdependence on the basis of the economic. This has deeper repercussions for the Jagannath culture. Unlike the earlier moment of democratisation where Jagannath culture expanded thanks to his presence in the newly constructed local Jagannath temples, he is now present in the temples of other gods' and goddess'. Added to it, he has also entered households through the basil leaf of the *prasad*. Jagannath has truly become the *Jagat ra nath* (Lord of the Universe) as he is available to everyone, devotee or otherwise. Thus, it is apparent how the traditional has been altered, thanks to the demands of the consumerist economy and has become part of, what may be called, 'spiritual economy'.

Spiritual Economy

Characterising spirituality's nexus with the capitalist economy in *Selling Spirituality*, Jeremy Carrette and Richard King contend, 'The "spiritual" becomes instrumental to the market rather than oriented towards a wider social and ethical framework, and its primary function becomes the perpetuation of the consumerist status quo ...' (2005: 23). Such an accommodation of the capitalist ethos and rebranding of religious ethics towards 'spirituality' is what may be termed as 'spiritual economy'. However, keeping aside the authors' somewhat extreme claims of takeover of religion by corporate capitalism, what is important for this chapter is their detection of the interrelation of spirituality and the economy of the contemporary world.

These new spiritual economies are based on the idea of 'therapy, peace and self-help' (Turner 2011: 152). Its main features are non-interference or little interference with the normative, the promise of mental and spiritual wellness of its participants, the unending desire and consumption of its products and a belief in individualism (every individual's needs need to be attended to) which ensures the achievements and furthering of community goals. One of the cornerstones of this economy is the assurance of the seeming inexpensiveness of the wellness programme. In India, the spiritual economy has made huge inroads. Various *gurus* and godmen have monetised their *bibhuti* (sacred ash), belongings, *prasad*, etc. with Patanjali, the brainchild of Ramdev, being the leader. Ramdev is both spiritual *guru* and brand ambassador of Patanjali, which has set its sights on being a 20,000-crore rupee company and claims a customer reach of five crore people in India.[10] Patanjali's emphasis on the 'commitment to a healthier society' demonstrates the salient features of the spiritual economy which is driven towards the betterment of individual and family health—both mental and physical.

It is important at this point to remind that this is not to posit an equation of equivalence between Patanjali's success and the *prasad* culture. Ramdev's success, putatively, is of a different order. The Jagannath culture is of recent origin, unlike the Patanjali group/ Ramdev. However, I argue that they are part of the same environment of spiritual economy that is prevalent in India. Both the food economy evinced in the *prasad* culture as well as the Yog economy of Ramdev partake, constitute and sustain the larger spiritual economy. By consuming the *prasad*, the devotee (or the non-devotee) is partaking of the value of the lord, just like someone buying a Patanjali product is participating in the Yog economy. Modernity in this case is signalled by the usable: what could be the immediate use of godliness and Ayurveda. Is it readily available and packaged so that it can be reused or reconsumed? In other words, the Jagannath culture has modernised itself whereby the devotee has 'also' turned into a buyer and consumer. The lord in various forms was already present in the households: as deities in the puja rooms, in calendars, in the names of their children, etc. Now the god and godliness has entered the households in the form of food. Thus, the economy is sustained by the same thing which engenders it: god's blessing through *prasad* also ensures the importance of *prasad* as the proof and existence of blessing. If one is not devotional enough, they will not get to have the *prasad*, is a common saying in Odisha. Hence, the *prasad* ensures blessing and the blessing can be thought of in material terms as *prasad*: the affective and the material going hand in hand with each other.

This paradoxical equilibrium of commodification and religiosity is manifested in the *prasad* culture's dovetailing into the eating habits of the Odias. The *prasad* is not only a sacred victual anymore; it has become a replacement to vegetarian food. More than 80 per cent people who were interviewed during the fieldwork, agreed to the fact that the *prasad* is the ideal lunch on days when they did not cook at home. One sees the mushrooming of smaller places selling '*prasad*' in various parts of Bhubaneswar whose *satvik* value or 'authenticity' is doubtful. In most cases, these places prepare a menu similar to the one in the temples or a simple *khichdi* and sell it under the name of '*prasad*'. I came across such places along the roadside, on the road connecting Vani Vihar and Acharya Vihar, Firestation and Baramunda, near Jaydev Vihar where the owners claimed that they cooked the food in their houses. These places do not sell *prasad* on a daily basis but on special occasions such as Purnima (the full moon day) or Ekadasi (the eleventh day of the Odia month) and other auspicious days. Mostly, this *prasad* is offered to the local/family deity and sold to people. The emergence of such contingent spaces that sell these facsimiles of *prasad* only underline its popularity.

In contemporary times where ordering food in or eating out has become a part of daily life, Odia households and the *prasad* culture have exploited it well. Data from temples across the coastal belt acknowledge that sales were normally high on Monday, Tuesday, Thursday and Saturday, the days when Odia household prefers *niramish* (vegetarian) food. *Shani* temple (Vani Vihar) had the following figures: On the *niramish* days of Monday, Tuesday, Thursday and Saturday they sell around 120 to 150 meals. On the *ainsha* (non-vegetarian) days—mostly Wednesdays and Sundays and also Friday in some households—it can go down to 50 meals. Banthia Jagannath temple administration also provided similar figures. On *niramish* days, they sell around 200 plates; it goes down to 120 on other days. On auspicious days, the sale could range somewhere between 300 and 500 meals. Thus, *prasad* has gradually become part of or a replacement for the usual vegetarian lunch. This underlines *prasad*'s participation in the spiritual economy that is dependent on the welfare of the modern subject, both mentally and physically. In the process, it has led to the rise of a new subjectivity that does not view the spiritual and secular as binaries. The sacred is not anymore a specialised vocation that remains aloof from daily life rather *prasad* has ensured that the sacred has become a part of the living. The sacred does not have to be 'practised' anymore; it lives with and in the modern Odia. The marketisation of Jagannath culture in no way has devalued the importance of the lord rather the Odias are happy to have the blessing of the lord recurrently in the form of *prasad*.

The prevalence of this eating culture would be incomplete without factoring in the spatial arrangement that facilitates the easy availability of the *prasad*. Among the temples which are selling *prasad* in the Balasore, Bhubaneswar, Cuttack and Baripada the location of the temple was an important consideration. The *Shani* temple at Vani Vihar is located next to Utkal University and is at an important junction of the city. Chandni Chowk temple at Cuttack relies on its proximity to the Odisha High Court and SCB Medical College. Dakshinakali temple is located adjacent to the Baramunda Bus Stand. The Laxminarayan temple in Balasore is located near the ITI chowk, in front of educational and business enterprises. Similarly, the Radha-Krishna temple is located in the middle of Balasore so that it is equidistant from the Railway station, Balasore court, medical college and the bus stand. Banthia Jagannath temple is close to the market and the hospital which provides it with a regular supply of customers. It is important to note here that the old temples like Banthia Jagannath in Balasore or Chandni Chowk temple in Cuttack, which thanks to the geographies of urbanisation have remained in the 'old' cities, harp on the idea of the 'authentic' *prasad,* use of 'indigenous' vegetables and sanctioned ways of sanctification to turn the cooked food into *praṣad.* Since, these temples cannot change their location to suit the needs of the customers they have tried to base their saleability on their authenticity and age-old tradition. However, neither the authenticity nor the availability of a strategic location is the sole determiner of higher sales.

The priest and the manager of Dakshinakali temple narrated an interesting story in this regard. The temple instituted Radhakrishna idols within the temple premises in 1994 when the new bus stand near Baramunda was coming up. The idols facilitated the preparation of the *prasad* as described earlier. Soon, the buses were parking themselves from the Firestation chowk to Baramunda. Thus, the temple became a popular eating place for the bus staff and the passengers and others associated with the business. The temple then expanded its premises to accommodate the rush and prepared a separate hall to consume *prasad.* But with the recent change in traffic rules, the buses are unable to park by the roadside and that has led to a loss of business for the temple.

Such material considerations highlight the various facets of the spiritual economy that the *prasad* is part of. Three important elements of this economy emerge through the previous discussion: strategic location, constant evolution of the menu according to the taste buds of the consumers on the one hand, and the discourse of sacrality as its unique selling point on the other. Temples have been built around localities of worth, menu is tweaked according to the taste buds of the consumers and *prasad* is marketed as a sumptuous yet inexpensive vegetarian meal. This demonstrates that in this second wave of democratisation, the temple has reached out to take in many (the non-devotees) into the fold of the culture, in the form of customers. In other words, this is a movement from 'below', much like the earlier one detailed by Kulke, that has ensured the pervasiveness of the culture and delimited the scope of the temple and religion itself (Kulke 1993: 90). Thus, like the *mahaprasad*, *prasad* has been able to open doors of the Jagannath culture to many outside it.

The Transformation of Temples

Jakob Roesel argues that with the emphasis on eating, each new devotee got added to Jagannath. Emphasising the role of food in the culture, Roesel writes:

> Food becomes the social coin of ritual interaction. The spatial arrangement of the Puri district, the architecture of the entire temple compound, the ritual itself, all have one basic purpose, that is, to procure food for the daily consumption of the God. The structure of the economy is geared towards one goal, and this goal is 'incorporation' in the original sense of the word. (1983: 58)

Roesel alerts us to the crucial part played by *mahaprasad* in the formation and sustenance of the culture. His contribution is important as it highlights that the food economy as a process needs to be analysed vis-à-vis the sociopolitical realities of temple and that the food economy has been one of the governing structures of the culture for centuries now. Following Roesel, I have argued that the food economy is not only a facet but is at the centre of the culture.

The spiritual economy of the temples through *prasad* has ensured that eating occupies an important focus in the daily functioning of the temple. Many new temples that are coming up in urban centres are constructing their premises keeping in mind the space that needs to be earmarked for the mini *Ananda bazaars*. This should not lead to a somewhat reductive conclusion like Roesel's that the temples have turned into bazars but to emphasise the new avatar of the temples. This juggernaut of the spiritual economy has ensured that there are two kinds of temples to be found around coastal Odisha: '*mandir*' and spiritual centres. The former is only a place for worshipping and the latter ones are becoming spaces where devotees and non-devotees are spending longer durations of time. Hence, these centres respecting the temporalities of the modern societies are offering more than just scope of worshipping; embellishing their premises with various other spaces like prayer halls, eateries, gardens and parks. Instead of the Puri temple, the ISKCON temples which are a place of outing have become the model.

Since these temples require a huge area, they have to move out of the cities and towns and moving out of the city means that only by sparing a few hours people can reach there. And once people/pilgrims/devotees are spending their time to reach these places, they need to be entertained not with just a place of worship but also a place which has multifarious avenues for every member of the family. The new Jagannath temple in Balasore is constructed on the outskirts and now enjoys the status of a tourist attraction. Similarly, another Radha-Krishna temple constructed on the outskirts of Balasore in Laupalgadi has ensured a perfect outing experience. The temple is situated on a water body where one can enjoy boating facilities. Also available is a park of sorts surrounding the water body, with animals like rabbits on display. The temple, too, is constructing lodging facilities along the water body (Figure 5.3). Needless to say that *prasad* is available but along with it, one can find fast food stalls (albeit vegetarian, and sans onion and garlic). In such ways, along with being places of worship, the temples are becoming marriage halls, food courts, kids' parks, etc. They are attempting to become the wellness centres that offer respite from daily chores and a perfect spiritual atmosphere for a break. Thus, the spiritual economy of the *prasad* has led to the transformation of temples and in the process, intertwined religiosity and market economy.

Figure 5.3 Radhakrishna temple, Laupalgadi, Balasore
Source: Author.

Conclusion

To sum up, I argue that Jagannath culture is still a religious cult whose religiosity is reinforced via its food economy by coupling the sacred and the commercial. Moreover, this food economy gradually is paving way for participation in larger spiritual economic practices by offering the temples as places worthy of the urban gateway. Thus, it is generating an interesting circularity where devotion and commodification are partaking of each other and are redefining urban living in significant ways. It has resulted in the formation of a new subjectivity that is not creating the binaries of the spiritual and the commercial; rather it is transforming the modern Odia living where religion is influencing eating habits not in coercive ways but by intertwining consumerist practices with religious ones. Such an exploration into the materiality of Jagannath culture fills the gap in the existing scholarship which has not emphasised the role of these everyday practices in the furthering of the Jagannath culture. It highlights and opens possibilities of other kinds of study on Jagannath's prevalence in everyday Odia culture.

Acknowledgements

I wish to acknowledge the contribution of the following for their help: Sumanyu Satpathy, Jatindra K. Nayak, J.P. Das, Aruni Mahapatra Monu Rajan, Nitya Datta, Jyotirmayee Ojha, Niroj Sethi and Subash Chandra Patra; temple administration and priests of all the temples listed in the chapter, especially Banthia Jagannath temple in Balasore.

Notes

1. Jagannath's food culture in certain ways defines the deity. According to the popular folklore, among the *char dhams* (four highest religious places associated with Hinduism) Vishnu eats at Puri. Therefore, justifying the elaborate food preparations where over 56 different dishes are prepared in the huge kitchen that houses around 279 hearths. For a detailed discussion of the *mahaprasad*, see Mishra (1984).
2. *Prasad* generally refers to any victual that is offered to any gods or goddess. By *prasad*, I refer to the local version of the *mahaprasad* of Puri Jagannath temple.
3. *The Cult of Jagannath* edited by Hermann Kulke et al., *Nabakalebara Bichara* edited by Mahimohan Tripathy and Asit Mohanty (2015), Jakob Roesel's essay on the food economy of Jagannath focus on the *mahaprasad*. Seminal works like K.C. Mishra's *The Cult of Jagannatha* has a brief appendix on the *mahaprasad*. However, this focus on *mahaprasad* itself is pretty scant when one compares it to the entire body of scholarship available in Odia and English.
4. Hermann Kulke's essay 'Ksatriyaization and Social Change: A Study in Orissa Setting' in *Kings and Cults: State formation and Legitimation in India and Southeast Asia* argues that Jagannath temple in Puri which had symbolised royal authority underwent a drastic change after the fall of the central dynasty in 1568. New Jagannath temples were constructed in various parts of Odisha which symbolised political independence.
5. The use of commodification and consumption are not used pejoratively but to suggest the economy built around the trade of *prasad*. Hence, it is technical than to rob the *prasad* or the process of consumption of any of its religious valence.
6. The list of temples which were part of the fieldwork: Banthia Jagannath, Laxminarayan, Emami Jagannath, Radhakrishna, Rameswara in Balasore; Radha-Krishna temple at Laupalgadi, Balasore; Jagannath temple in Baripada; Jagannath temple at CDA and Chandni Chowk in Cuttack, ISKCON, Dakshinakali, Shani, Ananta Basudev, Lingaraj, Ram Mandir in Bhubaneswar; Jagannath temple at Rourkela.
7. *Nirmalya* is part of the *mahaprasad*. It is the left over rice which is dried and is sold later in Puri. Odias keep it in their households and consume it as a religious victual which ascertains lord's blessing.
8. Potala is the Odia for pointed gourd. It is a popular vegetable that is used with potato or chole. Chole is known as 'sola' in Odia.
9. See K.C. Mishra's (1984) for a detailed description of the preparation of the *mahaprasad*.
10. See Patanjali's website http://patanjaliayurved.org/ for further details.

References

Appadurai, Arjun. 1987. *The Social Life of Things: Commodities in Cultural Perspective*. Cambridge: Cambridge University Press.

Bala, Nandakishore. 1927. *Kanakalata*. In *Nandakishore Granthab ali*, 752–824. Cuttack: Friends Publisher.

Carrette, Jeremy and Richard King. 2005. *Selling Spirituality: The Silent Takeover of Religion*. New York: Routledge.

Connolly, William E. 2011. 'The Complexity of Intention'. *Critical Inquiry*, 37(4): 791–798.

Eschmann, Anncharlott, Hermann Kulke and G.C. Tripathy. eds. 1986. *The Cult of Jagannath and the Religious Tradition of Orissa*. New Delhi: Manohar.

Figlerowicz, Marta. 2012. 'Affect Theory Dossier: An Introduction'. *Qui Parle*, 20(2): 3–18. Available at https://www.jstor.org/stable/10.5250/quiparle.20.2.0003 (accessed 21 November 2018).

Kulke, Hermann. 1993. 'Ksatriyaization and Social Change: A Study in Orissa Setting'. In *Kings and Cults: State formation and Legitimation in India and Southeast Asia*, 82–92. New Delhi: Manohar.

Leys, Ruth. 2011, 'The Turn to Affect: A Critique'. *Critical Inquiry*, 37(3): 434–472. Available at https://www.jstor.org/stable/10.1086/659353 (accessed on 25 November 2018).

Mahapatra, Kedarnath. 1977. *The Jagannath Temples in Eastern India*. Bhubaneswar: Sri Sarada Press.

Mishra, K.C. 1984. 'Bhogas of the Jagannath Temple, Dress and Ornaments'. In *The Cult of Jagannath and the Religious Tradition of Orissa*, edited by Anncharlott Eschmann, Hermann Kulke and G.C. Tripathy, 193–204. Calcutta: Firma KLM Pvt. Ltd.

Roesel, Jakob. 1983, 'Landed Endowment and Sacred Food: The Economy of an Indian Temple'. *European Journal of Sociology*, 24(1): 44–59. Available at http://www.jstor.org/stable/23999213 (accessed on 29 December 2017).

Senapati, Fakir Mohan. 2014. *Fakir Mohan Granthabali Galpamala*, 5th edition. Cuttack: Students Book Store.

Stietencron, H.V. 1986. 'The Jagannatha Temples in Contemporary Orissa'. In *The Cult of Jagannath and the Religious Tradition of Orissa*, edited by Anncharlott Eschmann, Hermann Kulke and G.C. Tripathy. New Delhi: Manohar.

Tripathy, Mahimohan and Asit Mohanty, eds. 2015. *Nabakalebara Bichara*. Bhubaneswar: Aama Odisha.

Turner, Brian S. 2011. *Religion and Modern Society: Citizenship, Secularisation and the State*. Cambridge: Cambridge University Press.

6

DOMESTICATION OF JAGANNATH TEMPLE RITUALS IN ODIA HOUSEHOLDS: A SOCIOLOGICAL UNDERSTANDING OF THE PANTHEISM

Pranaya Kumar Swain

Introduction

The emotional integration of the Jagannath culture in the everyday life of Odia household is unprecedented by any stretch of the imagination. From *Puranic* texts to contemporary Odia literature, the corroboration can be located overwhelmingly through history. It is believed that Jagannath represents an assimilation of all the religious cults, creeds and sectarian philosophies that come under the purview of Hinduism in the broadest sense of the term. It will be a revelation to many that Jagannath is worshipped as Narayan or Visnu when he is on the *Ratnavedi* (dais) in the sanctum sanctorum, as Ganesha when on the Snanavedi (pedestal for bathing) during the *snana* (bath), as Rudra (expression of Shiva) during the Navakalevara ceremony, as Durga in the Sayana festival and as the Sun when on the chariot during the rath yatra. Taking this as a point of departure, here is a modest attempt at a pantheistic understanding of the daily rituals at the Jagannath temple and also at locating their domestication along the lines of metaphysical understanding of metaphors and metonymy as in Jacques Lacan's psychoanalysis (Schutter 1983). Drawing empirical evidence from Odia households through qualitative research using grounded theory as a tool for collection and validation of data, this chapter argues that Jagannath goes beyond the surreal and the divine and assumes a symbolic presence in Odia households, 'humanising' the divine in the process. This conceptualisation is instrumental in forming the Odia identity.

None has guided the psyche, the sociocultural and the emotional fabric of Odisha in the way Lord Jagannath has done. From naming newborns to naming businesses, from posters on the household walls to the stickers on the vehicles, from advertising hoardings to a mobile phone cover, from greeting salutations to the display picture of people's Facebook and WhatsApp profile, Jagannath has long been a captivating agency in the history, geography, culture and economy of the state. The realisation goes deeper than human imagination when it comes to the reach of the Lord transcending the hitherto existing political boundaries. The entire state takes refuge in the Lord when it comes to the metonymy (metonymy in the sense that the state of Odisha is closely associated with and is attributed to the name of Lord Jagannath that would be discussed in detail later in the chapter). The representation of the Lord establishes the union of the God and the people, rendering any relationship between the signified and the signifier meaningless. There is no way that the Odia identity and the way of life can be determined, let alone be understood by isolating any association from Lord Jagannath. Even Odia diaspora across the globe wears the metaphor on their sleeves. As the etymology suggests, Jagannath is the 'lord' of the world, exemplifying the meaning 'people's god' in every sense of the term.

Jagannath temple is a peculiar Hindu shrine where Vaishnavite, Shaivite and Shakta elements have been embodied in a ritual system (Mohapatra 2013). As corroborated in the Puranic texts, Jagannath was originally a deity of the aboriginal tribes and was known as Nila Madhav. Later, the god manifested himself in the form of four wooden images that we worship now and came to be known by the present-day name in an atmosphere of Vedic reorientation. Thus, Jagannath is equally claimed by the aboriginal tribes and the Vedic Hindus to be their original deity of worship. When one thinks of the Puri temple, one also thinks of the presiding deities therein, as well as the pattern of cultural life that is in practice, which, in turn, inspires the pilgrims with a lofty ideal of emotional and spiritual allegiance. Hence, the culture of Jagannath, as it is called (by way of translating the words Jagannath Dharma), has to be understood, interpreted and appreciated with all its social, cultural, religious and spiritual implications. The everyday rituals of Lord Jagannath are believed to be symbolic representations of everyday life of an Odia household.

The significance is appreciated even more when we realise that the Lord has been made to lead a life of a commoner.

Lochtefeld's (2010) conceptual differentiation between the Ganges and the Ganga, when he describes the former as a moving body of water often filled with contaminants and pollution and the latter a purifying goddess and an object of worship finds a striking parallel in the way Lord Jagannath, as the leading deity in the temple at Puri, and the religious, social, cultural and spiritual implications of the pantheistic significance of the culture that He represents. The gap between human and the Divine is bridged in Jagannath culture because Jagannath is a highly humanised deity. He brushes his teeth, takes a bath, changes his clothes, wears out robes and gold ornaments, is studded with diamond and sapphires to suit festive occasions and seasons, enjoys 56 varieties of food (*mahaprasad*) and 36 categories of servitors pay their '*Seva Khatani*' (duty) according to their '*Khatani* routine' for the daily duties relating to the worship of Lord Jagannath (Mohanty 2005).

The acculturation of the metonymy provides a gateway to Odisha, its people and the values and the ethos that they embrace. The Lord and the state have long been used as synonyms for each other. Odia identity is not much different from the identity of its presiding deity—Lord Jagannath (Das 2016). The domestication of the Lord manifests the pantheism as elucidated earlier in the chapter. The deity is humanised as He is made to practice the daily chores as much as the other household level activities that bear semblance of the *nitis* of the temple. Jagannath, as has already been stated, goes beyond the surreal and the divine and assumes symbolic presence in Odia households. While men continue to be recognised as the religious specialists among Hindus, women are active practitioners at home albeit having little religious authority on orthodox and textually sanctioned Hinduism. Women are essential to most yearly calendric (as per the local almanac) rituals and follow a large number of them in both rural and urban India (Wadley 1977). Hence women folk were purposefully chosen for the purpose of understanding the rituals in Odia households in this engagement.

In the process of analysis of data the chapter tries to superimpose the rituals of Lord Jagannath and those occasional and specific ones that have strong traditional associations with the Lord, especially those observed in Odia households to understand the unique semblance and how they intersect one another. However, the biggest festival of the Lord—the rath yatra—has been purposefully kept outside the purview of this attempt so that Jagannath as a practice moves beyond its institutional articulations and finds validity in people's daily life practices. Many of the historical and mythological texts such as *Kanchi Kaberi*, *Neela Saila*, *Niladri Bijaya*, etc. and the popular bhajans (songs with religious themes and spiritual ideas) that form integral parts of Odia folklores depict a humanised and domesticated God. One such text is quoted below where a commoner draws an analogy between his life's rituals and those of Lord Jagannath, establishing a clear link between the divine and the mundane lives.

> *To aaga re kichhi dhupa, mo aaga re kichhi dhupa*
> *to deha re kichhi phula, mo deha re kichhi phula,*
> *to paain deepa tie, mo paain deepa tie*
> *to beka re maala tie, mo beka re maala tie*
> *tu bada dande jibu , mun bada dande jibi*
> *tate taani taani nebe, mate bohi bohi nebe*
> *nadighosha re tu jibu, mun je kokei re jibi*
> *sri gundicha ku tu jibu, mun je swargadwara jibi* (Odia bhajan album, Mayura Chandrika, Srikanta Gautam, translated by the author.[1])

(They burn incense sticks in front of you, they will do so for me
They decorate your body with flowers, so will they do to me
They light oil lamps for you, they will do so for me
They put garlands around your neck, so will they do for me
They drag your chariot along the grand road, I will be lifted on their shoulders
You will be abode nandighosh for your trip to Gundicha temple, however, I will be placed in a coffin during my last journey)

Methodology

This chapter borrows extensively from the available literature on Jagannath culture, the temple rituals and the sociocultural history of the state of Odisha. For empirical data, qualitative methods are used to obtain relevant information. The sampling method is selective and the tools that are used are semi-structured guidelines. The sampling framework is fairly detailed in Table 6.1.

Table 6.1 Information Matrix

Type of respondents	Number	Research tool used	Key information area	Objective
Sevayats and *pujapandas*	10	Focused Group Discussion (FGD)	Temple rituals and their significance	To understand the rituals and activities concerning Lord Jagannath and their sociocultural significance
Women	30	FGDs (three groups of ten respondents each)	Performance of temple rituals at the households Manabasa Gurubar and its association with Lord Jagannath	To find out the rituals performed at the household and understand the pantheism
Widowed women	10	FGD	Insights into *Habisha* festivities	
Households	5	Case study Semi-structured interview		To gain a deeper understanding of daily and special rituals performed at the households

Thirty married women between the age group of 35 and 60 were purposively selected for three FGDs with ten participants in each group. The groups were fairly representative of the three socio-economic stratas: urban, rural and rurban (an area close to the country with the amenities of a city; an equivalent to a semi-urban area). Snowball method[2] was used to select the sample respondents.

Since the questions in hand were related to rites and rituals of Lord Jagannath, purposive sampling was adopted to include only Hindu married women. We also resorted to case studies of five households to gain deeper insight into the household level rituals particularly the daily, occasional and specific ones. Another FGD was conducted among ten widowed women to capture the rituals that are very specific to *habisha* (the ritual that they observe during the holy month of Kartik, which generally overlaps with the English months of October and November). Similarly, FGD was conducted with ten *sevayats* and *pujapandas* of the Jagannath temple, Puri. The analyses of the empirical data obtained through the interviews and FGDs have been presented in the subsequent sections.

The Superimposition: A Typical Day at the Temple and in the Odia Households

Historically *dharma* has been the central principle to understand indigenous religion. *Dharma* is closely associated with the duties regarded as sacred and which are to be performed in accordance with one's caste or sect. The constituents of *dharma* are: conformity to ritual duties, social obligations and the norms of family and caste behaviour as stipulated in the religious texts (Ahuja 1993). Home is the place where most Hindus perform their worship and religious rituals. For most of the Hindu households, the day begins when the women of the house offer puja to the household deities after finishing their morning chores and after they take a bath. The central concern here is ritual purity. For more orthodox families, dawn and dusk are greeted with recitations from religious texts. More elaborate practices include the lighting of lamps, offering food to the deities or to their images and performing prayers.

Hindus are polytheist devotees worshipping one or many of the vast pantheons of deities. However, in Odisha many households have the practice of worshipping their *ishta-devata* (desired god). The deities are kept either on a pedestal or in a miniature temple made of wood or stone at the most sacred corner or place in the household.

The metaphorical presence of a temple in Odia households appears to be a continuation of the long tradition of idol or totem worship. It may actually be a futile exercise to locate the exact origin of such a practice. However, most *puranic* texts do acknowledge the presence of a 'temple' in households of upper caste Hindus. Jagannath being the ultimate reference point for Odia culture naturally occupies the metonymic space where both Jagannath and Odisha are used and understood almost interchangeably. It is not possible to imagine the sociocultural landscape of Odia households without symbols associated with Jagannath.

The presence of the puja space in the households essentially requires the ritual offerings and prayers typically performed either daily or on special days before an image of the deity that may be in the form of a person or a symbol of the sacred presence. In its more developed forms, puja consists of a series of ritual stages beginning with personal purification and invocation of the god, followed by offerings of flowers, food, or other objects such as clothing, accompanied by fervent prayers. The content analysis of the FGDs with the respondents on the rituals of the Jagannath temple and their domestication is elaborated in Table 6.2.

Table 6.2 Daily Rituals of Lord Jagannath

In Jagannath temple*	In households**
5:00 AM: *Dwaraphita* (opening the door) and *mangal arati* (offering of sacred lamps to deities)	Most of the respondents confirmed performing of *mangal arati* at home, but not on a daily basis. *Dwaraphita* was found to be irrelevant as the deities at households are not kept in the confinement of a room as it is in a temple.
6.00 AM: *Mailam* *Mailam* means a change of dress used by God in the night. After removal of night dress, the deities are made to wear a new set of clothes called *tadap* and *uttariyas* for taking bath in the morning.	None of the respondents reported this ritual being performed at home. In fact, most of them confided that they did not change the dresses that the deities were made to wear.

In Jagannath temple*	In households**
6.00–6.30 AM: *Abakash* It means brushing of teeth and bathing of deities. Just like the morning chores done by the human beings, this includes cleaning of teeth, scrapping of the tongue and taking a bath. All these are done symbolically through the bronze mirror placed in front of the deities. Soft twig and tong cleaners are shown to the deities with appropriate *mudras* (postures) as if they brush. After that, along with chanting of *vedic suktas*, water mixed with camphor, *amla*, *sandle* paste, milk and curd is poured on the reflections of the deities on mirrors and it is considered as if the deities are taking a bath. During this *niti* (ritual), the astrologer of the temple reads out the *tithi* (date) and other astrological information of the day.	*Abakash* ritual was not reported to be performed at home. However, the respondents did say that as a symbolic representation of bath they would sprinkle water on the deities.
6.45 AM: *Besa Mailam* During this ritual, the deities change their clothes and wear a new set of clothes as human beings do after taking a bath. For seven days of the week, the deities are dressed in seven different colours. For Sunday, the deities wear red coloured *Pata*, for Monday black and white, for Tuesday *Barapatia Pata*, for Wednesday *Pata* of blue, for Thursday *Pata* of yellow, for Friday *Pata* of white and for Saturday *Pata* of black colour. From the colour of the dress of deities one can understand the day of the week.	This was not found to be a practice at the household level. Though deities are dressed, it is not according to specific colours on specific days as practised in Jagannath temple.

In Jagannath temple*	In households**
8.00–8.30 AM: *Besha ulagi niti* starts in the morning. During this *niti* the deities are dressed with the specific colour of the day and gold ornaments studded with precious stones and are decorated with scented flowers.	This ritual with actual elaboration was not reported to be a daily practice at home. However, deities are decorated with fresh flowers every day.
8.30 AM: *Rosa Homa* During this ritual, fire is sacrificed to the temple kitchen before initiation of the cooking process for the day. It was learned from the respondents that as per the temple traditions, the *deula purohit* (chief priest) performs this ritual. However, nowadays the *pujapandas* (other priests of the temple) also perform the ritual. *Rasa Homa* ritual is followed by Surya puja (worship of Sun God), Dwarapala puja (worship of the gatekeepers of the Lord) and Garuda puja (worship of the charioteer of Lord Jagannath).	The respondents were of view that such rituals were practised at home too in earlier days when cooking used to be done in traditional ways in earthen hearths. Since the cooking is primarily gas-stove-based now, the practice has mostly stopped. The rituals of Surya are still done in most households. However, Dwarapala puja and Garuda puja are not done at home as these deities are to be found in the temple only. But at the household level, other deities are worshipped after worshipping Lord Jagannath.
9 AM: *Gopala Ballav Bhoga* This refers to the breakfast *niti* of the Lord in the morning. The priests pointed out that one must have breakfast after taking a bath. So, the Lord must have his bath. The breakfast includes *khai*, *ukhuda*, ripe banana, etc.	Though none the respondents associated the breakfast at home with that at the temple, they were of the view that family members generally have their breakfast after their bath. The time for breakfast and also the type of food that one takes for breakfast varies as every member has his/her specific time for office or school or any other work.
10.00 AM: *Sakala Dhupa* The offering of a morning meal is also known as *kotha bhoga or raja bhoga* (the royal food). After the offering to the Lord, the *prasads* are distributed to the temple *sevayats*.	Such things are done at home but the respondents are not so specific about the way these rituals are performed at Jagannath temple. After worshipping the deities at home, the *prasad* (food offerings, generally in the form of fruits and sweets) are distributed to the family members.

In Jagannath temple*	In households**
11.00 AM: *Bhoga Mandap Bhoga* The large-scale food cooked for the general public including rice, daal, vegetable curries of various kinds and pancakes/cakes. This food is cooked in large quantity by the *suaras* (a certain caste group with *bhoga mandap* cooking as their traditional profession) on a commercial basis and is sold to the general public at the designated place inside the temple premises. On festive days due to high demand *bhoga mandap bhoga* is cooked multiple times	All the respondents claimed to have been purchasing *bhoga mandap bhoga* from Puri temple on many auspicious occasions, including those of birthdays, weddings, etc. Some respondents while putting things in perspective also pointed out that food for family members is cooked in the home kitchen. However, if there is a feast or a party involving a large number, the same is either bought from outside or a catering agency is hired to cook the food in a larger quantity making specific reference to how the food for the deities and general public has to be cooked separately and by different sets of cooks.
2.00 PM: *Madhyanha Pahuda* The mid-day rest, as explained by the priests of the temple, is considered to be ideal for their sound health as it is also prescribed for human beings. As a symbolic measure *ratna palankas* (beds) are brought to the sanctum.	No such ritual was found to be in practice at the household level for the deities. However, most of the respondents confided that they indulged in afternoon siesta themselves primarily to take some rest. The Lord's *pahuda* ritual can also be attributed to people resting.
Sandhya arati Evening lamp offering is performed after the mid-day rest. The *sevayats* said that the deities changed dresses and would be decorated with scented flowers and *tulsi* in large quantity.	Most of the respondents confirmed offering evening lamps to the deities at home. This is generally performed after sunset.
10.00 PM: *Mailam and Chandanalagi* After the evening meal, the dresses of the deities are changed again. Sandalwood paste mixed with camphor, *kasturi* and *kesar* is applied on the body of deities.	Most of the respondents agreed that though they did not perform such rituals for the deities at home, they do clean themselves up and change to their night gears and get ready to retire for the day.

In Jagannath temple*	In households**
11.45 PM or thereafter: *Khata Seja Lagi* Beds are made ready for the deities to rest. Before going to sleep they are offered green coconut and betel seeds in a similar manner to how people take mouth fresheners after dinner. The temple is vacated and all the doors are closed.	Gods are covered with clothes symbolising rest time for God. The respondents related this to their household activities of making the bed for everyone in the family and closing the gates and door of the house before retiring to the bed.

Notes:

* FGDs with the *sevayats* and *pujapandas* of Jagannath temple, Puri.

** FGDs with the 30 married Odia women.

Source: Mahapatra (2009) and author.

Temple rituals like *Sahanamela* (during which public are allowed close *darshan* of the deities), *Dwiprahara dhupa* (mid-day meal), *Sandhya dhupa* (evening meal), Badasinghar *besa* and Badasinghar *dhupa* (grand decoration of the deities) were reported not to be in practice in the households.

Specific Festivals

Apart from the daily rituals, there are certain specific festivities that are widely observed in Odia households whose magnitude and significance are attributed to the principal deities of the Jagannath temple. Manabasa Gurubar and *Habisha* are two such festivities that are observed in most of the Odia households. We handpicked these two and took a deeper look at them to understand how they constitute the metonymy of the household as the temple. The FGDs with the sample respondents captured the mythological narrations of some of the specific festivals that bear huge testimony to the impact of Lord Jagannath on the everyday practice of the people of Odisha. Here, we present the content analysis of the FGDs.

Manabasa Gurubar

Manabasa Gurubar is an annual festival for almost, if not all, all Odia households. It is the worship of Goddess Lakshmi in the month of Margasira as per traditional Odia *panjika* (calendar). The festivities of Manabasa Gurubar are based on the ancient scripture *Lakshmi Purana* and the story goes like this. The untouchables were not allowed to pray, worship and perform rituals to God in ancient times. At that time Shriya, a woman from an untouchable caste, dared to pray and worship and win over the support of Goddess Lakshmi. But the real story began when Lakshmi got evicted from the temple by Lord Jagannath at the behest of his brother Balabhadra because she had attempted to end the discrimination on earth by encouraging all untouchables to conduct rituals and worship. As Lakshmi moved out of Jagannath's house, both Jagannath and Balabhadra had to undergo immense suffering to the extent that they starved without water and food.

The curse of Lakshmi had a severe impact on both the brothers for 12 years and they had quite a difficult time. Soon they realised the importance of Lakshmi and were keen to bring her back to their home. Lakshmi returned to Jagannath's house on one condition which is that there will be no discrimination along the lines of caste and creed on earth. This unique story highlights the fact that everyone irrespective of one's caste and creed was equal before the God. Besides, it reflects the reforms and progressive stance of gods from ancient times. Only in the end through Narad it is revealed that he himself had set up these series of events to send out a bigger social message. The story not only draws our attention towards casteism but also sets an example for women's empowerment.

During this holy month of Margasira, the houses are kept neat and clean. *Chita* (*alpana*) is drawn to welcome Goddess Lakshmi and special pujas are offered to her. According to the respondents, Lakshmi is worshipped on every Thursday during the Odia month of Margasira by Odia women with the prescribed ritual methods. The women wake up very early in the morning and clean the house with broomsticks. It is believed that Goddess Lakshmi never visits a house if it is untidy and dirty. The doorsteps, as well as the entrance, are decorated with artistic *chita* (traditional Odia decoration of walls and floor by using rice flour as well as other dry colours). The decoration also includes a pot made of bamboo canes used in the earlier days for measuring paddy (known as *mana*). It is filled up to the brim with newly harvested paddy. It is believed that Goddess Lakshmi visits every house during the puja. This is observed on all the Thursdays of the holy month of Margasira (four to five such days depending on the occurrence). Special food items like *manda pitha*, *khiri*, *kakara*, *chitau*, etc. are prepared and distributed among neighbours. *Lakshmi Purana* is read by women folks and the auspicious ambience is maintained throughout the month.

The Rituals of Habisha

Habisha is a set of rituals that widowed women (called *Habishyali*) practice in the month of Kartik with all religiosity and sincerity to provide homage to the soul of their deceased husbands and their piousness. It is considered to be sacred as it is performed by elderly and windowed women who have crossed their normal cycles of menstruation and are believed to be pious.

The ritual is initiated with some preliminary act of purifications like trimming fingernails and toenails a few days before the month of Kartik. When the month of Kartik starts, widowed women have a pre-dawn bath in chilling winter. After their bath, they take up a handful of mud, make *Balugan* (dough made from sand and earth) and turn the mud into images of various forms of Lord Vishnu, worship it with water, flowers and pray to the Sun God and the basil plant and then go to the temple to offer prayers. They again undergo purification process in which the priest sprinkles cow dung water on them and by drinking '*panchagavya*' (made from milk, butter, honey, cow-urine, molasses and dung). Then they wear new clothes and offer the priest some gifts. These women carefully follow the instruction of the priest. They read and listen to the sacred book of *Kartika Mahatmya* and vow to fulfil the rituals of fasting, purification and sexual abstinence. They worship the Indian gooseberry tree and the cows during the days of rituals.

There are rituals like abstinence from combing or using hair oil, trimming of nails and not talking while preparing food or eating food. Food is to be prepared by using the clay pot. They are forbidden to touch others and try to maintain purity to the fullest extent. They eat only boiled food that includes *Habisha anna* and *Agasti saga* with no use of spices, once a day before the sunset. After the meal is cooked, they offer it to Lord Jagannath near a basil plant and then eat the food silently without uttering a word. They draw the picture of Lord Jagannath, Balabhadra, Subadra and various motifs associated with Odia myths and folktales around the basil tree with coloured powder and other symbols of Lord Jagannath and start praying to the basil plant and the sun with *hulahuli* (a shrill of varying magnitude that the women folks produce by horizontal movement of their tongue, usually accompanied by the blowing of the conch shell to symbolise auspiciousness; a very popular practice in Odisha). They also play act the legends of Lord Krishna and milkmaids and start dancing, singing, clapping joyfully near the basil plant. They put Akashdeepa (offering of lamp placing it on an elevated pedestal; generally done in open air) in the evening. Most *habishyalis* travel to Puri to offer puja to Lord Jagannath on the last day of the month as a mark of their celebration of piousness and celibacy.

From the discussions with the respondents, it was discovered that on special occasions like Ekadasi, Dwadasi, Purnima and Amavasya, the rituals are a bit different than that of the daily ones. On the day of Purnima or full moon days, people worship the deities, offer *kheeri* or other foods to the Lord. On the days of Amavasya, no special ritual is followed by people. On days of solar and lunar eclipse, deities are not worshipped because everything is considered impure. After the day of solar or lunar eclipse, people get purified and then start worshipping the Lords. On the day of Indu Purnami, *arati* is done, along with that special foods are offered. Deities wear new clothes on that day. On the days of Ekadasi, the same ritual follows and some women including the widows keep fasting and eat their food after offering it to God. On the days of Chandan Purnima, *kheer* is offered to God. On Kartik Purnima, the rituals that are followed are more systematic. Arati is done in the morning, and then reading of *Bhagabat* is done. After that, the entire day is spent on worshipping and reading the religious scriptures. Bamana Janma, Radha Ashtami, Janmashtami are observed by reading *Bhagabat*, fasting and worshipping. On Gahma Purnima, special *pithas* and *kheeri* are offered to God. *Tulsi* is not plucked on this day. Deva Snana Purnima and rath yatra are special rituals that are celebrated by doing *arati* and offering *bhoga*. On the day of Dola Purnima, the deities are decorated with flowers and worshipped with colours.

Case Studies: On Jagannath and More

Attempts were made to understand up-close some of the rituals as they are practised at the household level. Five households of varied socioeconomic background were handpicked for the purpose and a conscious attempt was made to understand how deep Lord Jagannath has gone into people's daily lives. The respondents belong to different districts with different family size and diverse backgrounds to make the samples representative and data more inclusive. The diversity of socioeconomic backgrounds of the selected family also reveal the varying degree of vigour in terms of the festivities as observed at the individual household levels. Observing the variations in sociocultural practices under an overarching paradigm has always been a sociologist's delight.

Case Study 1

Type of Location: Rural (Village-Bhatimunda, District-Cuttack, Odisha)

Type of Family: A nuclear family of four consisting of elderly parents, two married daughters, one younger daughter who is working as a teacher in a college and the youngest son who is studying in college.

Profession of the Head of the Family: Retired from government service.

Daily Rituals: The day starts with *snana* (ritual bathing) of the gods (varied photos and figurines which include the revered Jagannath) and subsequent offerings of flower, sandalwood paste, *tulsi*, *ghee*, *mishri*, sweets and fruits (if available). The figurines are kept on a mud *pinda* (earthen elevated platform) located in a small deity room of the house. Camphor and *jhuna* (a plant extract generally burnt to offer the haze aroma to the deities) is burnt. Here the Puri temple rituals are not strictly adhered to and they are often subject to situational exigencies. The holy *Bhagabat* is read in the evening by the father every day.

Specific Festive Days: Gamha Purnima (birthday of Balabhadra/ Raksha Bandhan): This year (2018) it fell on 26 August of the English calendar. Since Balabhadra is represented by *hala langala* (tillage equipment carried by bulls), the bulls are tied a *rakhi* (a cotton bracelet, considered sacred, that a Hindu girl/woman ties around her brother's wrist hoping for his well-being) and are offered *pitha* (pancake) by the family. On such occasion *arua* (non-boiled paddy) rice is cooked and eaten.

Janmashtami: The birth of Lord Krishna (avatar of Jagannath/Vishnu) is celebrated by the extended reading of *Bhagabat* from early morning till the part in the scripture which leads to the birth of Krishna. It takes about six to seven hours with intermittent breaks. One member of the family is required to fast compulsorily. The said person cannot eat any cooked food (food cooked on fire) and eats only fruits at night.

Pana Sankranti: Pana bhoga is made of coconut, banana, yoghurt, etc. The street in front of the house is cleaned and wet cow dung is applied on the street in a circular fashion which when it dries, the *bhoga* is kept on top of it. The *bhoga* is offered to Lord Jagannath before being consumed by the family members.

Lakshmi (wife of Jagannath) puja during Manabasa Gurubar: As explained in the earlier section it falls on *Marghasira* month of the Odia calendar. The five Thursdays of this month are considered auspicious. The women of the house clean the house the night before (Wednesday). Rice paste is used to make *chita* (a form of motif/ rangoli) on the floor and walls of the house. *Gendu* (marigold) and *padma* (lotus) flowers are offered to Lakshmi. In a special *khatuli* (wooden pedestal) betel leaves, paddy grains, *gua* (nuts) are kept in reverence to Lakshmi along with her small figurine. *Pitha*, *chhena* (homemade cheese), fruits etc. are offered as *bhoga* which is eaten by the members of the household except the married daughters (for its believed that Lakshmi will leave the house if the *bhoga* is consumed by a married daughter). *Lakshmi Purana* is recited depicting the story of Goddess Lakshmi and Jagannath that led to the goddess leaving the temple and the ordeal that the Lord and his brother Balabhadra had to go through due to the wrath and curse of Goddess Lakshmi.

Case Study 2

Type of Location: Rural (Village-Adampur, Jajpur, Odisha)

Type of Family: Joint family involving four married couples

Profession of the Head of the Household: Agri-business/government service

Distinct Tradition: Worship of *salagrama* stones (representation of non-anthropomorphic symbol of Vishnu). The largest and heaviest *salagrama* is found at Jagannath temple in Puri. These fossilised sea-shells were collected by the forefathers of the household from river beds.

Daily Rituals: The morning ritual of opening of the *pahuda* (a piece of decorative cloth which screens the wooden *khatuli* on which the stones are placed) resembles dwaraphita, the ceremonial opening of the door of the Jagannath temple in Puri before the dawn.

The day's worship is done in three stages:

1. Following the age old *jajmani* system, a *purohit* (Brahmin priest) is engaged by the family to carry out the rituals. The opening of the *pahuda* symbolises the waking up of the Lords. The stones along with the bronze figures of Jagannath and other Indian Gods are then bathed in milk. They are then offered flowers, *chandan* (sandalwood) and *khai ukhuda* (roasted puffed rice grains mixed with jaggery).
2. In the afternoon lunch is cooked in *chulha* (earthen stove) for the Gods by the priest. Proper *neeti anna bhoga* (cooked rice) is made which also happens in Puri—a la *abadha*. The difference being, as opposed to the *arua* (non-polished) rice offered in Puri, the said household traditionally cooks *usuna* (polished) rice, *dalma* (an Odia dish with pulses and vegetables as main ingredients) and other vegetables in desi ghee and other condiments sans onion and garlic.

On certain days due to paucity of time and prior engagement of the priest the *khichdi* (rice and pulses cooked together) is made. The lunch is then served as *bhoga* to the Gods. The remaining food is eaten by the family as well along with other food items cooked in the household kitchen.

3. The day's ritual ends with the priest coming at night to pull down the *pahuda* so that they can go to sleep.

Special Festive Days: A few decades ago the celebration of rath yatra involved pulling of a small chariot by the extended family. The family also owned gold jewellery for the deities, the whereabouts of which have been lost by the current generation of the family. Now the eldest head of the household makes it a point to visit Puri every year along with his wife on *bahuda* (last day of the 9-day long rath yatra festivity) and other days associated with rath yatra.

Case Study 3

Type of Location: Urban (Bhubaneswar/Vishakhapatnam)

Type of Family: Nuclear. Old couple with married children living elsewhere

Profession of the Head of the Household: Officer retired from the Indian Revenue Service. Post-retirement he has been actively involved in several charitable trusts and temple committees. He has also built Lokanath temple in his village.

Distinct Factor: Chairperson of the Jagannath Temple Committee (since 2001) in Vishakhapatnam.

Daily Rituals: The head of the household wakes up at 4 AM in the morning and prays for a few minutes in his home temple and then heads out for a walk. He stops nearby the Jagannath temple and chants a few lines of *Geeta Gobinda*. The two home temples that he has in Bhubaneswar and Vishakhapatnam are taken care of by family members or house help in his absence.

Special Festivities: As chairperson of the Jagannath temple in Vishakhapatnam he has looked after the SOPs during rath yatra.

A total of 110 *padiharis* (servitors) are engaged in the temple to carry out the detailed procedures relating to Jagannath. To carry each statue out of the temple to the 'chariot' requires at least four servitors who carry it in exact angles to prevent the deities from falling. One of the servitors lays down a *dhoti* (traditional attire) for the Gods to be laid down and carries *chamar* (fan) to comfort the Gods from the heat. Almost 500 people are provided with *prasad* daily. The food is made in two ways, either with *Vanaspati* ghee (pure homemade ghee is hard to come by these days) or without (not many prefer the Vanaspati brand of ghee). Donations are collected for the same. On *bahuda* almost 4,000 people are fed. The Gods are clothed daily for different rituals. The servitors who in earlier times were provided land titles are now given salary/share of the donations in lieu of their work. The rituals followed are in tandem with what happens in Puri with digressions in cases not plausible to imitate.

Case Study 4

Type of Location: Urban, Bhubaneswar, Odisha

Type of Family: Nuclear family of four members

Profession of Head of the Household: Tax firm owner

Distinct Factor: Highly spiritual and ardent ISKCON temple members.

The family doesn't have a Jagannath idol at home for that would require offering *anna bhoga* that is daily cooking of proper lunch for the God and following articulate rituals. They have pictures of Jagannath but would rather worship *Krishna.*

Daily Rituals: They make it a point to read the holy *Bhagabat Gita* and chant *Geeta Gobinda* as most Jagannath followers do. They use the *japa rudraksha maala* to meditate and reminisce in the memory of the Lord chanting *Hare Rama Hare Krishna* (a very popular chant attributing its origin to the bhakti traditions of Chaitanya).

Special Festivities: The couple visits and stay in Nadia (Mayapur, West Bengal) which is a religious congregation for the followers of

Krishna. While in Nadia they, along with the devotees, wake up at 4:30 AM for the *mangal arati* (symbolic of what happens in Puri) which is performed to celebrate the waking up of the Gods. This *darshan arati* follows at 7:30 AM and the couple goes around the sanctum symbolising a *parikrama*. *Tulsi* and flower offering is pertinent. Dola Purnima, Radha Ashtami and Chandan Jaatra are celebrated by them with a festive rigour too. On those days, the couple follows all the rituals that are performed in the Jagannath temple at Puri.

Case Study 5

Type of Location: Urban, Cuttack, Odisha

Type of Family: Nuclear family of three

Profession of the Eldest Member: Government service

Distinct Factor: The eldest lady of the house is a prominent religious commentator on state television channels. She does voice-overs especially on rath yatra and conducts spiritual workshops apart from managing her day job of being a Sanskrit lecturer in a college.

Daily Rituals: As the lady grew up in an extremely religious family, she is particular about daily worship and traditional festive occasions. On most days she has simple food without onion and garlic. Since Jagannath personifies human conduct, bathing, getting dressed and having *anna aahar* (eating rice as most people of Odisha do) the same is translated in her morning puja. On waking up, the deities at home are bathed as is done in Puri. A mirror is reflected on the image of the Gods and they are symbolically bathed with water being put over a conch shell. To protect the Gods from rising temperatures sandalwood paste is applied to the deities.

Special Rituals: The *shraddha* (after-death rituals for the salvation of the departed soul) follows from the *shraddha* done by the Jagannath servitors. On Diwali, three *shraddha* rituals are performed by the priests for Basudeb-Debaki, Dasaratha-Kaushalya and Nanda-Jashoda (mythological couples from Hindu scriptures). *Pinda daana* (paying homage) done for humans follows the same ritual from Jagannath culture.

Discussion and Conclusion

The metonymic realisation of Lord Jagannath for the contours of Odia identity, both local and global, stems from the deployment of Jagannath in Odia people's everyday lives. The realisation runs deeper than the idea of a religious cult as can be understood from various texts that have attempted to establish the superiority of Jagannath over other Gods on the basis of His exclusiveness and philosophical speculations woven around the name Jagannath (Tripathi 1986). Such ideas are not inherent in the things themselves, but ascribed by people's agency and reinforced by culture and behavioural patterns (Lochtefeld 2010) through history. As found in this empirical study, the daily rituals of the Lord symbolise the activities that are associated with any common human being: brushing the teeth, taking a bath, having breakfast, lunch, evening snacks and dinner, taking an afternoon nap, having mouth fresheners after a meal, changing clothes, etc.

The real-life image makes the Lord more accessible and easy to connect with the people. The festivities of Manabasa Gurubar revolve around the central idea of non-discrimination of people along the lines of caste and creed. The bowing down of the Lords to the uncompromising determination of the Goddess Lakshmi goes a long way in inspiring empowerment of women, capturing the pantheistic imagination of the Lord like nothing else does. The experiences of the *Habishyalis* reveal how the activities associated with those of the holy month act as a code of conduct for the old widowed women to lead peaceful and pious lives. Given that the temple and households are different social agencies located in different landscapes, the rituals observed at respective places are bound to be different. However, the pantheism, as this chapter has argued, stands out incredibly in the way the rituals are conceived and practiced.

It is beyond any dispute that Odisha has changed incredibly in past couple of decades paving ways for changes in people's ideas about Puri as a pilgrim centre and the rituals as such. As put forward by an old lady, one of the respondents in an FGD during the empirical study,

> In [the] old days, people used to do their daily activities by keeping in mind the daily rituals of Jagannath temple, but now a days, the time schedule for every work has changed. The only thing that has survived is the daily worship of Lord Jagannath and other deities during the morning hour, along with offering some food and in the evening. Previously, people used to eat vegetarian food keeping in mind the rituals of temple, where, there was no provision of non-vegetarian food in the temple. The food items in breakfast, lunch, dinner used to be like those of temple, which are the traditional food including *pakhala, khai,* etc. But now the variety, diversity in food items have reduced a lot.

Though some rituals are being followed in the households on specific festivals, the intensity and rigidity are gradually loosening their grips. Only the elder populations, who are more religious, have been able to keep these rituals alive. Still, people are gradually forgetting the sense of strong religiosity and ritualism. Women staying in cities like Cuttack and Bhubaneswar were of the view that on a daily basis none of the rituals of the temple are followed by them. But on some special occasions, they do worship and offer food to God. The observance of rituals also has a gender aspect, where it is the women who are more conscious about the rituals, whereas male members of the family, as confided by the respondents, are not that much aware of the rituals that are followed, which dismisses their legitimacy as sole religious specialists. However, men continue to remain the caretakers of the temples and dominate most forms of public rituals.

New interpretations of the rituals traditionally associated with and attributed to Lord Jagannath have made those rituals understood, practised and passed on differently. As evident from some of the respondents' experiences, the socioeconomic and attitudinal changes are affecting the rituals for want of continuity and some of those are falling prey to ever changing consumerism. Though taking part in cooking and distributing *mahaprasad* is an important sacrament of Jagannath culture (Mohanty 1982), the *pandas* (the priests) have been transformed from ritual guides to tourist guides and the *ananda bazaar* has visibly turned into a mere congregation of shops selling *mahaprasads.*

Recent times have seen the emergence of community temples, where Lord Jagannath and other deities are worshipped. These centres have become the place of worship during the holy months and other festivals related to Lord Jagannath. Another noticeable thing is setting up of Sai temples, Hanuman temples, etc. in Odisha in the late twentieth century. These go on to imply that the people have accommodated the assimilation of various non-native Gods. Despite these recent adoptions, Lord Jagannath still remains the iconic deity of the state. The recent sociopolitical churning of the state, the growth in the upwardly mobile service sector, growth in the number of public funded educational institutions of national repute, the advent of IT and financial sectors have rendered Odisha a new look altogether. It is no longer a 'siesta state' as tagged by the BBC correspondent in India Daniel Lak a few years ago. Both the resident and non-resident Odias still, with loads of pride, associate themselves with Lord Jagannath and that reinforces Dash's (1978) conceptualisation of Oriya (now spelt Odia after the State was officially renamed as Odisha) nationalism, because of the intimate relationship that Jagannath automatically occupies the central position in the thought process of every Odia.

Notes

1. Available at https://www.youtube.com/watch?v=iYcUme5sof4 (accessed 21 July 2019).
2. In snowball method, as the name suggests, once you set the ball rolling it picks up more snow along the way and grows bigger. Snow ball technique is used when the researcher recruits participants from references from other people and acquaintances of already recruited participants.

References

Ahuja, Ram. 1993. *India Social System*. Delhi: Rawat Publications.

Das, R.N. 2016. *The Changing Contours of Odia Identity*. Available at https://www.dailypioneer.com/2016/sunday-edition/the-changing-contours-of-odia-identity.html (accessed 20 June 2019).

Dash, G.N. 1978. 'Jagannatha and Oriya Nationalism'. In *The Cult of Jagannath and the Regional Tradition of Orissa*, edited by Hermann Kulke, Gaya Chàran Tripath and A. Eschmann. South Asia Interdisciplinary Regional

Research Programme, Orissa Research Project. New Delhi: Manohar Publication.

Gautam, Srikant. 'To aga re kichhi dhupa', in album *Mayura Chandrika*. Available at https://www.youtube.com/watch?v=iYcUme5sof4

Lochtefeld, James. 2010. *God's Gateway Identity and Meaning in a Hindu Pilgrimage Place*. New York: Oxford University Press.

Mahapatra, B. 2009. 'Daily Rituals of Lord Jagannath'. *Orissa Review*, 84–87. Available at http://magazines.odisha.gov.in/Orissareview/2009/June/engpdf/84-87.pdf (accessed 20 June 2019).

Mohapatra, P. 2011. 'Daily Rituals of Sri Jagannath Temple'. *Orissa Review*, 22–26. Available at http://magazines.odisha.gov.in/Orissareview/2011/july/engpdf/22-26.pdf (accessed 20 June 2019).

Mohapatra, S.C. 2013. 'The Ritual System'. *Odisha Review*, 28–31. Available at http://magazines.odisha.gov.in/Orissareview/2013/jul/engpdf/29-32.pdf (accessed 20 June 2019).

Mohanty, J.K. 2005. 'Influence of Jagannath Culture on People of Orissa'. *Orissa Review*, 27–32. Available at http://magazines.odisha.gov.in/Orissareview/dec2005/engpdf/influence_of_jagannath_culture_on_people_of_orissa.pdf (accessed 20 June 2019).

Mohanty, Surendra, 1982. *Lord Jagannath*. Bhubaneswar: Orissa Sahitya Akademi.

Schutter, Dirk De. 1983. 'A Study of Metaphor and Metonymy in Lancan'. *Auslegung: A Journal of Philosophy*, 10(1): 65–74.

Wadley, S.S. 1977. 'Women and the Hindu Tradition'. *Signs*, 3(1): 113–125.

7

CONTEMPORARY BANGLA SONGS ON JAGANNATH: A HERMENEUTIC FOR BHAKTI AND COMMUNITY OF *BHAKTAS*

Sreejit Datta

Introduction

The fact that most search results for the keyword 'Jagannath bhajan' return Odia songs and/or music videos—except for a mere two to three Bangla and Hindi songs and music videos—on both YouTube and Google, gives one considerable ground to think that the phrase exclusively implies an Odia subgenre of the 'bhajan', which is the most well-known Indic genre of devotional music. 'Indic genre' means that bhajan refers to a specific form of Hindu/Jain/Buddhist/Sikh devotional music. The word 'bhajan' itself is a generic term, used across several modern Indo-Aryan languages like Punjabi, Bengali, Odia, Gujarati, Hindi, etc. because it encapsulates various subcategories of Indic devotional music, such as *kirtan*, *shabad* and *agomoni* and several others which have locally flourished all over the Indian Subcontinent but not in complete isolation from each other. The word is derived from Sanskrit word '*bhajana*' which is a noun denoting actions such as worshipping, chanting and singing praises to some form of the Divinity or other. This array of connotations of the word has been retained in the various modern Indo-Aryan languages, with only slight alterations in the pronunciation of the word across such languages; although in most cases bhajan would denote the contracted sense that is 'devotional music' when it is uttered in our contemporary popular contexts.

The scenario of devotional music in the Bangla language has undergone a sea change both in terms of quality and quantity in the last two decades. With the advent of digital technology in music production and dissemination a decade earlier (the first compact disc or CD player was launched in India in the year 1989 [Vasuki 1989]) in the Indian market and with the digital techniques starting to replace the previous analogue techniques in a wholesale manner for both producers and consumers of music in the country from around the year 2000, the quantity of Bangla devotional music has seen a sharp rise in its volume. However, in terms of quality, the songs, barring a few exceptions here and there, have failed to make any lasting impact in the minds of music connoisseurs/critics and the general audience alike. The same observations apply to Bangla songs devoted to Jagannath, which constitute a subset of the vast corpus of Bangla devotional music.

This shift in music production as well as dissemination techniques help us distinguish two (almost) clearly-defined periods in considering the songs composed on Jagannath-bhakti. It is rather difficult to associate these songs, which provide some form of expression to the devotional fervour of many Bengali supplicants (and even the non-Bengali ones on certain occasions), to any one particular sect or, as is frequently called, 'cult'. As such, unlike in Odisha, there has been a conspicuous absence of a 'Jagannath cult' in Bengal despite the strong devotional fervour displayed by an average Bengali devotee of Jagannath. The chief reason for this is the blurring away of rigid sectarian identities (like Shaivite, Shakta or Vaishnavite) in the Bengali Hindu society ever since the advent of Chaitanya Deva ('Deva' is Sanskrit for 'God'; it is frequently used as an honorary appellation) in the spiritual and cultural life of Bengal and the rest of Eastern India. It is because of his tremendous impact on almost every aspect of Bengal's culture: the language, sacred or profane performances, and in the way Bengalis perceive matters spiritual and divine (Ghosh 2007).

Chaitanya Deva has not remained a mere mediator between the individual devotee or a group of devotees of Jagannath and the deity of Nilachal (alternative name of Puri) Himself, instead he has transcended his role as a mediator. He has been a bridge between these two, as also the usherer who leads the devotee across that bridge. Thus, Chaitanya Deva has been the chief catalyst in forming a community of devotees around Jagannath in Bengal, across time and space.

It is difficult to draw divisions such as sacred or profane across performative elements found in Bengal or elsewhere in India, as far as the customs and practices of Indic communities are concerned. However, what started only as a gradual process of softening sectarian divisions and cult identities among Hindus of Bengal at the time of Chaitanya Deva, gained considerable pace in the nineteenth century and afterwards. The pinnacle of this process was reached at the time when spiritual movements led by Sri Ramakrishna, Swami Vivekananda and the Brahmo Samaj manifested in Bengal, and each in their own way left an indelible mark in the formation of today's spiritual and cultural landscape of Bengal. One of the many results of that long process, as it stands today, is this: Jagannath's famed shrine at Puri has become a major centre of pilgrimage for almost all the sections of Bengali Hindus, cutting across classes and castes, and irrespective of their distinctive *ishta-devata* or the deity of one's own preference and *kula-devata* or the deity who is traditionally worshipped by a family (and who, in many cases, have been forgotten by the later generations of such families, resulting in zero discrimination towards various deities by such families).

In the field of devotional music, however, this process has manifested as a most peculiar admixture of tunes. Many popular tunes that were traditionally associated with songs of devotion towards a particular deity, have presently found their way into the corpus of devotional songs dedicated to Jagannath. To cite just one such case, many popular (some would say 'folk') tunes associated for long with the Shakta sect, that is the fold of those Bengali Hindus who have traditionally worshipped the Divinity in Its feminine form, predominantly as Kali/Durga/Jagadhatri, have sneaked into contemporary devotional songs hailing Jagannath. Many such examples abound. Not only with tunes; this phenomenon has been observed in the way lyrical forms and tropes of songs, organically sprung and developed within deity-specific and historically distinct sects, have made their way into the songs of other sects as well. We will cite such examples in a more formal and organised manner in this chapter.

And yet, we would resist the temptation of labelling this phenomenon as 'syncretism' taking place in the sphere of cultural production—in this case music—for this musical amalgamation may or may not have taken place inadvertently. Whether this process has taken place with its facilitators remaining completely unaware of it, or whether they were forced to borrow the tunes of sect-specific devotional songs into their own musical expressions of devotion to the divine, is subject of further investigation into the matter. For instance, there may have been an absence of the creative impetus within a particular sect in some cases, in which scenario the process of borrowing—if not plagiarising—could be understood as a conscious attempt at a devotional music-making transaction. The present exercise will attempt to partly address this issue within its limited scope.

This study aims to initiate engagement on a few questions of bonding and belonging, if not fully answer them. The questions that guide this engagement are: How do these songs and singers create an idea of bhakti that unites Bengalis and how do they place Odia claim over Jagannath, that is to say, how do they relate to a God who is outside the state border? Has there been any noticeable change in the theme of Bangla bhajans and their sale/circulation etc.? How are 'being' and 'belonging' imagined, if not explicitly defined, by these songs? Does Jagannath transcend the differences in Odia and Bengali culture and identity or does the deity merely help to transcend those differences by providing a bridge between these two cultural universes? How impregnable are these two cultural spheres from each other's influences? Do cross-cultural transactions between them reflect on these songs in some way? The following sections address these questions by critically engaging with them. The first of these, 'Towards a Classification: Scope of the Study' discusses the bases of categories through which the theoretical framework is built and understood, and also defines the scope of the present study. The second, titled 'Bangla Songs of Bhakti on Jagannath' describes the centrality of Chaitanya Deva in Bangla Jagannath bhajans, and situates the latter in relation with Jagannath bhajans in Odia and other Indian languages. The next section, 'Discourse of Bhakti and Dynamics of Interaction between Odia and Bengali Cultures' traces the reception of the bhakti tradition in the contemporary Bangla Jagannath bhajans and delineates the position of the deity as depicted through such songs. Finally, the conclusion addresses the dynamics and anxieties of cultural differences between Bengal and Odisha and shows how the songs affect the same.

Towards a Classification: Scope of the Study

In this section, we offer definitions of key categories on which the survey and its arguments are based. To begin with the title itself, 'contemporary Bangla songs', wherever it occurs, would imply the songs which were composed between the year 2000 and the present day, that is mid-2018 (including each end) and/or rehashed from a much earlier version, and subsequently published during this interval. Compositions that occur previous to this period would bear other labels (for example, 'songs composed and/or published during the second half of the last century'), as and when required. Likewise, the phrase 'Bangla songs' would denote those songs whose lyrics are penned either in the standardised Bangla language or any of its variants. 'Songs on Jagannath' would imply such songs as referring either explicitly or implicitly to the Hindu deity Jagannath, or any of the festivals/rituals/incidents associated with the deity, or the sacred city of Puri (along with its metonyms, like Nilachal) which houses the deity. There are plenty of examples where artists of Bengali origin have performed and recorded devotional songs, like bhajans on Jagannath in Odia language.

We shall not consider such songs, despite their remarkable similarities with Bangla devotional songs about the *Prabhu*—the Lord—in both lyrical and melodic aspects, in this survey. The formulaic nature of songs, which consist only of repeated cycles of various names of the *Prabhu*, renders the actual lyrical content to be rather brief. This blurs the finer differences between the Bangla and Odia languages in the lyrics of such songs when they are performed or recorded. For this reason, it is not unusual to wrongly perceive an Odia devotional song on the *Prabhu* as a Bangla one and vice versa either at the first hearing or by an unsuspecting listener. As an illustration of this phenomenon, let us take the refrain of one such famous song, which goes like this: '*jaya jaya Jagannatha, trilokeri pati*'; and it becomes virtually impossible to determine whether the song is composed in Odia or Bengali unless the listener pays close attention to the words in the whole of its lyrics.

At the moment there is little scholarly literature available on the subject of Bangla songs on Jagannath, much less on contemporary songs of the kind. This could be due to lack of interest, resources and/or proper investigative orientation in reading such songs as a cultural phenomenon that contributes to building bonds between individuals and ultimately creates a community. This could also be attributable to the scarcity of aesthetically appealing songs on the subject—the reasons could be many and subject to speculation. Therefore, the present study, which is perhaps the first of its kind in the field, is expected to break fresh ground in Jagannath studies from a musicological approach that also caters to the needs of identifying processes of community building through the medium of music. Due to lack of existing literature on the topic, most of what follows is based on the primary empirical evidence of the songs selected for the present survey and subsequent analysis of the same. The analytical method employed here entails the close reading of contemporary (the term 'contemporary' has been defined and contextualised earlier in the chapter) Bangla songs on Jagannath, cultural as well as performative texts, in comparison to similar songs from the period preceding the chosen time frame. The comparison between these two sets of songs, belonging to two different periods, is based on multiple factors such as theme, lyrics, tune, instrumentation, etc. which have been expounded in the subsequent sections. The distinction between these two periods is made for the occurrence of a shift in the techniques of production and dissemination of the songs

At this point, it will be pertinent to note that several Bangla devotional songs on Jagannath, which were composed and subsequently published in the various analogue formats previous to the year 2000, have been given a new lease of life in the last two decades thanks to the promulgation of digital recording technology and the easy accessibility of songs in digital formats. It has been achieved not so much by remaking or rerecording the songs by new artists and recording companies as has been by simply bringing the old song, as they were, from analogue to digital media. Digitally restored devotional songs are a great favourite among devotees. The very popular Odia song '*jaya jaya Jagannatha, trilokeri pati*' is a case in point. This particular Odia song was recorded as far back as 1977, the singers being Nirmala Mishra, a renowned Bengali playback artist who had received much acclaim in the 1960s through 1980s, and Bhikari Bal, who had earned the epithet '*Bhajansamrat*' (literally 'the emperor among singers of bhajan') among his Odia listeners. And yet it still enjoys considerable popularity among Bengali and Odia devotees of Jagannath alike to this day, especially due to dissemination via various platforms on the Internet such as YouTube. As such, many of these songs are frequently used on various occasions, festivities and pilgrimages. Such songs have been referred in this survey only in comparison with the songs from the selected period since the chapter's focus is on songs that have been composed and primarily recorded within the period spanning from 2000 onwards.

Traditionally, devotional songs associated with the Vaishnavite sects are categorised as either *nama-kirtan* or *leela-kirtan* (Sarbadhikary 2015) depending, respectively, on whether the subject matter of the song relates to repeated melodious chanting cycles of the deity's many sacred names (that is *nama*) or whether the song concerns itself with the divine playful activities (that is *leela*) partook by the deity/an avatar/a saint. The generic names attributed to devotional songs across all sects are *kirtan* and bhajan. These names are also used to refer to two different, but related, genres of Indian music in their own right. Those genre-names apply equally to all deities/sages in Hinduism, irrespective of sects or *sampradayas*, and are also used to refer to devotional music practiced by the Sikhs to this day. These two names, having been derived from Sanskrit, are ubiquitously found in almost all the major modern Indian languages like Hindi, Bengali, Odia, Telugu, Kannada, Punjabi, Rajasthani, Gujarati, Assamese, etc.

Coming back to the songs used specifically by the various Vaishnavite *sampradayas*, it is to be noted that the act of performing any of these two types of devotional songs (viz. *nama-kirtan* and *leela-kirtan*) for a long period of time (ranging from 3 hours to 3 days; even at times as long as a week) without break on some special occasion is known as *sankirtan* (the added Sanskrit prefix *san-* sanctifies the performance of *kirtan*; connoting the *kirtan* to have been performed well). Sri Chaitanya was a pioneer of this type of devotional musical performance (Pandey 1996). Interestingly, this twofold division of Vaishnavite devotional songs is conspicuously detectable in Bangla devotional songs dedicated to Jagannath. As a result, it is possible to think of a twofold categorisation of these songs: one, where mainly the name of the *Prabhu*, along with a select few other names of

Vishnu/Krishna are chanted in the song with patterns of a melody improvised over time; the second consists of lyrics that describe incidents related to the lives of Sri Chaitanya Deva or Sri Nityananda Prabhu, especially the phase of their lives that was spent in Srikshetra Puri, that is Nilachal, in the vicinity of the temple of Jagannath. This observation holds true for the songs that are drawn from the period we have chosen for the present study, for there has been little variation in the variables that demarcate either category for such songs.

Bangla Songs of Bhakti on Jagannath

One of the most conspicuous features of Bangla devotional songs on Jagannath is the invocation of Chaitanya Deva and Nityananda Prabhu at the beginning, typically that of a *kirtan*/bhajan, for obvious reasons. Indeed, together they have acted as a point of departure—and not merely as some passive beacon of inspiration—from the themes, motifs and even forms of musical expressions of bhakti involving Jagannath in the Bengali cultural sphere. They are ever present in those songs—sometimes as a mediator, and sometimes even merged with the deity and his various aspectual markers. Thus, the duo has been animating these songs with the force of their living spiritual presence every time such songs are performed, or even merely played, in a sacred sphere; such as inside the temple premises or in the course of a pilgrimage to Puri. Innumerable songs recount their journey to Puri, their *leela* or divine play with the *Prabhu* and His devotees. The songs enliven the journeys of pilgrims to Puri by helping to visualise and thus bring back to life the ecstatic dances of the duo at the time of the *Prabhu's* rath yatra. This is achieved via the lyrics, rhythm and melody—all necessary ingredients of these Bangla devotional songs on Jagannath. These two sacred figures have functioned as a link that connects generations of Bengali devotees to their Lord Jagannath, and they continue to serve as that link to this day.

The invocation of Sri Chaitanya and Nityananda (and the other key associates of the duo) is often found to be composed in Sanskrit, typically sung *ad libitum* at the beginning of the song and usually without a rhythmic cycle; or, at any rate, with minimum use of musical instruments at that phase of the song. This is a traditional formula, found frequently in Bangla hagiographical texts written on highly exalted spiritual figures like Sri Chaitanya and Bangla hymns, such as those composed in the *panchali* form (*panchali* is a Bengali narrative form in verse with a distinct metrical structure). It demonstrates the close connection between the structures of Bangla devotional songs and longer Bangla narratives like eulogies of deities or hagiographies composed in the *panchali* form. The former can be seen as a veritable case of our contemporary reception of the latter, more archaic (but by no means outdated) texts. The rider 'but not outdated' is intended to stress the fact that those archaic texts are still very much in use, especially for sacred rituals associated with daily and occasion-specific pujas (ceremonial worship) within the Bengali Hindu context.

Coming back to the discussion of Chaitanya Deva/Nityananda Prabhu's influence in the Bangla musical expressions of bhakti towards Jagannath, it must be said that the duo, and especially the former among them, is easily identifiable as the major factor in binding *bhaktas* (devotees) of Jagannath into a community, which is, more often than not, a community in transit, usually to be found en route to Srikshetra Puri. The Bengali *bhakta* must make a pilgrimage to Puri at least once in their lifetime, and not merely because it is one of the *char dhams* or four principal Vaishnavite places of import. The importance of Puri for the Bengali *bhakta* is corroborated by the fact that Chaitanya Deva had spent a very significant part of his life in Puri until his demise. The fact that Chaitanya Deva had 'chosen' Srikshetra Puri to be the place where he would bring his earthly *leela* to an end makes the place culturally and emotionally charged region for the average Bengali *bhakta*—imbibing more levels of divine meaning into the place. It is interesting to see that the road to Puri from Nabadwip, Sri Chaitanya's native town, passes through Maahesh; and all these three centres along the path happen to be sacred spaces. This is one of the typical examples of the entire path of a pilgrimage being dotted with sacred centres, a theme that Chris Park brings up in his discussion of sacred spaces and pilgrimage (Park 1994). Jagannath's territorial identity as the eponymous presiding deity of Puri is thus corroborated by Chaitanya Deva's presence in (and continued religious association with) Puri.

Now the fact that Jagannath, the deity of Srikshetra Puri, is metonymic of Odia culture can hardly be characterised as disputable. However, the same cannot be said about the contiguous cultural sphere of Bengal, despite Bengal and Odisha's intimate religio-cultural correspondence across history and Jagannath's tremendous popularity among Bengali *bhaktas*. But it can certainly be said with a fair degree of confidence that Chaitanya Deva, the fifteenth-century Bengali Vaishnavite saint, had almost single-handedly determined the contours of Bengali Hindu culture for the centuries succeeding his temporal presence (Bhatia 2017). And it is Chaitanya Deva who remains the ultimate point of reference for the Bengali *bhakta* of Jagannath.

A cursory look at the music stands and charts of our time would reveal that the most sought-after singers of today have hardly recorded devotional songs dedicated to Jagannath. However, this does not so much reflect the apathy towards devotional songs as it reflects a more general trend in the Indian music scenario, wherein capital investments—and as a consequence the big names of the music industry—continue to move away from more traditional forms of Hindu devotional music. The situation is even bleaker when it comes to the Bangla music industry, compared to its Hindi counterpart. In Hindi, as well as in Odia, at least top playback singers such as Anuradha Paudwal, Jagjit Singh, Suresh Wadkar and alike have recorded a few songs on Jagannath in the recent times; but hardly any artist of comparable clout had recorded similar songs in the Bangla language. A contemporary Bengali playback singer Babul Supriyo (who is also a sitting member of the Parliament and a Minister of State in the current Government of India) has indeed recorded several bhajans that refer to Jagannath in the last two decades, but those songs are in Odia and Hindi, not in Bangla.

Due to geographical, historical and cultural reasons, the Odia and Bangla languages have together garnered a greater number of devotional songs on Jagannath than any other Indian language possibly could. Thus, devotional songs about Jagannath in Hindi—or in any other language in which such songs are being recorded with ever-increasing numbers—often tend to sound like literal translations of existing Bangla and Odia songs on Jagannath. What is true about their lyrics holds true for their musical form as well. In many cases, a typical Hindi song devoted to Jagannath would be found borrowing copiously from the *raga* (scale), *tala* (rhythm), and musical instrumentation of Bangla and Odia Jagannath bhajans. In some other cases, Hindi songs on Jagannath borrow tunes of Bangla Vaishnava *nama-kirtan* songs; or at times they would borrow even from a common *baul* (Bengali mystical folk music) tune or from an Odia folk tune. The number of songs that belong to the second type is not by any means statistically insignificant. For example, the reader may refer to the album titled *Jai Jagannath*, published by the highly sought-after recording company T-Series in 2016. Most songs included in that Hindi devotional music album would clearly illustrate this point. This lack of originality and creativity, and an excessive reliance on the corpuses of the more common Odia and Bangla songs on Jagannath have undoubtedly affected the literary quality of the lyrics of those songs in Hindi and a few other Indian languages. Despite this, such songs, mostly in Hindi, continue to thrive and gain popularity among devotees across India and abroad. This may constitute the subject matter of a separate study on the reception of Odia and Bangla devotional songs in general into the lyrical and musical traditions of other Indian languages in our contemporary world.

As a result, the scene of Bangla devotional music dedicated to Jagannath is currently dominated mostly by amateurish or inadequately trained singers, songwriters and small-time music producers. This has no doubt affected the melodic as well as the lyrical quality of the songs. But on the other hand, it has radically democratised the field of devotional songs about Jagannath in Bangla, albeit with the aid of increased ease and accessibility of digital recording techniques. The arena is now more open, and it offers a more or less level playing field to many hitherto unheard-of names (such as Rudra Ray, Sumitra Pal Some, Shilpi Das, Satyakam and alike) who would stand no chance if the field of Bangla devotional songs on Jagannath had still been trodden by such artists as those who have been regularly recording and performing Jagannath bhajans in Hindi and Odia. Consequently, more and more new entrants, many of whom are completely new to the field, have come up to try their luck in the musical profession. It is interesting to note that they have chosen to begin their careers with the music of a sub-genre that is barely touched these days by eminent names of the music industry.

In this regard, it may be added that several remakes of Bangla devotional songs on Jagannath, which were earlier performed or recorded by the eminent artists, have been pulled off by the new generation of artists who frequently bank on a number which had already been a favourite of the Bengali devotees of Jagannath, or of a typical connoisseur of Bengali music. Mention can be made, for example, of a rather recent remake of the hit song '*Jagannath Swami, Nayanapathagami*', recorded by Jhinuk Gupta in 2018. The singer, though an obscure name until quite a recent past, happens to be a relative of the legendary Bengali composer and music director, the late Pankaj Kumar Mullick, who had set this very song in tune for a film many years ago. The song, though its lyrics are in the Sanskrit language, is a favourite with the Bengali Hindu populace, as it is based on a series of *shloka*s (a type of Sanskrit poetic meter)—a veritable hymn in Sanskrit—which is believed to have been penned by no less a person than Chaitanya Deva himself. The hymn is known as *Sri Jagannathstakam*. It depicts Chaitanya Deva's yearning for Jagannath. The refraining part of the *shloka* literally prays for Jagannath to be the constant object of the devotee's (in this case, presumably, Chaitanya Deva's) vision.

Such feelings are reflected in several Bangla Jagannath bhajans composed and/or recorded by contemporary musicians. For example, '*Jagater Nath Tumi Prabhu Jagannath*' is a Bangla song that was recorded by Sri Satyakam under the recording company RDC Media in 2014. The lyrics of this song literally plead with Jagannath, along the lines of Chaitanya's Sanskrit hymn, to dwell in the pleader's (that is the singer's) memory forever. At the same time, the lyrics emphasise the devotee's agency in constantly remembering their Lord. Therefore, the song simultaneously highlights Jagannath as well as His devotee. This is a new element in Satyakam's song, as the Sanskrit hymn does not foreground the devotee in a pronounced manner.

Another Bangla Jagannath bhajan, recorded by Swarup Damodar Dasa, uploaded on YouTube in 2011 by the YouTube channel 'Krishna Bhakti Art', directly equates Jagannath with his most famed devotee Chaitanya Deva. Its lyrics include the following lines:

nilachale sankha-cakra-gada-padma-dhar
nodiya nagare danda-kamandalu-kar

Translation: In Nilachal He holds the conch shell, disc, club, and lotus flower, while in the town of Nodiya (the town in present-day West Bengal state in India where Chaitanya Deva was born) He holds a *sannyasi*'s (renunciate) staff and water pot.

This direct equivalence drawn between Jagannath and Chaitanya Deva in a Bangla Jagannath bhajan is profoundly interesting, and it is a common feature in several songs in the category. It is interesting because it reinforces the idea that for the Bengali *bhakta* of Jagannath, Chaitanya Deva acts not only as a bridge to access the Lord, but also as a signifier of the Lord Himself. Thus, Chaitanya Deva being a historical character hailing from Bengal adds to the sacred appeal of Jagannath and His abode at Puri for the Bengali Vaishnav *bhakta*. This equivalence also bespeaks the legend of Chaitanya Deva merging with the deity's image at the Puri Jagannath temple; in fact, the drawing of such equivalence in contemporary songs reinforces the old legend. Apart from the themes and motifs associated with the rath yatra festival, this equivalence is the most commonly visible trope across the sub-genre of Bengali Jagannath bhajans.

Discourse of Bhakti and Dynamics of Interaction between Odia and Bengali Cultures

All bhakti songs are meant to imply something beyond their mere literal meaning, especially those that consist of repetitive cycles of name, that is the *nama-kirtan* songs. The popular *nama-kirtan* '*Bhajo Gourango*', for example, mentions:

je jana Gourango (that is Chaitanya Deva) *bhaje,/*
se hoy amar pran re

This means 'the one, who worships and chants *Gourango*, becomes my life'. The implied suggestion here is: Chaitanya Deva is equivalent to Krishna. This is because there existed another *nama-kirtan* before the one just mentioned, which had the same wordings except that the name 'Krishna' appeared in place of '*Gourango*'.

This feature is in keeping with the concept of *vyanjana* (suggestive signification) in traditional (or, as some would say, classical) Indian aesthetics and poetics. As such, the songs associated with the deity Jagannath, especially those which were composed and/or published within the last two decades, present a subset of discourse before us. The entire corpus of bhakti music can be seen as the universe from which this subset has been taken. Following a frame analytical line of enquiry, we may ask the question: What are those activities and who are the ones who participate in this (subset of) discourse? Indeed, it is held by the tradition of Vaishnavites that the *nama-sankirtan* is an act of union with the *Prabhu*, and the space in which the *nama-sankirtan* takes place becomes a veritable abode of the *Prabhu*. He Himself participates in the *nama-sankirtan*, basking in the shared joy, uniting with the devotees, transforming together with them through the *hladini* (the joy-rendering *shakti* or energy of Sri Krishna according to several Vaishnava traditions, ascribed to Sri Radha) aspect of His essence, experiencing His own *madhurya* (aspect of sweetness) with them and becoming *ananda*, that is Bliss Absolute (Dasgupta 1975). Thus, both bhakti and the object of bhakti are embodied in the act of *nama-sankirtan* (Holdrege 2015). They transform together, as a community, and attain transcendence during the *nama-sankirtan*—that is the essence of bhakti (Prentiss 1999).

A recent Bangla album (published in 2017) consisting of devotional songs on Jagannath is titled *Dehi Padam*. It is published by Raga Music Communications, a Kolkata-based recording company. The title ostensibly refers to the *madanamohanashtakam*, a beautiful Sanskrit hymn devoted to Vishnu/Krishna and ascribed (by Vaishnavite legends) to an anonymous Odia author who is believed to have been alive in an era before that of Chaitanya Deva. The intertextuality between that hymn and Bangla devotional music, in general, is a rather old affair because the same hymn has been used for the soundtrack of a Bangla movie named *Bhagavan Sri Krishna Chaitanya* (released in 1953). The movie was a biopic based on parts of Chaitanya Deva's life. The fact that that movie and the recent Bangla album both draw upon the *madanamohanashtakam* is a testimony to the *madanamohanashtakam's* significance in Vaishnavite tradition, Gaudiya or otherwise.

Indeed, the *madanamohanashtakam* enjoys considerable popularity across the length and breadth of India, and not just within West Bengal or Odisha. Numerous compositions and covers/remakes have been made and are being made by musicians as diverse as Stephen Devassy (a new age composer of film soundtracks from Kerala) and Sreemoyee Bhattacharyya (a young Kolkata-based Hindustani vocalist). The album in which Bhattacharyya's rendition is included also happens to be titled *Dehi Padam*. Published by Cozmik Harmony in August 2018, *Dehi Padam* is an anthology of bhajans composed by an unusual collection of musicians, mystics and bards. Some of the bhajans happen to be by a few legendary composers and music directors of the Indian film industry, especially the Hindi film industry, such as Sachin Dev Burman and Ravindra Jain, while some others are traditionally attributed to the mystics who are generally clubbed together as poet-saints and bards associated with what is known as the bhakti movement. These poet-saints/bards/mystics include Guru Nanak, Sant Kabirdas, Tulsidas, Surdas and Mirabai. Although none of the bhajans included in this album are in Bangla, it is being referred to here because it helps us observe two things: one, the term 'bhajan' may include a wide range of literary and musical forms such as *shabad*, *doha*, *chaupai*, *ashtakam stotra*, etc. Second, it includes the *madanamohanashtakam*, and although that is in the Sanskrit language, the mere fact that the singer is a Bengali individual—with who lay the agency of deciding which types of devotional songs would constitute her album—points towards the centrality of the *madanamohanashtakam* in the sphere of Bengali devotional culture.

The musical component of the sphere of Bengali devotional culture is generically termed *bhakti giti* in Bangla. The above album is a good example of what an average Bengali consumer of music—who likes to think of himself as a connoisseur of music par excellence, regardless of his training in the subject—would imply by that very generic term. It is indeed a wide range of forms, taken from the pan-Indian lyrical-musical spectrum, that our average Bengali 'connoisseur'—or *samajhdar*, as they call it in Bangla—of music would include in the definition of *bhakti giti*. Let us claim that this Sanskrit hymn, the *madanamohanashtakam*, is a key to understand the nature of the Bengali sensibilities that determine the composition of a devotional song or bhajan dedicated to any form of *Bhagaban* (the blessed one, indicates Vishnu)—Vishnu in general and Jagannath in specific, on account of the fact that the *ashtakam* has endured a considerably long span of time in fascinating the Bengali imagination as much as it concerns music and poetry related to *Narayana Sri Hari* (names of Vishnu).

Descriptions of the attributes, rituals and stories associated with Jagannath are the dominant themes, if not the only ones, of Bangla songs on Prabhu Jagannath. Most of these songs consist of various attributes of the deity. While rituals, customs and stories become the *rohstoff* (that is raw material) of the songs when they specifically relate to a festival associated with the deity—rath yatra being the most notable of them all. Such is the importance of the rath yatra festival that recording companies often release their albums on or around the day of the festival. A recent album titled *Jai Jagannath Dehipodom* and published by the recording company Raga Music Communications was released (on 28 June 2017), as the description of the YouTube video based on the album proclaims, on the occasion of the rath yatra festival. There have been attempts, across a very long period, of not owning or claiming but replicating the rath yatra of Puri at various centres of Jagannath worship in Bengal such as Maahesh and Mahishadal. These replications seem to legitimise and consecrate the local expressions of Jagannath worship in and around the location of such replications. Notably, some of these centres are associated with figures who feature in stories and legends of journeys made to Nilachal. Maahesh is one such celebrated case of replication with a rich repository of stories regarding its inauguration as a replication. Such legends and the figures that feature in them provide the *bhaktas* with conceptual tools for imagining these different places as connected or even unified (Feldhaus 2003).

The one fact that stands out as common among almost all the Bangla devotional songs on Jagannath is this: the road to the deity—be it the metaphorical, metaphysical road of spiritual progress in bhakti or the actual, physical road that extends along the banks of the River Ganga from across Nabadwip and through Maahesh up to Puri—is through a lone figure, and that is Chaitanya Deva. It is not as if the Bengali *bhakta* were completely clueless about the deity, but they were certainly helpless without the reference to Mahaprabhu Chaitanya. In fact, the linguistic evidence for this dependence on Chaitanya Deva exists in the form of the word Mahaprabhu itself: it is an appellation, which is used interchangeably to refer to both Chaitanya Deva and his Lord, Jagannath Deva. It is highly unlikely that the saints/saint-poets, who created padas (couplets) and sometimes even biographies on Chaitanya Deva would inadvertently refer to him and the deity using the same appellation, or by a mere mistake. It shows that whatever access the average Bengali *bhakta* has into the sacred space around Jagannath is strongly mediated by Chaitanya Deva. This mediation culminates in the identification of Jagannath with Chaitanya Deva through the story of the latter merging with the form of Jagannath (Goswami 2004) inside the temple in Puri at the very end of his earthly *leela*.

What of those Bangla songs on Jagannath that make neither explicit nor implicit references to Chaitanya Deva in their themes, motifs, lyrical or musical forms? Though small in number, such songs have been composed during the chosen period for this survey. These Jagannath-bhakti songs, free from a palpable 'influence' of Chaitanya Deva, eulogise Jagannath as nothing short of Brahman, the highest truth according to Hindu philosophy. This is in keeping with the appellation Darubrahma (Brahman symbolised in a wooden image), which is how Jagannath is traditionally regarded in Odisha. The song '*lokkho manusher payer tolay*' from the album 'Jai Jagannath Dehipodom' demonstrates the above observations. The title of the song translates into English as 'the great road is trodden by a million feet'. This is an allusion to the overwhelming crowd that gathers in Puri during the rath yatra festival. The song further says:

Ved-purane tanr mohima lekha ache shoto shoto/
Bohu sadhoker onjoli dewa roktopodmo joto

These lines assert Jagannath as the 'Great God who has been described and praised in the *Veda*-s and *Purana*-s', thus foregrounding Jagannath as Brahman. The same claim has been made in a different, more literary way in another song titled '*debshilpi bishwakarma jaay je murti gorte*' (translation: the sculptor-god Vishwakarma goes to create images) from the same album. This song asks the rhetorical question 'how can man even think of creating His image when He is nothing but Purna-Brahma (the Absolute, abstract Brahman)?'

The concepts of Brahman and Purna-Brahma require one to use the neuter gender, as per Sanskrit grammar and usage, while referring to these words. This is because Brahman is indescribable and inconceivable in words, thoughts and form (Pandit 2001). The Vedanta Sutra describes Brahman as the one infinite substance and the underlying principle of the universe (Radhakrishnan 2008). Thus, it is impossible to determine its gender, and hence it should be referred to in neither masculine nor feminine pronouns. As such, the correct pronouns to be used in the question above would be 'Its' and 'It'. In any case, this particular song, like the previous one, mentions Darubrahma while describing Jagannath using various names in its refrains. Notably, the videos for both these songs have been shot on various beaches, presumably those located in West Bengal. This choice of location for shooting the videos of the songs in the album seems to be a deliberate attempt at evoking the images and memory of Puri, a pilgrimage that the Bengali consumer and/or spectator of this music video would seldom be expected to have missed. The last observation would be truer for the Bengali consumers/spectators belonging to the older generations, who are also more likely to buy or listen to this album and the likes of it.

Another song titled '*jai Jagannath jai Jagannath bol re amar mon*', recorded by a female vocalist named Sumitra Pal Some, from the 2016 Bangla album '*Jai Jagannath Jai*' laments about the fact that the *bhakta* has not yet succeeded in her attempts to secure Lord Jagannath's grace. The video which accompanies the song on YouTube shows snippets of the rath yatra festival of Puri and scenes around the Puri Jagannath temple. It is interesting to note that the album description uses the phrase 'Jagannath bhajan' in describing this song and several others included in the album, making it clear that singers, albums and recording companies have started to recognise 'Jagannath bhajan' as a sub-genre in the wider market-universe of bhajans.

Conclusion

Such songs, along with the ones discussed in the previous sections, constitute a considerable body of Bangla songs that can be brought under the label of 'Bangla Jagannath bhajan'. Indeed, recording companies and playback singers have already started to recognise this label (or part of it as 'Jagannath bhajan') as a market-driven 'legitimate' way of identifying this sizeable body of songs. The number of such songs clubbed together under this label will only increase, if the present rate of production of these songs is any indication of the future. This gives rise to a new and interesting genre-making phenomenon in the field of Bangla music and Bangla lyrics. John Frow, a critic and theorist who has worked on genology (a technical term borrowed from the lexicon of comparative literature theory, implying a systematic study of different genres of a kind, their formation and their uses) explains genre as 'a form of symbolic action' (2006: 1–2), that is formation of a genre (or a sub-genre) is nothing but a meaning-making process. Frow asserts that an agency makes use of this process and through it 'actively' (2006: 2) employs language, sound, images and gestures to organise objects, both tangible and conceptual, to make sense of the world. As a result, the agency ends up actively shaping the world it inhabits the way it understands that world.

This approach of understanding genres (and sub-genres, which are nothing but a second degree of derivative genres within an already-formed genre) appropriately fits into the framework that attempts to understand Jagannath through His usages in contemporary culture. Within that framework, these Bangla songs of bhakti on Jagannath—the deity of Puri, the deity who provides both uniqueness and a binding force to the Odia identity—expound the Lord's meaning in a neighbouring cultural region as a compelling spiritual force which has the power to drive the Bengali *bhakta* out of the borders of his familiar cultural, political and social sphere. Contemporary Bangla songs of bhakti on Jagannath repeatedly exhort the audience to undertake a pilgrimage to Nilachal or Puri. For example, at least two songs recorded by the child artist Shilpi Das contain such lyrics that indicate Jagannath's location at Nilachal and urge the listeners to visit it, if they want to receive the Lord's grace. Together, the music videos based on these two songs (viz. '*Chalore Sabai Chalore Nilachal*' and '*Nilachale Nilmadhab Prabhu Jagannath*') have garnered more than a million views on YouTube, indicating both the popularity of the young artist as well as the common Bengali devotee's craving of Jagannath for Jagannath bhajans in their native language. Here it may be noted that the tunes used in both these songs are palpably commonplace; having been drawn from popular Hindi/Bhojpuri bhajans and folk tunes that are often diluted in hastily made Bangla bhajan albums (vide songs by the Bengali folk singer Parikshit Bala).

But as soon as that same *bhakta* reaches Srikshetra Puri, all anxieties of the unfamiliar disappear. This is because that sacred town is the abode of Jagannath, the Beloved Lord and the '*nayanapathagami*' of his very own Lord Chaitanya Deva. At that sacred town where Chaitanya Deva had culminated his earthly *leela*, the Bengali *bhakta* feels at home. A question may arise: Is this an act of owning, or worse, an act of appropriation of either Jagannath who is an Odia national-cultural symbol or of Puri, a town located undeniably within the physical territories of Odisha, or of both?

Not so perhaps, because certain kinds of unfamiliarity would still exist for the Bengali *bhakta*, even if it does not cause anxiety as such. Such unfamiliarity, in the form of linguistic, cultural and socio-political elements, does exist and is strongly felt by the contemporary Bengali *bhakta* of Jagannath while he is in transit. But even that would be eventually eased by the familiar sound of the contemporary Bangla bhakti songs concerning the Lord; songs which accompany him in his journey towards the Lord, songs which use his familiar idiom to solicit the Lord's grace. He would listen to these songs, either all by himself using his personal portable music player (often the one that comes as a preloaded app in a smartphone) or in a group of pilgrims (perhaps by rather insensitively blasting the songs through a loudspeaker in a carriage), to supplicate, converse and establish personal relationship with Jagannath. That is the process through which, in this case, the text subtly rises and becomes a part of his lived experience and existence, becomes performance (Hess 2017).

Once he has returned home from a pilgrimage to Puri, the same songs would function as memorabilia of the journey and the culmination of the journey too. Thus, those songs would continue to bear the *bhakta's* reality and his truth, as experienced in private and within a group of fellow pilgrims—a group which often comprise members from his own family and the extended one—for some time, at least until new songs replace the ones which are presently in currency. This would further be established and at the same time somewhat glaringly highlighted by such tangible generic labels as 'Jagannath bhajan' in Bangla music albums in shops (real or virtual) or in Bangla music videos available aplenty on the Internet. Thus, the genre would legitimise the existence of a community of Bengali Jagannath *bhaktas* who peruse that genre, and vice versa.

Then, this community of *bhaktas*, created and held together by the binding force of spirituality expressed through songs of a common mother-tongue and fairly familiar tunes, as well as by the spiritual-cultural force exerted by the 'bridge' (and 'usherer/guide-across-the-bridge') metaphor already built around Chaitanya Deva, would have created the circumstances and resources to consciously use that body of Bangla songs on Jagannath for purposes of studying the phenomenology of the *bhakta* as well as the phenomenon of his close-or-loosely-knit community.

References

Bhatia, Varuni. 2017. *Unforgetting Chaitanya: Vaishnavism and Cultures of Devotion in Colonial Bengal*. New York: Oxford University Press.

Dasgupta, Surendranath. 1975. *A History of Indian Philosophy*, 4th vol. New Delhi: Motilal Banarsidass.

Feldhaus, Anne. 2003. *Connected Places: Region, Pilgrimage, and Geographical Imagination in India*. New York: Palgrave Macmillan.

Frow, John. 2006. *Genre*. Oxford: Routledge.

Ghosh, Ishani. 2007. 'Medieval Bengali Society and Culture as Reflected in Vernacular Literature of the 16th, 17th and 18th Centuries'. *Proceedings of the Indian History Congress*, 68(2): 1442.

Goswami, Shrivatsa. 2003–2004. 'Journey as Creation: Vrindavan'. *India International Centre Quarterly*, 30(3/4): 198–214.

Hess, Linda. 2017. 'An Open-Air Ramayana: Ramlila, the Audience Experience'. In *The Life of Hinduism*, edited by John Stratton Hawley and Vasudha Narayanan, 115–139. New Delhi: Aleph.

Holdrege, Barbara A. 2015. *Bhakti and Embodiment: Fashioning Divine Bodies and Devotional Bodies in Kṛṣṇa Bhakti*. New York: Routledge.

Pandey, Suresh. 1996. 'Journey of Devotional Music: From Brindaban to Bengal'. *Proceedings of the Indian History Congress*, 57: 387–389.

Pandit, Bansi. 2001. *The Hindu Mind*. New Delhi: New Age Books.

Park, Chris. 1994. *Sacred Worlds: An Introduction to Geography and Religion*. London: Routledge.

Prentiss, Karen Pechilis. 1999. *The Embodiment of Bhakti*. New York: Oxford University Press.

Radhakrishnan, S. 2008. *Indian Philosophy*, 2nd vol. New Delhi: Oxford University Press.

Sarbadhikary, S. 2015. *Place of Devotion: Siting and Experiencing Divinity in Bengal Vaishnavism*. Berkeley: University of California Press.

Vasuki, S.N. 1989. 'Bombay-based Bush India Launches India's First Compact Disc Player', *India Today*, 15 April. Available at https://www.indiatoday.in/magazine/economy/story/19890415-bombay-based-bush-india-launches-india-first-compact-disc-player-815955-1989-04-15 (accessed 30 November 2018).

Section III

Re-placing Jagannath

8

BECOMING JAGANNATH IN DRAVIDANADU: *KANCHI KAVERI* LEGEND AND OTHER POSSIBILITIES IN KANATHUR JAGANNATH TEMPLE

Jyotirmaya Tripathy

Introduction

The first challenge that confronts a Jagannath scholar is His very name, which betrays His supposed universality as well as obvious territoriality. In a literal sense, He is the *Nath* (Lord) of the *Jagat* (universe), which means He transcends geographical barriers and responds to grievances regardless of their places of origin. Though the universe here refers to a cultural and moral order rather than a spatial category, the idea of Jagannath is legitimised by the fact that He attracts devotees across places and cultures that once included Shankar and Chaitanya or the way His abode became a melting pot for multiple faiths such as Buddhism, Jainism, as well as followers of Ganapati, Shakti or even a subaltern faith such as *Mahima Dharma*. His devotees come from various religions and nationalities (such as the seventeenth century Muslim devotee/poet Salabega and the followers of ISKCON besides unaffiliated devotees from abroad) who unfortunately cannot get access to the temple and must fulfil their wish by looking at His image as Patitapavan (rescuer of the fallen) near the eastern gate or by waiting for the annual rath yatra to have *darshan*.

That universality, however, is impaired by His location in Puri, a sea-side town in the state of Odisha, which binds Him to that place and its people and where He is required to protect their interest as and when they come in conflict with the interests of others—those who do not belong to His land, language and culture. As we know, space has a special connotation in Hinduism, the reason why Jagannath is seen as an Odia god (Dash 1986: 362; Hegewald and Mitra 2008: 1). Thus, during the agitation over Odia language as a medium of education in late nineteenth century that challenged the hegemony of Bengali language, He is openly deployed as the protector of Odias. His territoriality was evident when a Christian lawyer Madhusudan Das in the beginning of the twentieth century invoked Jagannath for restoring the Gajapati king's rights. In recent times, the conflict over rasgulla and its place of origin brought Jagannath as the reference point of Odia claims over the sweetmeat.

To understand Jagannath's appeal across space and His physical location in Puri (one of the *char dhams* or four abodes of salvation) is a fascinating enterprise that becomes more complex while dealing with Jagannath temples outside Odisha. Jagannath's tribal origin, His mediation by Jainism and Buddhism in Odisha's layered history and His being an Odia god makes scholarly pursuit complicated when we deal with these temples. Though Jagannath temples are fairly common in Odisha, most of these temples have a link with the original Lord. During Islamic incursions, the servitors were always on the move along with the idols to escape the marauding forces and many such places of hiding later got converted to Jagannath temples. But a Jagannath temple in Chennai (my present concern) becomes a little more intriguing because Chennai did not have already-existing local devotees and so may have required justification for a non-local god.

The recognition of difficulties in Jagannath's travel and legitimation outside Odisha and His possible transferability defines the present engagement. The Jagannath temple in Chennai, more than thousand kilometres from Puri, offers a unique field view where contestations and negotiations around His universality and particularity, fixity and mutability, frozenness and expanse take place that in turn problematise Jagannath's being and becoming. The complexity gets even more pronounced when we understand that unlike Delhi that offers a neutral space for Jagannath's abode, the Chennai temple (in the outskirts of the city and under Kanathur village of Kanchipuram district) has an intricate history of domination and collaboration that makes Jagannath's seamless integration a spectacularly interesting enterprise. That is to say, the temple maintains a very precarious balance between identity and difference on the one hand and immersion and sameness on the other.

After this introduction, the first section highlights the meaning and significance of Jagannath temple in a culturally different place by playing around *Kanchi Kaveri* legend and how an alien God is imagined as part of Tamil Nadu's sacred geography. The second section traces the delivery of the temple and highlights the ways it maintains its distinct Odia character while engaging and appropriating local practices, thus, leading to a novel experiment in cross-cultural meaning-making. The concluding section focuses on the migrant Odia consciousness in Chennai and how they relate to the Jagannath temple for their place in Chennai's social imaginary.

The chapter draws from secondary material (both scholarly and experiential/*mahatmya* literature) as well as personal interviews with a cross-section of people such as present and past office bearers of Sri Jagannath Spiritual Education Cultural Trust that runs the Jagannath temple, members of Utkal Association of Madras, local people and devotees. This is supplemented by participant observation over a period of time during July–September 2018. The narrative constructed, thus, is based on my own independent assessment and may or may not find any institutional or popular sanction. All quotations from Odia texts and narrativisation of interviews have been translated by me and as such make no claim to have access to what the authors/subjects exactly intended.

Finding Kanchi in Kanathur

The Chennai Jagannath temple became functional in 1996 when the idols of Jagannath, Balabhadra and Subhadra arrived from Puri and adorned the meditation hall of the present temple before its formal consecration in 2001 when the idols were shifted to the sanctum sanctorum. The temple is located in a one-acre plot on the sea in a village named Kanathur in Thiruporur block along the East Coast Road that connects Chennai with Pondicherry (Figure 8.1). Built in Kalinga style architecture, the most important reason for the choice of Kanathur was the presence of the sea that ensured a Puri-like environment. Though the area is in the outskirts of Chennai, administratively it falls under Kanchipuram district. And that makes our narrative riveting given that Kanchipuram (or Kanchi) has a special place in the Jagannath *mahima* (glory) as well as in Odisha's modern historical narratives. The legend has travelled across time and has been variously represented as victory of Vaishnavism over Ganapatya faith or of Odia jati over its adversaries (Mohapatra 1996: 213) and during Odia nationalism phase, the legend became a national allegory (Dash 1986: 368; Samal n.d.: 8–11). The present temple is imbricated in that labyrinthine narrative and connects the Kanathur temple with the one at Puri, the latter being the ultimate signified of any discourse around Jagannath. This section revolves around the *Kanchi Kaveri* legend and shows how that legend is reactivated, re-narrativised and even transcended in Kanathur temple.

Figure 8.1 The Jagannath temple at Kanathur
Source: Author.

Purushottam Dev, the Gajapati king of Odisha during 1467–1497 had expressed his wish to marry Padmavati, the daughter of Saluva Narasingha, the ruler of Vijayanagar. Everything was on course until the Vijayanagar king came to know that the Gajapati king performs *chhera pahanra* (ritual sweeping of the chariot) during rath yatra and so he declined to give his daughter's hand in marriage to the Gajapati king. The infuriated Gajapati took it as an insult to Lord Jagannath and ordered a military takeover of Kanchi, the seat of the Vijayanagar king. In the first attempt, the Gajapati king is squarely defeated and returned to Jagannath for help. The latter asked the king to prepare for another strike and assured him that both He and Lord Balabhadra will join the Gajapati's army. In the second attempt, the Vijayanagar king is vanquished but the anger of the Gajapati king had not subsided yet, the reason why he took Padmavati captive. After reaching Odisha, he ordered his minister to marry the Kanchi princess to a sweeper to avenge the earlier insult. The responsible minister waited for the next rath yatra and when the Gajapati king was preparing for his ritual sweeping, asked Padmavati to garland the king thereby finding her a perfect sweeper match.

The story has some historical validity and the Gajapati king had indeed defeated the Kanchi king, though layers of imagination have been added to the skeletal story over centuries. These layers bring out interesting facets and complicate this straightforward narrative. In popular folk tales, after assuring Purushottam Dev of help, Jagannath and Balabhadra marched riding white and black horses towards Kanchi and stopped on their way to drink buttermilk from a milkmaid named Manika, who demanded coins after feeding the thirsty brothers. Jagannath gave His ring in pledge and asked Manika to collect the coins from his king who will pass by shortly. When the King reached the spot later and was confronted by Manika with the ring, he knew that his Lord has come to help him. The enthused king went on to pay the milkmaid and win the battle. The spoil of the war was not just Padmavati but also Kanchi's titular deity Ganesh.

In one narrative popularised by Ram Shankar Ray (n.d.) in his drama *Kanchi Kaveri* written in 1878, the battle was as much between Kanchi and Odisha kings as it was between their *kula-devata*s (family deities) Ganesh and Jagannath. In Ray's drama, the Kanchi Ganesh is called *bhanda* Ganesh or fraud Ganesh whose idol shows his trunk inside the vagina of his consort Siddhi Devi. This was the sign of the decadence whereas the evolutionary superiority of Jagannath is visible all over, not the least in His tribal origin and His chief servitor the Gajapati king becoming a sweeper performing *chhera pahanra*. Thus, the victory of the Gajapati king was the victory of egalitarianism over degenerated faiths, the reason why removing Ganesh along with the princess is the ultimate revenge that the Gajapati king could have extracted. This narrative however does not explain as to why Purushottam Dev installed the Kanchi Ganesh in a temple inside the Puri Jagannath temple premises or why he accepted Padmavati in marriage if he was determined to humiliate her father.

That gives birth to a competing narrative of collaboration rather than conquest (Patnaik 2016: 29–30). Since Siddhi Devi was on a spree to produce more and more number of soldiers through her vagina to replenish the dead soldiers and until that stopped, Gajapati king could not win the battle, the King (prodded by Jagannath) prayed Ganesh and convinced Him that *dharma* will prevail only with Gajapati's victory. Thus Ganesh placed his trunk inside Siddhi Devi's vagina to stop the endless birth of soldiers, and when the battle was over, He decided to join Padmavati in moving to Puri. His temple inside the western side of the Puri temple establishes the understanding between Jagannath and Ganesh and helps devotees see the divine plan behind the story. If one narrative pits Jagannath against Ganesh and holds them in an antagonistic relationship, the other narrative sees them as participants in the general drama of *dharma*. If one sees the story as one of conquest, the other sees it as a site of collaboration. If one sees Kanchi as the negation of Puri or Vijayanagar as the negation of Odisha, in the other both the places appear as different names of one sacred geography. S.N. Majhi, a former Professor and one of the leading champions of the Kanathur temple, cites scholars who believe that it was Padmavati who requested the Gajapati king to take Ganesh along with her and that Ganesh chose Puri temple as His residence (2008: 6).

The Kanchi story became a metaphor of Odia pride during *bhasha andolan* (demand for Odia language textbooks) in the last decades of nineteenth century when Jagannath was invoked to protect Odia interest. Ray's *Kanchi Kaveri* had converted the story into a tale of Odia valour in the face of adversity and had iterated Jagannath's direct involvement in Odia struggle against the imposition of Bengali language on Odia students. Thus Jagannath became a secular symbol and provided the glue to Odia nationalism in its formative years; he was not 'merely a Hindu deity but also the embodiment of Oriya nation' (Dash 1986: 368).

The reality of ignominy in the hands of Bengali administrators and the pride of a glorious past found an outlet in Ray's text and gave Odia consciousness a historical validity. Here Jagannath is not a passive God but an angry one who can decimate the adversary's army, as in Ray's drama that pitted the *Gana Gana* (hail Ganapati) slogans against *Jay Jagannath* (victory for Jagannath). By associating Jagannath with Odia language, the drama not only secularised Jagannath, but also made Odia sacred. The sacral nature of Odia because of its association with Jagannath offered a psychological immunity from defeat and a spiritual amulet to Odia nationalists. It also consolidated the idea of Jagannath as an Odia and territorial God who will save His people from others. But while valourising Jagannath and His power, Ray's narrative and its resonance among people also limited Jagannath's power, who after all was just an Odia god. That said, Jagannath's territoriality is one side of the story. During the independence movement, there were frequent references to Jagannath in various anti-colonial speeches (Nanda 2008: 388); it was also believed that Lord Jagannath was accompanying Gandhi in his nationwide tour (Acharya 2008: 67).

The historical connection of Kanchi with Jagannath cannot be missed in the Kanathur temple. The temple is located in Kanchipuram district (if not Kanchi town) and makes a conscious effort to highlight that connection. One of the first temples built in this temple premises is Kanchi Ganesh for which the idol was gifted by the Kanchi seer. One of the founding members of Kanathur temple S.N. Majhi devotes the first chapter of his *mahatmya* to this episode, thus, reiterating the centrality of Kanchi in Jagannath *mahima*. In a re-enactment and near-divine emplotment, Ganesh complements Jagannath, both then (during Kanchi battle) and now. Kinsley believed that 'Hindu pilgrimage often involves a self-conscious attempt to cultivate a rapport with Indian geography that establishes, reaffirms, or transforms one's religious identity' (1998: 228). Thus, Ganesh in both the temples (Puri and Kanathur) creates a pattern that links Odisha with Tamil Nadu and Kanchi with Puri. Like most Hindu pilgrimage sites, which create their own *sthala* puranas or place narratives,

Kanathur temple has stories connected with past events and reminds them to the devotees.

Other facets of *Kanchi Kaveri* legend can be found in the Jagamohan/ audience hall of the Kanathur temple that carries four wall paintings depicting various phases of the legend. In the first, Lord Jagannath is shown pawning his ring with Manika after drinking the buttermilk. In the second we see the Gajapati king recognising the Lord's ring. The third shows the journey of Padmavati and Ganesh to Puri along with the victorious Odia soldiers. Here the journey appears voluntary and both the princess and the God are not presented as captives. The fourth one shows Padmavati (guided by the minister) garlanding Purushottam Dev during his *chhera pahanra*. It must be mentioned here that when the office bearers of the temple administration were looking for someone to paint the inner wall of the Jagamohan in Odisha *patachitra* (Figure 8.2) (originally cloth-based painting, but also any painting with natural dye) style before the grand consecration ceremony in 2001, there was an incident that established the power of Jagannath to facilitate desired things. A deaf and dumb boy came to the temple and after initial interaction introduced himself as Sriharsha Shukla from Odisha and a trained painter, and agreed to do the painting for free, with the help of his brother, who was also physically challenged like him (Majhi 2008: 45–49).

Figure 8.2 *Patachitra* adorning the interior wall
Source: Author.

The fact that the two painter brothers appeared when nobody expected them establishes that Kanchi was the divine reference point for the Kanathur temple. If the painting established Kanchi as optical conscious (represented in paintings), the Ganesh idol (miraculously sourced from Kanchi) made Kanchi the temple's unconscious. Schmid tells us that artefacts should be evaluated in contexts in which 'objects were produced, distributed and utilized' (2001: 297) and 'that we must study things in motion in order to grasp their human and social context' (2001: 297). The production and reception of these images in Kanathur temple make them an endless site of negotiation, normalise the conflictual relation between Puri and Kanchi and facilitate expected responses to legends.

Kanchi Kaveri paintings are also found on the walls of Jagamohan of the Puri temple (Das 1982: 157). But there is a difference between the significations of these motifs in Puri and Kanathur. If in the former the note of triumph may seem harmless, its depiction in Kanathur (Kanchi) may complicate the temple's place in Kanathur. Interestingly, the *chitrakara*s (traditional painters) in Raghurajpur (the artisans' village in Odisha) believe that Brahma is the original painter of the first *pata* depicting the Jagannath triad. If that be the case, even the Kanchi paintings betray a divine scheme. The Kanathur temple creates a novel idea of Kanchi that binds it to a past when its only hope for salvation was its association with/surrender to Jagannath. It was not Kanchi in itself; it was Jagannath's Kanchi. The paintings freeze that moment of history and expect the viewer to see Kanchi as Jagannath's *leela bhumi* (land of divine play). The temple, through these pictorial representations, establishes Kanathur as Kanchi and makes a conscious effort in making the devotees see that connection.

The Kanchi paintings in the Puri temple refer to a far off place, which was just a medium through which Lord's *mahima* was played out. Kanchi is the other place, which was subjected to the Gajapati king and Lord Jagannath. Yet it was the same place, which was the stage for the Lord's *mahima*, something which the Odia devotees only heard about but were not witness to. In contrast, the defeated subjects of Kanchi were the ones who in their loss were blessed with the *darshan* of the Lord in physical form. That makes Puri the experiential other of Kanchi. Thus, Kanchi occupies the mental space of an Odia devotee as an ambivalent space, which in its defeat created conditions for the Lord to save the Odia king. By subjecting themselves to defeat, the soldiers and people of Kanchi legitimised Jagannath and His power, one who protects His devotees by appearing outside His abode and truly becomes *Jagat Nath*.

Kanathur temple is not a lack in the sense that a Jagannath temple in Bangalore is. Puri is only the seat of Jagannath whereas Kanathur is the site of his *mahima*, something only people of Kanathur could see during the Lord's Kanchi victory. That means devotees of Kanathur are closer to the Lord in a way devotees at Puri are not. If Kanathur temple is a lack, it is also a space of fulfilment and plenitude. That makes Kanathur not an incomplete Puri, but a bountiful and an abundant one. Without Kanchi victory, Jagannath will be less powerful; without Kanathur temple, the Puri temple will be without its past glory. Jagannath, thus, creates a wave of bhakti where Puri and Kanathur complement each other in ways not experienced by other temples outside Odisha. For Majhi, Kanathur is an already always sacred place as 'Deva Balabhadra and Sri Jagannath might have passed through these seashore areas during their legendary Kanchi Vijaya Expedition' (2016: 15). There is also a historical link between Puri and Tamil Nadu, manifest in Alarnath temple (*apabhramsha* or deviation of Alwar nath) frequented by Alwar saints in earlier times. It is also believed that Puri Gundicha temple is derived from Tamil word *gudisa* or *gudisai* meaning cottage, as claimed by Mahatab (in Dash 1996: 120).

Kanathur's is not an ordinary Jagannath temple; it is located in a place supposedly vanquished by Lord Jagannath and the paintings in the audience hall may refresh that unpleasant past. However, interaction with locals establishes that it is not the case. Unlike monotheistic religions with a clear division between the sacred and the profane, a place like Kanchi establishes the futility of that binary. The land of Kanchi is incorporated into Jagannath's grand narrative by appropriation, which was confirmed when Kanchi Ganesh became a resident deity in Kanathur temple. In the absence of a clear division between the pure and the impure, the *pata* paintings create and reiterate one simultaneous moral order where Ganesh and Jagannath are actors in a *dharmic* play. They are not competing gods any longer; even during Kanchi battle, there was a collaboration between them without which the war would not have ended the way it did.

Kanchi's relationship with Puri goes beyond one of domination and subordination and becomes one of consensus. That is the reason why Majhi was so confident (in my interviews with him) that Kanathur is *apabhramsha* of *Kanha atura* (eager for Kanha). That means the people of this area were pleased to see the Lord (Jagannath/Kanha) when He was returning to Puri after Kanchi victory and were eager to see Him again, a wish fulfilled in the presence of Jagannath in Kanathur temple. This interpretation may be just an ascribed meaning and has no historical validity but it establishes the imaginary connect of the devotee to the Lord's residence. Tuan's observations, thus, define Indian sacred where experience is not defined by the geography of the existing shrines but by the experience such as wholeness and connectedness that is different from ordinary and commonplace experience (cited in Park 1994: 250). In the end people of Kanchi remain Ganesh worshippers and the victor takes Ganesh to worship Him alongside his titular deity Jagannath. The present Kanathur temple, thus, complements and completes that narrative (Ganesh travelling to Puri) by bringing Jagannath to Kanchi.

Jagannath in Dravidanadu

What are the textual and performative practices that integrate Kanathur temple with the larger religious landscape of Tamil Nadu and what are the transcripts that keep Jagannath away from integration? What are the microsites of conformity and resistance and how do they articulate themselves? These questions do not have definitive answers and in the absence of that certainty, we encounter interesting possibilities where sameness is mediated by difference as much as the difference is normalised by sameness. The whole project of meaning-making, thus, becomes a slippery exercise where identity and immersion consolidate and weaken the project. For Lochtefeld, people's agency is key in transforming space into a place that connects that place with notions of identity for both individuals and groups (2010: 4). No doubt Kanathur temple went through a process of induction as an abode of Jagannath, but it continues to be Kanathur Jagannath temple.

Though both Kanathur and Puri contribute to Jagannath's grand narrative, the Puri temple remains the ultimate signified for Jagannath Dharma; other temples only imitate the ways of Puri to become authentic. Most Jagannath temples are operated in correspondence with the main temple in Puri (Stietencron 1986: 469). Thus, the temple of Kanathur is both a presence and absence of the Puri temple. It does not come as surprise that in its zeal to imitate Puri, Kanathur temple is called Dakshina Kshetra (sacred site in the South), in line with Puri as Srikshetra. Similarly, like Aruna stambha (Sun pillar) outside the Puri temple, the Kanathur temple has a pillar called Kshetra stambha (the pillar of sacred site). Thus, the moment of sameness that connects Kanathur to Puri, the very same moment, differences are generated. If we selectively use Bhabha's vocabulary (1994: 86), Kanathur temple is repetition with difference, that is to say while trying to be the same like Puri temple, it produces slippages (such as local conditions). In the act of doubling, Kanathur temple both complements and destabilises Puri temple.

Hegewald and Mitra have spent a considerable amount of time in describing what they consider the reuse of sacred sites in Hinduism (2008). Though the site of Kanathur temple is not erected on some other older shrine, its relationship with Kanchi King and Ganesh cannot be underestimated. Though the authors bring to light an interesting site of power, that is reused sites, they limit the promise of their enterprise by defining reuse as 'the attempt by conquering groups to appropriate the sacred sites' (2008: 1). This project excludes imaginary sites; it also binds reuse to one of domination and subordination. We have seen how unlike the conventional reuse through force and the replacement of sacred icons, the presence of Kanchi Ganesh in both Puri and Kanathur (Figure 8.3) establish a philosophy of reuse that is complementary.

Figure 8.3 Kanchi Ganesh in the Kanathur temple premises
Source: Author.

For Odias living in Chennai, the Kanathur temple offers a place to imagine themselves as Odias. But while being a bridge that connects them with the land they have left behind, the temple also connects them to the new land, which is different yet the same (by being an abode of Jagannath in Kanathur). The Navagraha temple in the Kanathur temple complex carries *Parsva Devis* (Figure 8.4) or supplementary deities (such as Samaleswari, Cuttack Chandi, Berhampur Thakurani) who create not only an imaginary Odisha in Kanathur but also an Odisha that is coherent and unified. A *pradakshina* (circumambulation) around the temple acts like an imaginary *pradakshina* around Odisha's map that reactivates Odias' memory with their land and makes one imagine Odisha as a singular whole. Integrating goddesses from various regions of Odisha

Figure 8.4 *Parsva Devis* around Navagraha temple
Source: Author.

neutralises the internal contradictions within Utkal Association of Madras or between western Odisha and coastal Odisha. This is how an Odisha without internal inconsistencies is symbolically performed.

A visitor to Kanathur temple is often greeted with Odia bhajans (devotional songs) that makes one mentally migrate to Puri. The recorded bhajans (or sung by some ardent devotee) connect Odias to the real places in Odisha. In his study of Tamil migrants in London, Hornabrook talks about 'song pathş' and 'metaphorical pilgrimages' (2018: 107). Similarly a song like '*thaka mana chala jiba*' (a popular bhajan by seventeenth century poet Saria Bhika invites weary devotees to visit Puri Jagannath) is often sung in Kanathur temple and creates a sacred geography 'resulting in the song path as a sounded pilgrimage through songs' (Hornabrook 2018: 107). These song paths produce an Odia collective in Chennai and localise Jagannath and the diasporic community by means of spatialising 'religious identities and forms of belonging in that they mark urban sites as religious' (Burchardt and Westendorp 2018: 163).

If the performance of devotional songs in Odia leads to emplacement of Kanathur as Puri, simultaneous use of English/Tamil in the temple premises apparently problematise that imagining. The use of other languages is something that Rosowsky calls 'truncated repertoires' (2018: 91) that refer to a fragmented blend of language resources from a range of languages. Though the puja is performed in Sanskrit, non-religious communication is done predominantly in Odia but also in English, Tamil and Hindi to integrate everybody. The conversation among office-bearers and priests is done mostly in Odia, whereas the reception desk uses multiple languages; even some Odias prefer English and Hindi and communicate freely in these languages. Far from being a weakness, this 'truncated repertoire' of an Odia serves as an interesting survival strategy as well as a pathway to inclusivity and attracts non-Odia devotees.

Even then Kanathur temple makes no effort to disguise its Odia character, nor does it make any claim to be a part of the local landscape. It remains an island on most occasions though on some special days, the temple sees participation from local people. On a normal day, the local footfall is limited to 10 or 15, though the number swells on occasions like rath yatra that generates massive response from local people. The idols worshipped in the temple are made from the same neem tree log as the idols at Puri during the Navakalevar (re-embodiment) of 1996, thus establishing both physical and spiritual link with the Puri temple. The maharana (carpenter) who carved Kanathur temple idols also prepared the idols during 1996 Navakalevar. Before the ceremonial coronation of the Kanathur idols in 2001, a sacred permission was obtained from the Puri temple and the present Gajapati king of Odisha, Divyasingh Dev, witnessed this event. The daily puja in Kanathur temple is performed by four Odia priests as per Puri Jagannath temple traditions. The flag hoisted atop the *sanctum sanctorum* is also sourced from Puri and Shri S.J.N. Dev, a scion of Parala royal family of Odisha, performs the ritual *chhera pahanra* during rath yatra.

But then new territories offer new challenges and Kanathur temple has its share. It is understood that Kanathur temple cannot procure all the vegetables or flowers or specific types of rice for the temple, something which is taken for granted in Puri. But this deficiency allows its servitors to innovate and appropriate local customs. Freeman in his study of Kapileshwar temple shows how temple practices were transformed when they were subjected to rapid changes such as modernisation and urbanisation (1975: 124). Thus, Kanathur temple rationalises various services and the available priests multitask that is not difficult to manage in the absence of a large number of devotees. The rigidity of worship leads to flexibility and often a kind of jugaad (temporary solution) takes care of new situations. Since Jagannath is not an angry God like Shiva, His rituals are tweaked or blended with others thereby legitimising the appropriation of local practices into temple services. Vegetables prohibited in Puri temple (such as potato and tomato) are freely used in the *mahaprasad* (food offered to Jagannath) preparation in Kanathur.

In spite of being an Odia god residing in an Odia temple, the Lord blesses all in a substantive sense. Majhi's *mahatmya* makes a conscious effort not to use Jagannath as an Odia symbol: 'the Jagannath temple built on the sea at Kanathur is a matter of pride for residents of

Chennai' (2008: 19) and that 'getting the idols made from the same logs as Puri's idols was a matter of great fortune and blessing for the Utkal Association and the people of Chennai' (2008: 22). Similarly, Dr Kabi Prasad Mishra, who was instrumental in the conception, execution and completion of the Kanathur temple project and was also the President of Utkal Association of Madras (during 1985–1999), believed that Jagannath is for all people living in Madras: 'O God, if you do not bring yourself, we ordinary mortals cannot bring you to Madras' (2008: 21). Mishra is pleased with the fact that the Kanathur temple is open to all irrespective of caste, colour and creed and that everybody is allowed to pray or meditate: 'though people may think that this is in contravention of existing convention since ancient times, we feel that Lord's blessing and *darsan* should be open to all' (2008: 94).

If the design, resident gods and goddesses make Kanathur an Odia geography, to which Kanathur and its people can be co-opted, it can also be argued that it is a site of constant negotiation. While struggling to collect resources in the early days of construction, the champions of the temple met the chief priest of Ashta Mahalakshmi temple in Besant Nagar who advised them to take the blessings of Kanchi Paramacharya Chandrasekharendra Saraswati (Mishra 2008: 16). Mishra gives the details of his experience with the Paramacharya under miraculous circumstances and later with Paramacharya's disciples Jayendra Saraswati and Vijayendra Saraswati (2008: 18–19). Even the decision of building the temple on the sea in Kanathur (rather than in Mogappair) was due to the advice of Jayendra Saraswati. We also know that donations were received from various people, most notably famous and rich South Indians, which makes the Kanathur project a site of shared experience. Mishra acknowledges that the Kanathur temple represents an amalgamation of traditional and modern architecture and that Tamil Nadu's granite stones gave shape to Odia architectural style (2008: 70).

The team guiding the temple construction was led by South Indians such as Prof. Raju and Prof. Aravindan of IIT Madras. The Kanchi seer Vijayendra Saraswati sang Adi Shankar's *Jagannathastakam* (hymns of Jagannath) in the Kanathur temple; famous singer Vani Jayaram, a celebrated Tamil singer but not unknown to Odias due to her playback Odia songs, too performed in various languages including Odia. The priest of Saidapet's Karuneswara temple Mr Ramanathan performed the coronation ceremony of the idols. A team of 14 devotees had gone to Puri to collect the sacred permission for the coronation in Kanathur temple and many Tamilians were part of that group. The invite to obtain the sacred order was written in Sanskrit by Prof. Srinivascharia and was blessed by the Kanchi *Shankaracharya* Jayendra Saraswati. Similarly, when the *salagramas* (sacred fossil shell) were procured from Nepal, there was a discussion as to how best to place them. As per local convention, they must be worshipped every day and so cannot be buried under the *ratna singhasan* (throne decorated with jewels) as in Puri temple. So, it was agreed that they would be placed in the meditation hall right under the sanctum sanctorum that finds a balance between Eastern and Southern practices (Majhi 2008: 45).

Thus, the temple is a hybrid place, not an authentically imitative one. The hybridity is reinforced by local practices such as Pradosh puja being mainstreamed in the Kanathur temple. Here Narayanan's study of Sri Venkateswara temple in Penn Hills, Pittsburgh can offer a comparative template, where the temple remains faithful to the parent temple in Tirupati (Narayanan 2006: 232). At the same time, the Penn Hills temple takes liberty with the sacred calendar to coincide with holidays in the United States (Narayanan 2006: 232). This collaboration and consensus transcends linguistic/ethnic/regional barriers. When Kanathur village escaped nature's fury during 2004 tsunami, it was believed that Jagannath protected the village. The local character of Jagannath was confirmed when the Gajapati king declared that 'the Lord of the Universe is no longer confined to Sri *Purusottama-Kshetra* (Puri) or Odisha' (Souvenir 2016: 11). This institutional declaration by the king makes Jagannath universal and His presence in Kanathur confirms that universality.

Conclusion

The relative absence of Jagannath in the religious landscape of places outside Odisha and its contiguous territories, at least until recently, may be explained by the lack of economic and cultural power of Odias outside Odisha. In may be argued that it is not Jagannath who created a felt need outside Odisha but an increasingly visible Odias and their consciousness that established Jagannath, His temples and His power outside Odisha. At the turn of the century, Odias of Chennai were mostly invisible. Later, they would come as brick kiln and construction workers, security guards, etc. and that presence did not necessarily translate into visibility. Mohapatra rightly points out (in a different context) that Odias outside Odisha were only participants in 'belly politics' (1996: 219).

As more and more educated Odias came out of Odisha and became a significant part of the IT sector and were supplemented by Odia doctors, scientists, professors and administrators, as well as engineering students, their presence was successfully translated into some sort of assuredness, confidence and visibility. In the first decade of twenty-first century, Odia civil servants dominated Tamil Nadu administrative structure occupying high positions whose help would contribute to the making of Kanathur temple. But more than their financial contribution and administrative facilitation, it was their presence as high-ranking officials that changed the way Odias saw themselves, who so far were occupying the margins of the city. The temple was, thus, the expression of their arrival and visual proof of their presence, goodwill and even power. Building the Jagannath temple was the ultimate symbolic act of announcing and building a community (Pati 2011: 194). Pati shows how in different geography (in Merrillville, Northwest Indiana), Hindus built a temple called Bharatiya temple which carries complexity and diversity of Hinduism with various Hindu deities as well as Mahavira Jaina (2011: 192).

That does not mean that the Jagannath temple was an elitist and interventionist enterprise; these doctors, officers and professors symbolised Odia pride and made up for the decades-old humiliation as worthless Odias in the informal economy. These white-collar officers will channelise the desire for Odia-ness (to be distinguished from an assertive Odia identity) and a project that desire to Jagannath, a metaphor of believing and belonging. Imagining themselves as Odias through Jagannath was not an invented tradition, but an age-old signifier. It established that Tamil Nadu can be home and this alternative to the conventional idea of Odia-ness disavowed 'loyalty to territorial homelands' (Giri 2005: 215).

Waghorne in her fascinating work on contemporary temple-building spree in Chennai, sees such a desire in middle-class aspirations in a post-secular age (2004: 5) that also shows the agency of ordinary people to create their sacred geography, unlike earlier times when only kings could build temples. This traditionalisation makes the city something more than a space of economic activities and turns the idea of a secular soulless city on its head. However, she limits the scope of this traditionalisation by her focus on middle-class, whereas Kanathur temple offers an interesting constellation cutting across class and caste. That said, she gets it right when she argues that the devotees and donors of such temples are not dupes of priestly class but are agentic beings (2004: 17). She also refers to Kanathur Jagannath temple and the former President of Utkal Association (Dr Kabi Prasad Mishra), who believed that the Kanathur temple brings the conservative and the progressive together (2004: 33).

The Kanathur temple is representative of an ethical-territorial order, created and sustained by bringing all parts of Odisha so as to offset any claim of an Odisha that is divided. Jagannath provides a coherence strategy to Odias divided by region (such as the demand for Koshala state in western Odisha) and recreates Odia-ness through collective imagination. The celebration of Nuakhai is done with fervour, possibly to delegitimise the claims of *Juhar*, a rival group of western Odias to assert their difference from the existing Utkal Association. Similarly, the strong presence of western Odias in the Sri Jagannath Spiritual Education Cultural Trust, the worship of Samaleswari as *Parsva Devi* as well as the transcendent signified of Jagannath neutralise such fractures and makes Kanathur temple a symbol of internal consistency and stability. This firmness remains a precondition for Jagannath's negotiation with local practices and universalist claims.

Acknowledgements

I benefitted from multiple rounds of discussion with Prof. Surendranath Majhi, Prof. Ashok K. Mishra, Mr Panchanana Sahoo and Mr Bibhuti B. Bishoyi. This chapter is a tribute to them.

References

Acharya, Pritish. 2008. *National Movement and Politics in Orissa, 1920–29*. New Delhi: SAGE.

Bhabha, Homi K. 1994. *The Location of Culture*. London: Routledge.

Burchardt, Marian and Mariske Westendorp. 2018. 'The Im-materiality of Urban Religion: towards an Ethnography of Urban Religious Aspirations'. *Culture and Religion*, 19(2): 160–176.

Das, J.P. 1982. *Puri Paintings: The Chitrakara and His Work*. New Jersey: Humanities Press.

Dash, G.N. 1986. 'Jagannatha and Oriya Nationalism'. In *The Cult of Jagannath and the Regional Tradition of Orissa*, edited by Anncharlott Eschmann, Hermann Kulke and Gaya Charan Tripathi, 359–374. New Delhi: Manohar.

Dash, Kailash Chandra. 1996. 'A Study of the Origin of Rath Yatra in the Purusottama Ksetra'. *East and West*, 46(1/2): 117–125.

Freeman, James M. 1975. 'Religious Change in a Hindu Pilgrimage Center'. *Review of Religious Research*, 16(2): 124–133.

Giri, Bed Prasad. 2005. 'Diasporic Postcolonialism and its Antinomies'. *Diaspora*, 14(2/3): 215–235.

Hegewald, Julia A.B. and Subrata K. Mitra. 2008. 'Jagannath Compared: The Politics of Appropriation, Re-use and Regional Traditions in India', Working Paper No. 36, Heidelberg Papers in South Asian and Comparative Politics, University of Heidelberg.

Hornabrook, Jasmine. 2018. 'Songs of the Saints: Song Paths and Pilgrimage in London's Tamil Hindu Diaspora'. *Asian Music*, 49(2): 106–150.

Kinsley, David. 1998. 'Learning the Story of the Land: Reflections on the Liberating Power of Geography and Pilgrimage in the Hindu Tradition'. In *Purifying the Earthly Body of God: Religion and Ecology in Hindu India*, edited by Lance E. Nelson, 225–246. Albany: State University of New York Press.

Lochtefeld, James G. 2010. *God's Gateway: Identity and Meaning in a Hindu Pilgrimage Place*. New York: Oxford University Press.

Majhi, Surendtanath. 2008. *Prabhukrupa: Byaktigata Divya Anubhutimala*, translated by R.N. Mishra. Kanathur: Sri Jagannath Spiritual Educational Cultural Trust.

Majhi, Surendtanath. 2016. 'A Short History of Sri Jagannath Shrine of Chennai', *Sri Jagannath Spiritual Educational Cultural Trust Souvenir*, 14–23.

Mishra, Kabi Prasad. 2008. *Baisi Pahacha*. Bhubaneswar: Mahavir Prakashan.

Mohapatra, Bishnu N. 1996. 'Ways of "Belonging": The Kanchi Kaveri Legend and the Construction of Oriya Identity'. *Studies in History*, 12(2): 203–221.

Nanda, Chandi Prasad. 2008. *Vocalizing Silence: Political Protests in Orissa, 1932–42*. New Delhi: SAGE.

Narayanan, Vasudha. 2006. 'Hinduism in Pittsburgh'. In *The Life of Hinduism*, edited by John S. Hawley and Vasudha Narayanan, 231–248. University of California Press: Berkeley.

Park, Chris C. 1994. *Sacred Worlds: An Introduction to Geography and Religion*. London: Routledge.

Pati, George. 2011. 'Temple and Human Bodies: Representing Hinduism'. *International Journal of Hindu Studies*, 15(2): 191–207.

Patnaik, Janakiballabha. 2016. 'Chennai SriJagannatha Mandira: A Different Tradition', *Sri Jagannath Spiritual Educational Cultural Trust Souvenir*, 29–30.

Ray, Ramashankar. n.d. *Kanchi Kaveri*. Cuttack: Books and Books.

Rosowsky, Andrey. 2018. 'Globalisation, the Practice of Devotional Songs and Poems and the Linguistic Repertoires of Young British Muslims'. *Culture and Religion*, 19(1): 90–112.

Samal, Baishnaba Charan. n.d. 'Grantha Prabesh', in *Kanchi Kaveri*, edited by Ramashankar Ray, 1–26. Cuttack: Books and Books.

Schmid, Anna. 2001. 'Lord Jagannatha in Pictorial Representations: A Collection of Cloth Paintings (*pata citras*)'. In *Jagannath Revisited: Studying Society, Religion and the State in Orissa*, edited by Harmann Kulke and Burkhard Schnepel, 297–316. New Delhi: Manohar.

Souvenir. 2016. *Sri Jagannath Spiritual Educational Cultural Trust*. Chennai.

Stietencron, H.V. 1986. 'The Jagannatha Temples in Contemporary Orissa'. In *The Cult of Jagannath and the Regional Tradition of Orissa*, edited by Anncharlott Eschmann, Hermann Kulke and Gaya Charan Tripathi, 469–475. New Delhi: Manohar.

Waghorne, Joanne Punzo. 2004. *Diaspora of the Gods: Modern Hindu Temples in an Urban Middle-Class World*. New York: Oxford University Press.

9

DELHIWALLAH JAGANNATH AND THE ODIA DIASPORA: NOTES TOWARDS A SOCIAL HISTORY

Gautam Choubey

By focusing on the two oldest among the seven Jagannath temples in Delhi and the centrality of the Jagannath culture to the sociocultural imagination of Delhi-based Odias, this chapter attempts a brief social history of Delhi's Odia diaspora. The study addresses, inter alia, the structural and the evolutionary challenges of such transplanted communities, questions of cultural acclimatisation and the dynamics of collective bargaining in a multiethnic ecosystem. Further, using diaspora as a study sample, an attempt has also been made to explore how autochthonous religious symbols and practices facilitate secular enterprises such as occupational migration, community formations and even cultural revival in a foreign environment.

Ever since their establishment in the late 1960s, Jagannath temples at Hauz Khas and Thyagraj Nagar have defined the possibilities and the limitations of Odia aspirations in the city. These temples, and their respective locations, underscore the glaring contradictions and the many commonalities that characterise the constitution of nearly 1.3 million Delhi-based Odias.[1] Hauz Khas is an upscale neighbourhood and its temple is well-funded. Thyagraj Nagar, by contrast, is a working-class settlement and its temple—although the oldest in the city—often runs into budget deficits. Over the decades since the arrival of the first Odias, the diaspora has grown in number and diversified significantly. As expected, diversification opened up fault lines in the social makeup of the community, and the emergent classes started drifting apart.

In electoral politics, the community becomes a site of mobilisation and affirmative initiatives (Fazal 2016: 107). Its prospects are linked incorrigibly to its numerical strength and internal cohesion. This is particularly true of a diaspora situation, where the community is in minority, and therefore, vulnerable. Outnumbered by other contending ethnicities and factions, Odias of Delhi seem to have realised that fragmentation might soften their bargaining capacity with the powers arrangements in both Delhi and Odisha. Consequently, over the past two decades, several attempts have been made to bridge the widening class divide and bolster the community's image. What were these initiatives and were their outcomes true to the original purpose? What role did the temples play in these endeavours? Did diversification diminish the temples' hold on the community?

A diaspora's yearning for a space that recreates the milieu of its homeland bears a positional relationship with the cultural ecosystem of the place of migration. In what ways does Delhi catalyse the very enterprise of building a Jagannath temple and such other communal projects? What are those geocultural elements which influence preservationist manoeuvres of a transplanted community? What negotiations allow Hindu subcultures to subsist, and even flourish, within a pan-Indian Hindu landscape? Sociologists believe that in Delhi, state intervention in the disposition of urban spaces and management of the migrant influx is unprecedented (Baviskar 1998: 3101–3102). What are the achievements and promises of the state-politics nexus in the life of diaspora?

The chapter begins with an examination of the Odia diaspora's formative years and then moves on to its contemporary conundrums. Besides responding to the aforementioned questions, in the same order as enumerated, the shaping influences of the two temples and Delhi's sociocultural ecosystem has been constantly foregrounded. In the penultimate section, to facilitate a deeper engagement with the dialectics of migrant-space interaction, Delhi's diaspora and the temples have been contrasted with those in Vadodara and Bokaro Steel City—one far from the Odia homeland and another in the neighbouring state of Jharkhand. Finally, by analysing the changing paradigms of community initiatives and state-community continuum, this study speculates on the diaspora's prospects in Delhi.

This chapter draws upon primary data collected during my fieldwork in Delhi and Bokaro, and over numerous interactions with the diaspora across the three cities. With the two Jagannath temples and the Odia cultural bodies listed on the website of the Delhi-based Resident Commissioner of Odisha (Government of Odisha) as starting points of this investigation, my pursuit brought me in contact with a diverse group of Odia forums and with even more diverse objectives. All the interviews conducted in this investigation were based on a non-restrictive use of questionnaire and the participants were encouraged to digress to aspects of their collective/individual memory not addressed by the questions.

Early Migrants and Their Challenges

The story begins in Mandapada, a village in Pattamundai block (Kendrapada district) of coastal Odisha. In the 1920s, a 20 something Choudhary Pradhan of Mandapada arrived in Calcutta and started working for Gammon India limited, a British construction company founded by John C. Gammon in 1922. By the 1930s, having mastered the craft of plumbing, Pradhan moved to Delhi.[2] Within a few years of his arrival, he became a plumbing contractor and started hiring people from his own region. In Pradhan's ascendancy, residents of the flood-stricken Pattamundai saw a way out of their miseries. Soon many flocked to plumbing and left for cites like Delhi and Calcutta. By late 1950s and early 1960s, the plumbers of Kendrapada district constituted an overwhelming majority among the earliest Odia migrants to Delhi. This serial migration was catalysed by several 'push' and 'pull' factors. If unemployment, chronic poverty, natural disasters and a sense of stagnation pushed them out of Odisha, an 'under-construction' Delhi attracted them with its abundant plumbing and labour-intensive assignments.

The network of friends and family members, who were beginning to find a firm footing in the city, provided a sense of security. In India, the process of migration and the choice of destination are largely influenced by the presence of such absorptive social networks of relatives and co-villagers (Banerjee 1983: 185–88; Ratnoo 2017: 60–62). These networks reduce the cost of relocation and strengthen kinship structures by rekindling regional ties in an alien environment.

By the middle and late 1960s, many had graduated from being manual labourers to contractors. This long-range mobility, from working class to the middle or the upper middle classes, mostly through intra-occupational transition, triggered a delayed family migration. By now many felt emboldened to fetch their families. Ravi Pradhan, the secretary of Hauz Khas temple, remembers how his father D.D. Pradhan (Chaudhary Pradhan's nephew) fought a surge of disapproving voices in Mandapada to bring his wife and children to Delhi. It was only after he promised to continue with his son's Odia language and script training—a non-negotiable condition set forth by the child's grandfather, that he could finally have his wish.

In a multicultural ecosystem like Delhi that seeks to homogenise its inhabitants through Hindi and a corporate calendar, this fear of linguistic and cultural dilution is real. Once family units were established and their numbers grew, they sought to allay these anxieties by devising ways of importing Odia customs in their new environment. It was under these circumstances that a *prerna* (divine inspiration) to build a Jagannath temple descended upon Pradhan's father. This was in 1962. Soon a trust was set up with an initial capital of ₹ 20,000, out of which ₹ 16,000 was donated by P.K. Deo, Maharaja (king) of Kalahandi. Most of the remaining 4,000 was donated by nearly 300 plumbers of varying financial status. Finally, in 1967, with the concerted interventions of R.N. Singhdeo, the then Chief Minister of Odisha and Delhi's first Lieutenant Governor Aditya Nath Jha, a plot was procured in Hauz Khas. The temple at Thyagraj Nagar has a similar story to share. A managing trust was registered in 1968 and a functional structure was ready by the end of the year. Here too, most of the founding trustees were plumber-turned-contractors.

The construction of a Jagannath temple was central to the attempts of the migrants who wanted to preserve the memories of their homeland and families. In other words, the pursuit of Jagannath was the very vehicle, and to some extent, the principal objective of this preservationist enterprise. It is for this reason that most managing trusts describe themselves as cultural bodies. The temple in Thyagraj Nagar is managed by a society named Sri Jagannath Mandir and Odisha Arts and Cultural Centre. Roger L. Henrie argues that all sacred spaces fall into one of the five categories: places of mystical manifestations, cultural homelands, places of historical legacies, functional religious places and places connected with purported fulfilment of prophecies (1972: 18). In Puri, at least the first three of these categories appear to converge. It is not just a place of divine revelation but is also cardinal to an Odia Hindu's notion of homeland. Compared to shrines such as Kedarnath, Badrinath and Vaishnav Devi that are located in geographically inaccessible terrains, the temple in Puri is situated in the middle of a city abuzz with human activities. It could, therefore, develop a set of rituals which mirrored the rhythm of everyday life in Odisha. Perhaps, this also accounts for Puri's attraction and its integrative character.

According to Frank G. Kirkpatrick, in an age where the very idea of 'objective reality' is a suspect, talking about God as a lived experience becomes a slippery task (1994: Preface). But Odias do not associate distant veneration with Jagannath, nor do they confine him to the plank of affect. He is humanised, domesticated and is the de-facto head of every Odia-Hindu household. As such, he not only commands their devotion, but incurs their displeasure too. Further, the Odisha-based Odias consider him a local deity and are least attentive to Jagannath's pan-Indian stature.[3] There is a saying: *sakala tirtha to charane, Badrika jibi ki karane* (all sacred shrines converge at your feet, why shall I to go Badrinath?) This localises their notion of pilgrimage. Instead of embarking upon a treacherous journey to a distant shrine, which may be potentially disorienting as it brings them in contact with the unfamiliar, every journey to Puri reaffirms their religio-cultural identity.[4] Moreover, as Rosel points out, a pilgrim's communion with Jagannath is uncomplicated and sensual (1983: 52).

For the diaspora, these temples localise the sense of both home and identity. By recreating the cultural geography of Puri, and by extension that of Odisha, the temples seek to truncate their sense of displacement. However, since Jagannath is an autochthonous deity and Delhi lacks both scriptural validation and territorial continuity, transplanting Puri's religious landscape becomes nearly infeasible. This necessitates resemblance at three levels: ritual, architectural and affective. To ensure architectural fidelity, the temples made it a point to hire only Odia architects and sculptors. As far as the rituals are concerned, their elaborate nature makes faithful adherence difficult. Consequently, they are miniaturised and modified. However, measures are taken to reduce the quantum of deviation and the *pandas* (priests) of Puri are routinely invited to counsel the servitors of the temples.

Displayed prominently in the two temples, the Odia sacred calendar ensures perfect temporal overlap between the original and its replica. In post-industrial societies, calendars are seen as sites where the sacred and the secular rhythms of life converge. Vasudha Narayan's study of Pittsburgh based Hindu community shows how the almanac is often re-calibrated to align with public holidays (2006: 233). Here, such liberties are strictly forbidden and the calendar elicits perfect compliance. The temple managing committees and the *pandas* are responsible for recreating Hindu Odias' religious experience and reaffirm the milieu that shaped itself around Puri. By attending to requirements such as horoscope surveys, marriages, holy thread ceremonies, etc., the *pandas* registered with the temple seek to ameliorate their sense of dislocation.

Over the decades since the first plumbers arrived in Delhi, the socioeconomic profile of Odias has changed considerably. In the 1960s, barring a few MPs and bureaucrats, plumber-turned-contractors constituted the only prosperous minority among the diaspora. Various factors explain this bleak picture. First, this was still an early stage of migration and the majority was confined to plumbing jobs. The entire range of occupational possibilities that Delhi opened up to them, was yet to be explored. Second, their integration with the locals, which was essential for the growth of the business, was still incomplete/far from complete. For the Odias, acquiring local texture in both food and language was slow and strenuous. Third, access to Delhi's state education system, including the city university, was proving to be a challenge. Evaluation patterns in Odisha were so stringent that students could barely meet the Delhi University (DU) cut-offs. Fourth (as several respondents pointed out), north Indians considered Odisha as a province of poverty, epidemics and famine. Conscious of this stigma, Odias became diffident about their ethnicity.

Fifth, the absence of a regional forum was acutely felt. The network of Delhi-based plumbers from Kendrapada and the neighbouring district of Jajpur, was circumscribed by professional and local ties.

Thus, the diaspora's struggle was not restricted to questions of social mobility and livelihood. It was also about announcing its arrival and carving a niche for itself in Delhi. The establishment of these temples, in conjunction with a few local factors, altered the community's self-definition as well as its fortunes. For several years, Delhi's education system thwarted the ambitions of Odia students. While it drew a huge contingent of livelihood seekers, students from well-established education centres such as Cuttack, Bhubaneswar, Sambalpur and Berhampur did not find the city's academic institutions too welcoming. These students needed support and positive discrimination, neither of which was available at DU. As mentioned earlier, an illiberal evaluation pattern followed by Odisha higher secondary board further jeopardised their chances; the cost of living in Delhi, which has always been extremely high, was equally discouraging. But the historical concurrence of Jawaharlal Nehru University (JNU) and the two temples proved to be a major turnaround. JNU was established in 1969 and in 1974 it introduced deprivation points for students from backward regions of the country. Several districts from Odisha were also notified in this list. Moreover, it assured heavily subsidised accommodation to all its students. Buoyed by these improved prospects, several students arrived in the city (Das 2014: 47).

Ravi Pradhan recalls how in 1977, over a hundred bright students from Ravenshaw College and Utkal University thronged the temple premises. Some of these were instructed by their local contacts to reach the temples as soon as they deboarded the Delhi-bound Utkal Express. The temples were ready for the challenge too. By the mid-1970s, arrangements had been made to accommodate medical tourists and job seekers from Odisha. At both the temples, *pandas* and caretakers welcomed these students with a homely ambience, accommodation at nominal charges and free *mahaprasad* (the great sacrament). The response from the now sizeable plumbing community and the government officials was equally enthusiastic. However, very few were familiar with the intricacies of the university system. Fortunately, the then recently established Delhi Oriya Students Association (DOSA, est. 1970) was beginning to spread its wings. Using its network of professors, researchers, students and union leaders, DOSA assisted these aspirants in the admission processes.

By the 1980s, the number of Odia students at JNU had increased considerably and some of them were even elected to its student bodies. Delhi's mushrooming UPSC coaching institutes did not go unnoticed either. Leveraging local contacts at the temples, JNU, DOSA and the plumbing community, several Odia students joined these coaching centres and many among them became civil servants.[5] This was in the late 1980s and 1990s. Around this time, there was a significant increase in the number of ICSE and CBSE board schools in Odisha. Once the Odia students started scoring at par with the national average, their intake at DU increased too. Most of those who graduated from JNU and DU became successful professionals. The epochal role which the temples played in the entire process goes to show that in urban multicultural spaces, religious institutions are much more accommodative of both individual and communal aspirations, than they are usually thought of. Further, trajectories of urbanisation in India are such that even in liberated cosmopolitanism spaces like Delhi, rural and regional ties remain the most significant social binder (Chatterjee 2017: 153).

In the meantime, India had liberalised its economy and the Odia working class had diversified itself. Although plumbing was still their preferred profession but it was no longer the only option available to them. Consequently, the number of Odia migrants surged and the areas adjoining the two temples became their favoured destinations. Chhattarpur, Shahpur Jat and Munirka near Hauz Khas and localities like Kotla near Thyagraj Nagar have a sizable Odia population. Over the next three decades, the socioeconomic profile of the Odias changed dramatically. The temples themselves were busy consolidating their fields of activity and expanding their physical infrastructures. The Hauz Khas temple added another floor and built rooms for visitors. In 1986, an eighteen-room *dharmashala* (sacred rest house) was built adjacent to the Thyagraj Nagar temple and in 1999, in the presence of Divya Singh Dev, the Gajapati king of Puri, the present temple was inaugurated.

Diversification, Fragmentation, Consolidation: Temples and Beyond

Diversification opened up rifts in the composition of the diaspora. Once class schism started widening, several class-based associations emerged in the late 1990s and the early 2000s. Broadly speaking, activities undertaken by these associations reflected their class-specific aspiration. The working-class groups were interested in organising health camps and celebrating local festivals, while the professional-class associations wanted Odia and Odissi lessons for their children. The business-class groups desired access to temple management committees, better ties with the political class and a community centre/auditorium.[6] The intellectual class sought to encourage Odisha-centric research and establish a research centre to promote Odia heritage. However, these forums had at least one of the three things in common: culture and language of Odisha was their favoured field of operation, even though they claimed to be apolitical, each appeared keen to woo the political class, and they are intemperately reliant on the temples.

Ethnic socialisations are known to translate into voting patterns (Birnir 2006: 32) and it is only through a sustained exhibition of such designs that political patronage can be earned. But diversification compromised diaspora's bargaining capacity with both local as well as the Odisha government. Although the annual rath yatra (chariot festival) remained the most popular occasion for ritual convergence, the hurried festivities around the event frustrated possibilities of further collaboration or transcendence of class division. Under the circumstances, temples provided the anchorage necessary to steer unificatory maneuvers. One of the earliest events, aimed ostensibly at integration, was sponsored by the managing committee of Thyagraj Nagar temple. In 2008, on Kartik Purnima (according to Hindu calendar, the full moon day in the month of

Kartik), a three-day *kirtan* (collective performance of devotional songs) extravaganza was organised at the Thyagraj Nagar temple. The event that was planned and managed by a Kotla-based *kirtan* group, demonstrated both resourcefulness as well as limitations of the working class.

According to Uddhav Senbahal, a young member of the *mandali* (troupe), there are 20 such groups of Odisha-born first-generation migrants. Most of them are based in working-class localities such as Kotla, Mandawali, Shahpur Jat, Chattarpur, Munirka and Jonapur Bhim Basti. It was through random meetings at the temples, a shared fondness for *kirtan*, association with village *mandalis* and regional ties that these groups came about. Temple directory and class networks were mobilised to invite 19 other *kirtan* groups in a customary fashion; each group was given a *dhoti* (Hindu male wraparound), a coconut and ₹ 501 as *baina* (advance). The event, as the group remembers, was a monumental success and close to five thousand Odias feasted on that day. The *mandalis* themselves were the greatest beneficiaries as they got the visibility and acceptance hitherto withheld from them. Soon, their calendars were full and they became the regulars at Odia cultural events across Delhi.

Jagannath culture and several of its rituals appear faithful to the rhythm of pre-industrial societies. It is believed that the spirit of Chaitanya descends on the *kirtan* performers. Uddhav pointed out that each year several 'big people' touch his feet. But deification of these working-class performers is restricted to the religious imaginary. In the social sphere, class dynamics remain intact. None from the *kirtan mandali* has ever been inducted in a temple managing committee. Evidently, solidarity remained a challenge too gigantic for the working class to surmount. The reluctance of the elite to associate with the working class is a reminder of the fact that most community initiatives are, in fact, class initiatives. And the ones that are more likely to succeed are those which are executed by the dominant class. It must also be emphasised that since Thyagraj Nagar does not enjoy the patronage of the elite the way Hauz Khas temple does, the majority of those who turn up for this annual event come from the working-class localities.

Figure 9.1 Kartik Purnima celebration at the Thyagraj Nagar temple
Source: Picture taken by the author with the permission of Manorama Puspalak, the proprietor of Sadgranth Niketan.

Reflecting on both rath yatra and Kartik Purnima celebrations (Figure 9.1), Debendra Rout (founder, *The Intellects*) argues that the Odias needed a more relaxed and sustained setting to intermingle. As far as the temple visitors are concerned, only a few among the regulars share a formal relationship with it, while the majority comprise a floating variety. In 2011, with the aforementioned challenges in sight, Rout organised a religious congregation around Odisha's most loved religious text—Jagannath Das's *Bhagabat.* Two of Odisha's best known *katha vachakas* (story tellers) were invited for a week-long event and Hauz Khas was the chosen venue. Proximity to the Hauz Khas District Park (one of the best-maintained parks in Delhi) and the circuit of exclusive eateries in Hauz Khas village make the temple a perfect destination for short recreational excursions. These locational merits complement the elite patronage which the temple enjoys.

Over the seven days, the entire political class and the elite among the diaspora turned up in huge numbers. Rout remembers how the elites shared the mattresses laid out in the temple basement without any class inhibition. This seating arrangement is standard practice across temples in India, and therefore, one must not read a lot in this overture. Yet, it is indeed remarkable that most of them had come uninvited. Further, the ambiance was such that people could hold long conversations on the sidelines and interact freely. For Rout, it was an occasion for the community to recognise its strength and diversity, and to revitalise its professional and cultural networks. However, even with the kind of resources which *The Intellect* could summon, bridging the class divide remained a tall order and almost unachievable in an experiential everyday sense. Thus, class unity stays a performative exhibit. In electoral politics, where a public exhibition of numerical strength is widely regarded as the most potent statement on solidarity, class unity has to have a strong performative dimension. It is perhaps in this limited yet decisive sense, that the event was a success.

Just as Uddhav and his troupe drew substantial dividends from the Kartik Purnima event, *The Intellects* benefited enormously from *Bhagabat* recitation. For an organisation's inaugural venture, the event gave it more visibility than the group may have hoped for. Post 2011, *The Intellects* emerged as one of the most active cultural bodies. Using contacts established during these seven days, the group diversified its areas of operation. Soon they were organising events at city's landmark venues such as India International Centre (IIC) and India Habitat Centre (IHC). This also goes to show how it takes an effort from the very top to accomplish even a semblance of class integration. Further, even within a community, which appears homogeneous with respect to its ethnic identity and religious practices, there is heterogeneity in terms of the 'most favoured' ritual. In other words, even among members of the same faith, religious practices vary with class. *Kirtan* is an important constituent of the Jagannath culture, but it doesn't find favour with the elite. Although it is performed every Sunday at the Thyagraj Nagar temple, participation is restricted to the performers and their friends.

The cultural events organised by and at the temples were well attended, but even a capacity to crowd at these venues is a far cry from a representative sample of Odia population. The basement at the Hauz Khas temple is huge, but many are opposed to the idea of attending sociocultural events on mattresses or plastic chairs in a non-air-conditioned environment. The 'auditorium like' Subhadra Kala Mandap at the Thyagraj Nagar temple can accommodate a maximum of 200 people. IIC and IHC are constrained by numbers too. Thus, stepping out of both the temples as well as the elite settings has now become imperative.

In a city which is bitterly divided along ethnic lines, it was important to assert one's identity. However, Gobardhan Dhal of Bal

Jagruti Association argues that Odias are generally diffident about their identity, and showed reluctance to move beyond their comfort zone—the Jagannath temples. From 2004, with an objective to draw them beyond their traditional environment, Dhal started organising *Boita Bandana* at Kalindi Kunj, Yamuna. The exhibition value of the event is comparable to Chhath celebration in cities like Delhi and Mumbai. Chhath is often linked to Bihari pride and is seen as an occasion to put the community's strength on display. The inaugural event was far from overwhelming, but in the subsequent years, it has caught up with all segments of the diaspora. In 2009, the annual event shifted to Delhi Boat Club at India Gate. Dhal argues that the growing attendance of top government functionaries and politicians attests to the strength of the Odias in the city and has emboldened the community.

Many felt that distracting the *Odias* away from the temples was not enough. Providing them with lasting alternative space(s) was equally important. For decades, the Odias have been lobbying and petitioning for a cultural centre in Delhi or at least an auditorium to support the soaring cultural and political designs of the community. Other than the *kirtan mandalis* and the temple management committees, almost every organisation interviewed in the present study lamented the lack of an auditorium. Many claimed to have endured great hardships and humiliation in their campaign.[7] Many rued the absence of an Odia medium school or one where Odia is taught along with other subjects. Although an Odia school was part of the original architectural design of the Hauz Khas temple complex and the Odisha government had promised to bear the operational cost of the school, but the help did not come forthwith. Another set of respondents appeared keen on contesting misrepresentations of Odia heritage and reclaiming its rightful position in the national imaginary. To this end, they hoped to establish a research centre in Delhi.

Since state patronage remained a distant dream, several 'inspired' individuals and groups have taken it upon themselves to carry out the preservationist enterprises. G.D. Pradhan's Kalinga Siksha Samaj has been sponsoring Odia language courses in the city for the past 26 years. Similarly, groups like Institute for Promotion and Research on Odisha Culture and Heritage (IPROCH) and *The Intellects* have been promoting research on Odia history and culture. IPROCH has been demanding classical status for medieval devotional songs about Jagannath and Krishna that accompany Odissi dance performances. They contend that these songs represent a distinct art form that cannot be subsumed under either of the two existing classical styles of music in India: the Hindustani and the Carnatic.[8] Such a claim to originality is also evident in the activities of *The Intellects*. In an event organised in January 2018, the group demanded recognition of the Paika rebellion (1818) as the first struggle for India's Independence.

Till the time such cultural centres and auditoriums are built, the community remains hinged to the temples. When the diaspora launched language teaching programmes, the temples became the favoured venues. Of the six Odia language training centres managed by *The Intellects*, three are based in Jagannath temples. Even the elite groups like *The Intellects* and IPROCH, that are gradually drifting away to other posh venues, recognise their centrality to the sociocultural life of the diaspora. However, one needs to ask as to how auditoriums, language training centres and research become so integral to the diaspora's notion of home. Here, the distinction which Eric Hobsbawm draws between imagination of home-based on individual/private memory (*heim*) and the public idea of home (*heimat*) may be useful (1991: 67). Taking a cue from Hobsbawm, one may argue that although cultural centres do not feature in recollections of the Odia home, they are central to the way communities in Delhi think of themselves. Justifying their demands for an all-Odia auditorium, the majority of respondents cited the presence of schools and auditoriums affiliated with other states of India.

The cumulative experience of the aforementioned integrative manoeuvres and the cultural projects underscore sharp ethnic rivalries in the city. Further, it underscores two distinct patterns. First, there has been a strategic appropriation of the sacred for secular reasons. *Kirtan*, *Bhagabat* and *Boita Bandana* serve a purpose beyond the religious. Second, the decline in the community's sacred commitment is matched by a surge in its secular concerns. Of late, the community has displayed a heightened awareness of its self-image and its own linguistic and cultural heritage. This necessitates an assessment of the diaspora's religiosity. While the temples are diligent in fulfilling their religious obligations towards the community, it may be worthwhile to ask if the diaspora too fulfils its religious commitments with a proportionate fervour. Chris C. Park proposes two conceptual models to analyse the relationship between migration and religious commitment: dislocation and adaptation models (1994: 153). While the dislocation model predicts a decline in religiosity, the adaptation model postulates variations in commitment depending on the norms of religious behaviours in the place of migration.

Using the adaptation model, the chapter proposes to examine the variations in diaspora's sacred/secular commitments concerning religious behaviours prevalent in Delhi. How does a place, so distant from the Odia homeland, offer to advance the diaspora's aspirations? What are the distinct advantages as well as the drawbacks of Delhi's cultural landscape? As a city of possibilities, how different is it from other metropolitan spaces? To understand diaspora's special relationship with Delhi in a comparative paradigm, I propose to examine Jagannath temples and the state of the diaspora in Vadodara and Bokaro Steel City. As pointed out in the introductory section, when compared to Delhi, Vadodara in Gujarat is remote from Odisha. Bokaro, by contrast, is located in the bordering state of Jharkhand.

Three Cultural Ecosystems and Electoral Politics

All the founding trustees of Bokaro's Jagannath temple (est. 2000) temple are Odias. The managing committee too, just like those in Delhi, is an all-Odia body. However, while raising funds for the temple, the entire city had come together. For a number of reasons, raising funds in Bokaro temple was relatively easier. Land is ample and affordable, Odia presence in the city is sizable and stable with respect to employment structures and Jagannath is extremely popular among the people of Bihar, Jharkhand and Bengal; the three dominant communities in Bokaro. Compared to Delhi, the dominance of tribal cultures in the east results in a greater acceptance of the Jagannath culture. Furthermore, for those living in Bokaro, Puri is not just a place of pilgrimage, but a popular tourist destination too. People from Bihar and Jharkhand find Puri hotels affordable and Odia food is extremely close to their own gastronomic preferences. Thus, even though Bokaro may not be entirely invested in the Jagannath culture, the city is indeed circumscribed by Puri's extended religious landscape.

It is worth noticing that even though its architectural design replicates Puri, the temple complex caters to sociocultural needs of the city's other communities too. Unlike the temples in Delhi, which are now opening up to the non-Odias, this inclusiveness was part of the original design and not an afterthought. The temple auditorium hosts religious, cultural, corporate and at times even private events like weddings. Besides, its pond draws thousands of devotees during Chhath. Bokaro too reciprocates this spirit of assimilation. In a state where Odia is officially recognised one of the 11 second official languages, Odias experience no cultural threat. While numerous Odias in Delhi expressed the need for an Odia school, no one in Bokaro feels that way. Bokaro's Jagannath temple does not host any language teaching programs. Instead, it organises essay writing competitions and debates; activities which anticipate an advanced degree of linguistic competence. As far as Odissi dance is concerned, it is taught along with Bharatnatyam and other contemporary dance forms in nearly a dozen dance academies in the city.

The industrial town of Vadodara in Gujarat offers a contrasting image. It is home to nearly 700 affluent Odia families which are strung together through Utkalika Seva Sangh—an 'exclusive' cultural association which celebrates a few Odia festivals. Its Jagannath temple is located within the premises of the royal palace of Vadodara. The queen's second husband was heir to the royal family of Rajkanika, a town located in Kendrapada district of Odisha. Following his death, when the queen returned to Gujarat, she built the temple to honour the memories of her late husband. As the temple is privately owned and managed, diaspora's desire for a cultural space commensurate with its economic stature remains unfulfilled. To this end, they have set up a trust (Jagannath Seva Sangh), which aims to raise ₹ 5 crore to build a Jagannath temple complex, complete with a crafts museum and a cultural centre.

Bijay Nayak, one of the founding trustees of Jagannath Seva Sangh, points out that even after three years of extensive reach-out drives, the temple continues to be a distant dream, restricted largely to its website. For a project this ambitious, enlisting local support becomes imperative; whether monetary, bureaucratic or political. Consequently, there is a concerted effort to abandon the insularity of their previous cultural association in favour of an assimilative approach. Although Nayak is hopeful, he admits that the project is ambitious and may take a long time to complete. This is notwithstanding the fact that the Hindus of Gujarat are deeply invested in Krishna worship. While rich and religious Gujaratis are recognised nationally for their philanthropy and for patronising temples, the Bokaro-scheme does not seem to work in Vadodara. The sluggish progress of the project is a reminder of certain insurmountable hurdles: linguistic barrier, absence of inclusiveness in the guest-host relationship, the modest numerical strength of the Odias, territorial distance and an attitude of indifference, if not outright hostility, towards Hindu subcultures.

Delhi, through both its locational possibilities as well as the lacunae in its cultural ecosystem, provides a fertile space for establishment and sustenance of various ethnic forums. The city has a rich past, and the presence of government-aided cultural and literary bodies such as Sahitya Akademi, Sangeet Nayak Akademi, National School of Drama, to name a few, makes Delhi the un-proclaimed cultural capital of modern India. Besides, the city is also known to host a number of secular events and cultural festivals such as book fairs and film festivals. However, this city of migrants lacks an equivalent of Mumbai's *Ganapati* festival, Kolkata's Durga puja or Chennai's Pongal; a cultural extravaganza which endows the metropolis with a distinct flavour (Baviskar 1998: 3012; Kumar 2013: 12–30). On the Delhi tourism website, geographical locators for each of the fairs and festivals celebrated in Delhi underscore their 'all India' character. Perhaps the three-day *Phoolwalon ki Sair* is the only religio-cultural event which is unique to Delhi. However, over the years, both state as well as popular support for *sair* has shrunk considerably. In fact, it has also disappeared from the official website of Delhi's tourism department. In both public imagination as well as the official calendar of the government of NCR, space for that quintessential tradition remains largely unclaimed.

The absence of a state festival triggers ethnic tension, if not conflict. Several Odia organisations begrudged Delhi government's decision to declare Bihar's Chhath as a state holiday (Ghosh 2018). To them it was not the chief minister of Delhi, but the remarkable assertiveness of people from Bihar as well as their leaders which swung the beam in their favour. But the tenor of Odia regionalism is relatively milder. Its narrative is different from regional nationalism in states like Tamil Nadu, Andhra Pradesh, Assam, Maharashtra and even West Bengal. Unlike people from these states, Odias have a little or no reservation against Hindi, the language of Delhi. In fact, a number of them attributed their socioeconomic progress to their ability to bond with the locals and to their acquisition of local tongue. Consequently, simmering anti-Hindi sentiments, which translates into pro-active state governments, and generous support for their respective diaspora's cultural aspirations, has been absent in this case.

To the working professional in Delhi, cultural and religious activities are largely restricted to the realm of recreation. Realising that it is generally difficult for individuals to summon the degree of commitment necessary for such enterprises, several groups have assumed the role of facilitators, while others are canvassing for a cultural centre in Delhi. But the completion of all or any of the projects outlined by the diaspora requires political will and federal coordination. For the major part of the last thirty years, successive political dispensations in Odisha have opposed the power arrangements at the centre. The period coincides with the brief history of post-liberalisation India and the establishment of the majority of organisations interviewed for this study. Without centre-state coordination, neither the Odia schools nor the proposed cultural centre could be established.

In the early 1970s, Odisha government started sponsoring a hostel for the Odias studying in Delhi. Two decades later, when this state patronage was suddenly terminated, many felt that the diaspora was gradually losing its relevance to Odisha's electoral politics. However, over the last two decades, owing to their increased strength and prosperity, the diaspora from east have emerged as a major force in Delhi's electoral politics (Kumar 2013: 15–17). The state governments too have been trying to woo the expatriates. In 2017, Odisha government sanctioned land for a multipurpose guest house near Bhubaneswar. The proposed facility will provide affordable accommodation to those non-resident Odias who visit the state for marriage, pilgrimage and other rituals. In Delhi, by contrast, such projects remain elusive. In and around the city, land is expensive. Moreover, the diaspora is yet to project itself as a formidable political force, which thinks and acts in unison.

As outlined in the previous segments, Odias have been trying to address these challenges by falling back on their cultural resources. Of late, there has also been an attempt to embrace the non-Odias who may have been alienated by the elaborate specificities of the Jagannath culture. As Manfred Hutter puts it, if homeward bound elements 'sharpen one's own identity, they on the other hand lead to religious differentiation within the Hindu community as a whole' (2012: 361). The experience of Bokaro and Vadodara suggests that syncretism and inclusivity are keys to the prospects of the diaspora. Now, the diaspora seems eager to recast components of its symbolic boundaries into vehicles of assimilation (Lamont 2006: 172). Once again, the Jagannath temples have become rostrums of these drives. Temple menu and food have now become important sites for integrative experiments. Paneer (cheese) and a few other food items, typical of north India, have been introduced in *mahaprasad* menu as well as the confectionery shops/eateries attached to the two temples. Temple facilities are being rented out to non-Odias for marriages, birthdays and other rituals.

It is interesting to note that even though the Odia cultural organisations of Delhi, including the Jagannath temple managing committees, consider themselves apolitical, yet they attributed both their failures and successes to the political class. While the community rues the failure of successive state governments in establishing an Odia school or a state auditorium, several respondents pointed out that the presence of Odias in the union cabinet has been a great enabler. There is indeed some truth to this perception. In 1982, when Braj Mohan Mohanty became the union minister of state for Works, Housing and Land, he sanctioned the plot for Thyagraj Nagar temple. Dharmendra Pradhan, the present union petroleum minister, is seen as the driving force behind the much-hyped Odisha Parba and the revival of several Odia associations in the city. Although rath yatra and a few other cultural events draw considerable participation from the political class, the community seems to lack a strategy to engage them in long-term projects.

Conclusion

For the Odias, Jagannath is not confined to the realm of affect or ritual.[9] He is a supreme historical agent and a potent cultural symbol. As a historical agent, Jagannath is largely responsible for the evolution of a distinct Odia identity. As a symbol, he becomes the custodian of that identity. Furthermore, since the symbol is autochthonous in nature, even in a metropolitan space like Delhi, regional affinities and shared cultural experiences of the homeland continue to be the most effective community binder. In a very concrete sense, the life of diaspora appears to undermine notions of community as an imaginary construct. These communities are forged through regional ties, shared cultural experience and compelling local symbols. Even among those Delhi-born Odias, who have distanced themselves from linguistic, culinary and social landscape of Odisha, the attraction of Jagannath and Puri remains intact.

Arjun Appadurai regards locality as an inherently fragile social construct and argues that even the most intimate and insulated of localities must be guarded against other odds (2005: 179). As this study demonstrates, transplanted communities exhibit a greater degree of fragility. The grafted homeland is a social construct based as much on the notions of community prevalent among rival ethnicities, as it is on the real memory of the home which a migrant has left behind. For the diaspora, home is conceptualised through urban components (auditoriums, cultural research centres and museums) and shifts in sacred authority (temple management). For the diaspora, religion functions as a proto-social institution. It not only endows religious and ethnic minorities with a distinct social status but also provides alternative avenues of articulation and activities. In electoral politics, these subcultural enclaves acquire legitimacy and agency through expressions of collective will. Although such expressions are either dominant class aspirations disguised as collective sentiment or largely performative, they are necessary for a useful state-community continuum. This chapter also contends that instead of perpetuating their cultural distinctiveness through exclusionary practices, these conclaves must find ways to accommodate other communities, specially the dominant ones. The brief social history of Delhi's Odia community suggests that even with the advantage of numbers and economic prosperity, it is only through assimilation that bounded communities may thrive.

Notes

1. Although the exact strength of the diaspora is difficult to establish, the figure is an average of the numbers suggested by several dailies and many Delhi-based Odia associations.
2. Pattamundai is home to India's only technical institute dedicated exclusively to plumbing. In recognition of the plumbers of Pattamundai and their contribution to Odisha, in 2010, Naveen Patnaik's government established State Institute of Plumbing Technology in Pradhan's native village.
3. For a descriptive typology of the shrines from the perspective of cultural geography, see Lochtefeld (2010: 171–203).
4. For a case study of pilgrim interaction and cultural exchanges thereof, see Bhardwaj (1983: 216–223).
5. According to Professor Jatindra K. Nayak, who remembers having spent time in JNU around this period, for every successful IAS aspirant, there were hundred others who failed and returned home to join the education system in Odisha as school teachers and professors. Many among these got drafted in the State Service Commission.
6. They rue the fact that while most other communities have auditoriums and cultural centres built by their respective state governments, no help has come from their own state.

7. Some even linked it with Odia pride and suggested that it was extremely humiliating to realise that while almost every community including the Bengalis and Biharis have an auditorium, they don't. This is an inescapable expression of intercultural rivalry.
8. To this end, members of the institute have published several research articles and have also produced a 72- minute documentary on the subject. Although this has been a long-standing demand among the Odias because such claims are confined to Odisha and the Oriya diaspora, little progress has been made in this direction.
9. This partial secularisation does not dislodge the deity from his sacred context. For a discussion on Hinduism, modernity and community formation, see Smith (2003: 1–33).

References

Appadurai, Arjun. 2005. *Modernity at Large.* Minneapolis: University of Minnesota Press.

Banerjee, Biswajit. 1983. 'Social Networks in the Migration Process: Empirical Evidence on Chain Migration in India'. *The Journal of Developing Areas*, 17(2): 185–196.

Baviskar, Amita. 1998. 'Towards a Sociology of Delhi: Report on a Seminar'. *Economic and Political Weekly*, 33(49): 3101–3102.

Bhardwaj, Surinder Mohan. 1983. *Hindu Places of Pilgrimage in India: A Study in Cultural Geography.* California: University of California Press.

Birnir, Johanna Kristin. 2006. *Ethnicity and Electoral Politics.* Cambridge: Cambridge University Press.

Chatterjee, Pritha. 2017. 'Embedded or Liberated: An Exploration into the Social Milieu of Delhi'. In *Marginalisation in Globalising Delhi: Issues of Land, Livelihood and Health*, edited by Sanghmitra S. Acharya, Sucharita Sen, Milap Punia and Sunita Reddy. New Delhi: Springer.

Das, Gopabandhu. 2014. 'Changing Perspectives of Odishan Historiography'. *Odisha Review*, 70(6): 44–48.

Fazal, Tanweer. 2016. 'Home and Politics: Bihari Labour in the Metropolis'. *Indian Anthropologist*, 46(2): 93–110.

Ghosh, Avijit. 14 November 2018. 'Sun Shines of the Fest of Migrants: How Politics has made Chhath Delhi's Own'. *The Times of India* (online). Available at https://timesofindia.indiatimes.com/city/delhi/sun-shines-on-fest-of-migrants-how-politics-has-made-chhath-citys-own/articleshow/66611802.cms (accessed 18 January 2019).

Henrie, Roger L. 1972. 'The Perception of Sacred Space: The Case of Utah and Other Sacred Places in Mormondom'. All Theses and Dissertations.

4786. Available at https://scholarsarchive.byu.edu/etd/4786 (accessed 22 July 2019).

Hutter, Manfred. 2012. 'Half Mandir and Half Gurudwara: Three Local Hindu Communities in Manila, Jakarta and Cologne'. *Numen* 59(4): 344–365.

Kirkpatrick, Frank G. 1994. *Together Bound: God, History and the Religious Community*. Oxford: Oxford University Press.

Kumar, Sanjay. 2013. *Changing Electoral Politics in Delhi: From Caste to Class.* New Delhi: SAGE.

Lamont, Michele. 2006. 'Culture and Identity'. In *Handbook of Sociological Theory*, edited by Jonathan H. Turner. New York: Springer.

Lochtefeld, James G. 2010. *God's Gateway: Identity and Meaning in a Hindu Pilgrimage Place*. Oxford: Oxford University Press.

Narayan, Vasudha. 2006. 'Hinduism in Pittsburgh: Creating the South Indian "Hindu" Experience in the United States'. In *The Life of Hinduism*, edited by John Stratton Howley and Vasudha Narayan. Berkeley: University of California Press.

Park, Chris C. 1994. *Sacred Worlds: An Introduction to Geography and Religion.* London: Routledge.

Ratnoo, Himmat Singh. 2017. *Migration of Labour in India: The Squatter Settlements of Delhi.* New York: Routledge.

Rosel, Jakob.1983. 'Land Endowment and Sacred Food: The Economy of an Indian Temple'. *European Journal of Sociology*, 24(1).

Smith, David. 2003. *Hinduism and Modernity.* Oxford: Blackwell Publishing Limited.

10

JAGANNATH IN TRIPURA: DISAPPEARANCE AND DISSEMINATION

Samik Malla

Introduction

The literal and metaphoric 'Juggernaut' that once conjured the darkest fears in the Victorian British imagination in referring to a ruthlessly devastating and unstoppable force, also emerged, as Dash (1986) has shown, into an undisputed, benevolent symbol of Odia nationalism. This trope can be further gauged by the building of Jagannath temples in the new urban centres outside Odisha that are home to an emerging diaspora. It is with this framework in mind that we need to examine the profoundly different stature of the figure of Jagannath in Tripura, a former princely state situated in Northeast India. Looking almost singularly at the temple of Jagannath in Agartala, built in the first decade of the twentieth century, this chapter traces the symbolic halt of the march of the unrelenting 'Juggernaut'. In an uncanny paradox to the uninitiated, the lord appears not to be at the centre of things in a temple named after him while undoubtedly occupying the prime locus for *darshan* in the sanctum sanctorum. The central problem I wish to explore here is the texture, meaning and consequences of what I term the 'disappearance of Jagannath'.

In what follows, I shall look into Jagannath's 'presence' in locating him in the religious and cultural history of Tripura, inquiring how it recasts our scholarly understanding of the concepts of bhakti (Sharma 1987) and *darshan* (Eck 1996) and go on to study the fabric of embodiment and emotion through the frame of *rasa-siddhanta* or the traditional Indian aesthetic theory (Lutjeharms 2014). Having mapped the experiential and affective reality of the devotional bodies, the chapter would then look at the emergence and circulation of

Jagannath's image in the secular sphere through the annual rath yatra (Chariot Festival). Dwelling upon the creation of cultural memory (Nora 1997), the chapter would attempt to understand how bhakti is transformed in the public space and would conclude by looking at the meaning of Jagannath's tryst with secular modernity in the light of a set of critiques housed under the rubric of 'post-secularism' (Habermas 2003, 2009; Mahmood 2005).[1] In so doing, the chapter seeks to ask how the aesthetic form and the political form exist in an ever-evolving, mutually-stirring synaesthesia.

This is an attempt to trace an alternative narrative of Jagannath that emerges from his eastward voyage, specifically in consonance with Gaudiya Vaishnavism and in morphing the so-called 'cult' of Jagannath to acquire new meanings in a society largely dominated by Shaktism and indigenous tribal rites. The case of Tripura certainly complicates this story, assimilating aspects of Hinduism from neighbouring (undivided) Bengal while retaining its own rich, popular traditions with distinct pre-Sanskritic roots. The matter of Hinduisation takes a curious shape in the case of the 'lineage cult' of the royal family which has, over time, identified its 14 deities with Puranic gods. Yet, it would be a mistake to assume that this is a clear instance of Sanskritisation since the worship at the temple remains in the hands of a section of the Tripuri community known as Chantai who belong to a hierarchy of priesthood independent of mainstream Brahmanism. Festivals surrounding these deities—known as Kharchi and Ker puja—have grown from strength to strength, attracting lakhs of devotees across the state and cutting across ethnic confines.

In mapping an uncharted territory, this chapter makes a limited attempt to capture a slice of the religious culture of Tripura in the wake of modernity and its vagaries. The preliminary observations were recorded through fieldwork conducted in October 2018, with further visits in December, supplemented by library work and museum trips. It involved unstructured interviews with devotees, monks and officials; participant observation of *sankirtans*, pujas, rituals and lectures; deep engagements with theoretical paradigms with sustained attempts to cohere theory with praxis. As ethnography recommends long-term engagement with the subjects, my findings do not lay claim to a complete grasp of the nuances.

The Disappearance of the Lord

The most striking finding and, perhaps, the provocative argument of this chapter is that Jagannath himself is strangely 'absent' from the daily affairs of the devotees at the Agartala temple, located near the Ujjayanta Palace. This section shall seek to clasp a unique dissonance in the performance of embodied bhakti. To be sure, it is a situation that has emerged out of distinct historic events and was not the case at its inception. Built in the year 1516 of the Tripura Era (1906–1907 CE) under the patronage of King Radhakishore Manikya, the Jagannath Temple saw its management pass into the hands of the *Debarchan Bibhag* (roughly 'department of worship') of the district administration after Tripura acceded to the Indian Union in 1949. The temple rituals lingered on with two Odia priests conducting the daily puja and the building itself was a modest single-storied edifice with a narrow veranda encircling the *garbha-griha* (inner sanctum). Devoid of the significance enjoyed by the 'lineage cult' of the Fourteen Gods (*Choddo Debota*) in Khayerpur or that of the tutelary deity Tripureswari in Udaipur, Jagannath was initially emblematic of the personal affiliation of the royal family with Vaishnavism who had converted to it at the beginning of the seventeenth century (Bhatia 2017: 26).

The situation took a new turn in 1976 when the supervision of the Jagannath temple was handed over to the Chaitanya Gaudiya Math from West Bengal.[2] The doctrinal framework that guides Gaudiya Vaishnavism considers Chaitanya to be the dual incarnation of Radha and Krishna in one body. So powerful was his impact that 'the radical newness of his large, public, and procession-like *sankirtan* soirees places him at the *origin* of a new kind of devotional collective' (Bhatia 2017: 9, emphasis mine). Chaitanya's followers in Vrindavan (the six Goswamis) who composed the theological exposition of his school, however, did not agree on the question of his divinity, promoting him instead as their *guru*. The epicentre of the school is the worship of Krishna, an *avatara* of Vishnu, through the *bhava* (mood) of Radha. The experiential reality of bhakti in this case, as we shall soon see, is markedly different from the understanding of bhakti in Puri.

It is crucial that we dwell upon what precisely is implied by the act of Jagannath's 'disappearance'. There seems to exist an inexplicable silence in the academic scholarship regarding the nature of Jagannath's position in the Gaudiya cosmological hierarchy or his sociocultural significance among Bengali Vaishnavites. It would be facile to argue that Tripura constitutes a veritable melting-pot of 19 different linguistic and ethnic groups when the truth is far more elusive. About 85 per cent of those from the various indigenous communities return themselves, in the census, as Hindus (Ghosh 2003: 226). Pre-Sanskritic deities, however, are still widely revered. This chapter, for reasons of feasibility, limits itself mostly to the Bengalis who usually frequent the Jagannath temple in Agartala (while Manipuris, for instance, tend to be overwhelmingly Vaishnavites, they have their own temples in the city).[3] This brings us to the pertinent question of divine embodiment and that of bhakti, for there are no other sanctums in the temple compound housing deities that compete with Jagannath.

Jagannath is, sans doute, corporeally present and the inner sanctum bears witness to his material embodiment along with that of Subhadra and Balaram. In fact, theirs are the largest images that immediately draw one's attention. His 'disappearance' then refers to his metaphorical eclipse by the overwhelming presence of Krishna in the affective reality of the devotees, particularly through the process of performative devotion that includes *japa* (chanting), *sankirtan* (communal singing and dancing) or more secularised inter-devotee interactions (Vaishnav-*sanga*, or keeping the company of fellow Vaishnavites, is considered an important part of the secular life of the devotees).[4] The *bhaktas* I met during the entire course of my fieldwork were never heard greeting each other with the name of Jagannath. If it happened at all, then the usual phrase to greet a fellow devotee or someone believed to be one, appears to be 'Hare Krishna'.[5]

To the uninitiated, the claim of Jagannath's 'disappearance' might come as a surprise, since all requisite rituals unique to the worship of Jagannath are followed in this temple as closely aligned to the temple at Puri as possible. It might even appear counter-intuitive to regular devotees unless they have engaged in a critical analysis of their religious experiences which, usually, is marked as a realm beyond the reach of reason. This, of course, is accentuated by the specific kind of bhakti taught by the Chaitanya school which is often summarised by the *gurus* as '*biswashe milay bastu, tarke bahudur*' (roughly, 'faith, not logic, brings you what you cherish') in reaction to the hair-splitting analysis of *Nyayayikas* (logicians) who dominated the intellectual climate of Nabadwip in fifteenth-century Bengal. It is this 'total dedication to a personal God' and 'a dissonance with the Advaita Vedanta and the path of jñāna' that leads modern scholarship to (somewhat imprecisely) define bhakti as 'a religion and a doctrine' (Sharma 1987: 255). Opposed vehemently to the impersonal notion of divinity, the quintessence of the Gaudiya sect lies in the philosophy of *parakiya prem* (Radha's 'illicit' love for Krishna as her paramour) and in transforming bhakti into a *rasa* of *rati bhava* ('erotic mood'). Chaitanya, in theological terms, vehemently rejected the notion of *svakiya prem* ('licit' love) between them, arguing that the condition of marriage would fail to capture the intense longing and overwhelming passion that stood testimony to Radha's love for Krishna, for whom she risked breaching all social norms. Consequently, Sharma argues, 'in no other religion, is the antipathy to the path of jñāna so noticeable, and dependence on mere emotion and faith, so complete' (1987).[6]

Several *bhaktas*, upon being asked about the 'marginalisation' of Jagannath in daily practice blinked in confusion, usually quipping 'but Krishna himself is Jagannath!' So complete was Jagannath's identification with Krishna that the very question appeared cognitively unsound to them. Yet, it is not a mutually interchangeable identity. The practice of Chaitanya's path, after all, requires one to immerse oneself in a sea of emotions overflowing with divine eroticism (*madhurya*), elevated by the sacredness of the object of desire. Radha's love, though theoretically illicit, is beyond the reach of profane law since it mirrors the ultimate devotion for Krishna. That very sentiment is at odds with the opulent (*aishvarya*) image of Jagannath who is flanked by his siblings.[7] Evening after evening, as I continued to participate in the *sankirtans*, it began to dawn on me that the devotees seemed to find no contradiction in their experience of *bhakti-rasa* during the frenzied dances at the Natmandir while facing the sanctum that houses Jagannath and whose devotion would generate anything but the ecstasy of *Radha-bhava* (the mental state of Radha in her 'illicit' longing for and union with Krishna). In fact, during the *sankirtan* which is overwhelmingly dominated by the *parakiya prem* of Radha, the devotees also briefly chant the names of Jagannath, Balaram and Subhadra without any apparent confusion or fear of inconsistency.

Frits Staal once argued, rather polemically, that it is not what one believes that makes him a Hindu but 'the ritual practices he performs and the rules to which he adheres, in short, what he *does*' (1989: 389). This warrants a careful analysis of the actual practices of the devotees who regularly go to the Agartala temple. Several devotees, by tradition, also maintain a small shrine at home. And while each of them most certainly has images of Radha-Krishna and Chaitanya-Nityananda, not all of them have Jagannath. The latter has never been at the centre of Gaudiya Vaishnavism and several of their temples never have had an image of Jagannath. Thus, Jagannath occupies a paradoxical space in the Agartala temple whereby he is accorded full ritualistic honour in the inner sanctum but has little presence in the actual spiritual praxis of the devotees. If Jagannath is the image they see, Krishna is the form they worship. Jagannath becomes the symbol through which devotees relate to Radha-Krishna. In other words, Jagannath is present in body but absent in spirit.

The equation of hierarchy in the sacred space of the sanctum is further complicated by the presence of smaller statues of Radha-Krishna at the altar, intriguingly placed at the feet of Jagannath. The visual impact of the *darshan* is certainly dominated by Jagannath, who is consciously paid obeisance to. But in the subconscious, the regular *bhaktas* seem to harbour no confusion about the theological unity of Jagannath and Krishna, nor do they recognise any competing sect of the former. No matter what the verbal texts (songs, injunctions or narratives) have to contend, the enacted text of 'rituals, customs, practices and techniques' produces what Pierre Bourdieu would call an embodied doxa, defined as an 'active presence in the world through which the world imposes its presence, with its urgencies, its things to be done or said' (1977: 96).

Perhaps, the inseparability of the discourse of Jagannath from the location of Puri might have played a part in the emergence of this situation. One must bear in mind the distinct ontological status of Jagannath in Puri. Flying straight in the face of postmodern theories as that of Baudrillard's hyperreal image which no longer retains an original, Puri Jagannath undergoes a ritual of *prana-pratistha* (animation) with the transference of *brahmapadartha* (the life essence) in secrecy each time there is a Navakalevar (in which Jagannath ritually assumes a new body carved from sacred neem wood). This marks the continuity of the life force through the transfer of the 'soul' and has been occurring since the beginning of the tradition.[8] No other image of Jagannath can, therefore, claim anything more than a derivative status, devoid of the *brahmapadartha* that animates Jagannath.

The figurative assimilation of Jagannath into the cosmology of Krishna in the Agartala temple has been at the level of abstraction. It is, however, consciously concretised at least in one case that emerged during the fieldwork. I refer here to the oldest Jagannath temple of Tripura situated in Udaipur and built in 1661 CE. With the old structure crumbling into a ruin, a new temple has been erected in the compound. And the fate of the images that must have adorned the sanctum of the earlier structure remains shrouded in mystery. The caretaker proudly claimed that the new structure is home to a Jagannath who has hands. The images, unlike those of the traditional Jagannath iconography, are fully anthropomorphised. Furthermore, the classic blue colour associated with Krishna has been substituted for the traditional black of Jagannath. The 'Krishnaisation' of Jagannath in his supposedly oldest abode in the state is complete.

An Aesthetic of Absence

If the process and the meaning of Jagannath's 'disappearance' has been demystified, we must now turn to the inescapable consequences of such a phenomenon. What, indeed, are the implications of the absence of Jagannath in the devotional experience of the devotees? Bhakti religiosity, as Aditya Behl reminded us, 'is strongly weighed towards presence: the presence of the Lord, the bearing witness to this presence on the part of the devotee' (2007: 319). This section, therefore, will look into the concepts of embodiment, *darshan* and affect through the prism of bhakti and how Jagannath's complex presence at the Agartala temple reshapes those experiences for the devotee. The section will draw from theologian Rupa Goswami to bring to light the aesthetic savouring of bhakti as a *rasa* (*bhakti-rasa* can be understood as the nectar of love) that overwhelms the Gaudiya mind and absorbs the image of Jagannath in its ocean of feelings.

The divine may be embodied in many ways, viz. prayers, songs, dances, rituals, chants, living beings or iconic and aniconic images; but it is through images that the *saguna* (with form) schools of Hinduism have fashioned divine bodies for over two millennia. As discourses of the body began to occupy a greater importance in bhakti, the allegorical divine bodies of the Vedic era were later replaced with material ones, embodying the divine in both time and space. But the concept of embodiment would be incomplete if we fail to factor in the 'devotional bodies' where bhakti is performed through the body of the devotee (Holdrege 2015; Novetzke 2007). In contrast to *Advaita* metaphysics that views the world as illusory and the mind as the sole point of focus, the bhakti schools affirm the reality of the world and fully integrate the body in devotional practices. As Karen Pechilis Prentiss shows, 'in actively encouraging participation… the poets represent *bhakti* as *a theology of embodiment*' (2000: 6, emphasis mine). And it is in this context that the *kirtan*, embodied by the devotees, comes to life.

Much against the tide of the time, Chaitanya never asked others to listen to him, but 'to enact, embody, experience, and mimic his devotion' (Bhatia 2017: 10). He made his path open to all, cutting across caste and community boundaries and initiated the forms of *nama-kirtan* (repeating Krishna's name) and *nagar-kirtan* (performing *kirtanas* in public spaces). *Sankirtans* constitute the daily gathering of the *bhaktas* to sing songs for the lord and praise the intensity of Radha's passionate love for Krishna. This helps in creating an affective symbolic community of devotees in the precincts of the temple. Led by one of the resident devotees of the temple, the devotees of the Agartala temple spring to their feet, swirl and dance with rhythmical moves in the accompaniment of barrel-drums and cymbals. Repeating '*Jai Jai Radha Damodar Bol*', '*Hare Krishna Hare*

Krishna Krishna Krishna Hare Hare', or simply '*Haribol Haribol Haribol Haribol*', they rise to a rapid ecstasy, raising their hands in the air in their quest to embody the *madhura-bhava* (roughly, 'the mood of intense longing and desire for one's paramour') of Radha. Towards the end of the *kirtan*, some of them seem to enter into a trance-like state, ceaselessly murmuring '*haribol*', eyes closed, still swirling, still with their hands in the air, a distinct impression of intense pleasure flooding their visage.

This promise of being able to directly experience the ecstasy of *ananda* (divine bliss), on the one hand, liberated one's need to either master forbiddingly difficult Sanskrit scriptures or hire the Brahmins for ritual propitiation of the deities; on the other, it introduced 'dangerous eroticism, with the body playing a key role in the devotional practice. The body, itself a medium of altered states of consciousness in Vaishnava *kirtan* sessions, served to turn *kirtan* into a practice that needed to be disciplined' (Bhatia 2017: 79). Marking a radical break from the tradition of *kirtan*, Chaitanya not only universalised but also sanctified the somatic materiality of devotion, requiring little more than absolute faith and complete surrender to the magnificent splendour of the lord. If bhakti for Jagannath can be said to mean 'devotion', in the case of Krishna it can be more accurately rendered as 'illicit passion' of the kind a cheating spouse feels for the paramour when they cannot meet but instead must long for a mere glimpse or the slightest touch. This expanded the concept of the term bhakti from the sense of 'respect' in the Upanishads to a form of '*yoga*' in the epics to the all-consuming, passionate ecstasy of Chaitanya's 'complete surrender' in the sixteenth century—'distinguishable on grounds of belief in a personal god, rejection of the monism of Advaita Vedānta, and an antipathy to jñāna' (Sharma 1987: 279).

Its implications for appreciating the absence of Jagannath are important. In the Hindu cosmology, praxis frequently trumps theory. Any symbol can be anointed with divinity if the popular faith believes it to be so. Devoid of the *brahmapadartha*, Jagannath's symbolic embodiment in the Agartala temple depends upon the act of being 'recognised' by the devotees. It is this affective validation that ironically leads to the abstract 'Krishnaisation' of Jagannath. It further inverts the causal relation between the devotee and the object of devotion. If the apparent image of the deity should normally cause the appropriate form of emotions in the heart of the devotee, then we have a situation at hand where the devotee conjures another dominant image (albeit of the same deity) and projects it back upon the visible image. In marginalising the presence of Jagannath in the experiential reality, the devotee identifies the locus of the cause of devotion not necessarily in the material image but in the immaterial affect within him and in the collective act of worship. The devotional body, in the process, turns into a site of spiritual causality.

We must, at this point, turn to the scholarly understanding of *darshan* and how that is recast in the event of Jagannath's symbolic disappearance. John Berger in his *Ways of Seeing* once insisted that what we know or believe in leaves a mark on the way we see things. In the Middle Ages, for instance, 'when men believed in the physical existence of Hell, the sight of fire must have meant something different from what it means today' (Berger 2008: 8). As Jessica Frazier has contended, of all the ways of communicating with the divine—be it the Vedic altar for sacrifices, through serving (*seva*), by anointing the god (*abhishek*), etc.—*darshan* or 'meeting of the deity's eyes' is most commonplace (2012: 5). *Darshan* is an act of worship and 'it is not only the worshiper who sees the deity, but the deity sees the worshiper as well' (Eck 1996: 6–7). This mutual beholding is essential to our understanding of the ritual worship of Jagannath in Puri. It is less certain as to how the devotees in Agartala make meaning of their visual interaction with the icon of Jagannath. Upon being asked, it so seemed that they were consciously praying to Jagannath as an incarnation of Krishna, with little interest in considering that they could be two competing images that command a unique and exclusive set of emotions. A more nuanced explanation is in order.

The affective disappearance of Jagannath, as we have earlier seen, is mostly in the realm of abstraction and experience, and might therefore exist in the subconscious where Jagannath is taken out of its context and rendered into a desemanticised signifier—one that is emptied of its original, dominant meaning and is infused with the signified 'essence' of another. As the referent continues to bear an outward likeness to the actual Jagannath, the conscious mind fails to take note of this shift. The *trompe-l'oeil* of sorts is reinforced by the discursive unification of the two images into one ultimate divinity. As a different register of worship, *darshan* does not require the active physical involvement that *kirtan* does and it is the latter which places Jagannath under erasure. It would, then, be more accurate to say that a stand-alone *darshan* at the sanctum at other times of the day would recognise the 'presence' of Jagannath. This would usually be personal and individual in nature and would not lead to the formation of a symbolic, affective community in the Agartala temple. Taking a cue from Stella Kramrisch, Eck argues that in India seeing is not only a kind of 'touching', it is also a way of knowing (1996: 9). *Darshan*, therefore, is not merely an outward gaze but also an inward introspection that leads to the truth. And this is why the Sanskrit term for the discipline of philosophy is *darshan* (or, in transliteration, *darśana*).

As we turn our gaze inward, we enter the sophisticated realm of *rasa-siddhanta* that was used by the Gaudiya theoreticians to illustrate the elevated emotional *bhava* (mood) of the devotees in the light of the aesthetic theories of *rasa*. In the light of Jagannath's emotional disappearance, we are faced with what can be argued as an 'aesthetic of absence'. To grasp how the act of devotion is distilled into an emotional mood that can be relished as a *rasa*, one needs to return to the concept of *bhakti-rasa* that was most consistently systematised by Rupa Goswami. He was one of the first six Goswamis of sixteenth-century Vrindavan who created the theoretical bedrock for the school of Chaitanya Vaishnavism. Rembert Lutjeharms argues that Rupa's theology is 'rigorously systematic and vigourously analysed', but it aims to intellectualise a personal and emotional feeling. He adds that, 'devotion (*bhakti*) is his central concern… [but] devotion is more than an emotion. It is a state of being that translates into action, and leads to a state of divine absorption in which God alone can be fully known' (2014: 175). And to this end, he drew from Sanskrit literary aesthetics or Rasa Theory from Bharata's *Natyashastra*.

To understand how bhakti gets recast as 'an emotional religion of love' (Bhaduri 1988: 378–379), one needs to gather how bhakti comes to be accepted as a full-fledged sentiment and, eventually, as a *rasa*. Rasa Theory, being historically associated with the appreciation of secular drama and poetics, had to be deftly manoeuvred by Rupa Goswami to make room for religious bhakti (Sharma 1987: 283). And even as the *Rasa-siddhantins* declined to accept the status of bhakti as one of the nine *rasas*, *bhakti-rasa* became a common trope for imagining bhakti as a religious sect 'of love and attachment for a personal god as opposed to the monistic Vedānta' due to influence of the Goswamis of Vrindavan (1987: 284). The bone of contention lay in the very assumption in Bharata's *Natyashastra* that 'certain bhāvas (human feelings and emotions) were common to all people… [and therefore] arouse universal response' (Sharma 1987). The trouble was that bhakti as a *bhava* was not universal in nature, nor did the theologians ever claim it to be so. Elaborate theses exist, *au contraire*, theorising why some people have bhakti and others do not. Edelmann, for instance, looks at the debate on the *adhikara* ('eligibility') of a person to feel bhakti, showing that in certain Vaishnavite traditions (such as those of Vallabhacharya and Madhvacharya), the highest forms of bhakti and moksha are forever closed to certain souls (Edelmann 2015: 49). It was, consequently, a tall order for a theoretician to transform *bhakti-bhava* into a *rasa*.

Rupa Goswami, at this point, wrote two significant treatises, the *Bhakti Rasamrita Sindhu* and *Ujjvala Nilamani*, declaring *bhakti-rasa* as not only valid but to be the only *rasa* by subordinating all other *rasas* to it, renaming *sringara-rasa* (the pleasure of love) as *madhura-bhakti-rasa*.[9] Curiously, while identifying *madhura-bhakti-rasa* as the supreme *rasa*, Goswami diminished the importance of emotions such as *vira-bhakti-rasa* (Sharma 1987: 289). Now, it ought to be kept in mind that the image of Jagannath is that of 'martial and universal sovereignty and one that is connected with the institution of divine kingship, the Gajapati dynasty' (Stewart 1991: 241). He symbolises Krishna's *aishvarya* (opulence). It is my contention that of all the twelve *rasas* accepted by Goswami, it is the *vira-bhakti-rasa* that most closely captures the essence of the sovereignty and lordship. On the contrary, Stewart argues that Krishna's image is focused on the love Gopinath (lord of the gopis) had for the cowherd girls. This stands for Krishna's *madhurya*, 'his loving sweetness, which is deemed the most desirable and indeed the ultimate form' of Krishna by Gaudiya theoreticians (Stewart 1991). This, I argue, most closely mirrors the processes leading to an aesthetic emptying of the icon of Jagannath in the Agartala temple of its *aishvarya* form by the intense flooding of *madhura-bhakti-rasa* in the affective experience of the devotees who, in their embodied bhakti, clamour for the nectar of *parakiya prem* that Radha feels for her divine paramour.

Into the Secular

The trajectory of this chapter up until now has witnessed the elusive presence of Jagannath in the religious lives of the devotees, referring to it as his figurative 'disappearance' in the Agartala temple. It would then seem likely that the secular public space would register a similar phenomenon. But as we shall realise, that is not the case. In what follows, I will look at the bleeding of the boundaries that carve out the sacred and the secular as autonomous spaces, arguing that the *locus standi* of Jagannath in public memory is in sharp contrast to his 'absence' in the temple. Beyond the precincts of the temple of Jagannath, the idea of the public undergoes an important shift. Bhakti is no longer confined to the devotional bodies that perform an act of synecdochical, ecstatic union with the lord. The conditions of modernity do not empty the public space of religion but compel it to come to terms with new realities.

In other words, I argue that bhakti evolves from being an act of embodiment to one of *bearing witness* (but not in Eck's understanding of *darshan*); and that the emergence of Jagannath's image into the open transforms the festival into a spectacle. Bhakti now requires a different kind of participation: it needs an 'audience' (Novetzke 2007: 256). To better understand the presence of Jagannath in the popular consciousness and his dissemination in the collective memory of Tripura, we must turn to the annual rath yatra or the Chariot Festival. The rath yatra in Agartala, initiated under regal patronage, dates back to the early twentieth century. And while it is neither the earliest nor the largest Chariot Festival in Tripura, its historical association with the temple of Jagannath in the city gives it a sense of enduring continuity in the public mind.[10] It must be pointed out that the rath yatra, at the time of writing this chapter, is still several months away. I have hence relied on my childhood (cultural) memory of growing up in the city, on print and digital media resources and on the interviews conducted along the course to analyse and understand its meanings and processes.

As a cultural icon, it is readily apparent that Jagannath's presence in the discursive and symbolic reality of the secular sphere is very limited. Agartala is dotted with small shrines and temples, sometimes literally impinging upon narrow public roads. But neither in the physical spaces of active sacrality, nor on commercial billboards, posters, calendars or print media can be discerned any significant presence of the iconic image or associated symbolism that reminds one of Jagannath. In fact, while inquiring for his photo at a shop dealing in images of Hindu deities near the Kasba Kali temple of Tripura, his absence became palpably visible. None was placed on display and it required the vendor a good few minutes to dig one up from his stock. He admitted that there is little demand for Jagannath's photograph, but quickly added that it soars during the time of rath yatra. In these conditions, the material engagement that Jagannath has with the sphere of modern urban life is through the spectacle of the chariot. It is through his cyclical return to the streets of Agartala that he emerges in the popular consciousness.

While religious processions can be said to ephemerally spiritualise the public space while confronting rational modernity, they are concomitantly being commodified by the omnipresent gaze of technological progress. Mediated by innumerable cameras, absorbed by the 'cloud' and transformed almost immediately into packets of data for consumption beyond the constraints of time and space, the immediacy of the felt experience is no longer what it once arguably was. Nor can it be denied that far more people can now virtually 'participate' in the spectacle of the rath yatra. In fact, some devotees, upon sighting the lord atop his *rath* on television, immediately bring their hands together in the posture of a prayer, bow their heads, and quietly transform the moment into that of a solemn, sacred *darshan*.

Every year in the month of *Ashadha* (June–July), flanked by his siblings Balaram and Subhadra, Jagannath embarks on his voyage to his aunt's place from the Jagannath temple. With thousands of people in attendance, including devotees and curious onlookers alike, the trio set forth on their tour of the cityscape. Given the modest economic conditions of the temple administration, they are not accorded the luxury of separate chariots, nor can the *rath* match the imposing magnificence of Nandighosa, Taladhwaja or Devadalana (as the three chariots are respectively called) in Puri (Dash 1996: 118). Nonetheless, the throng lurches ahead to take a turn at pulling the rope that carry the chariot ahead. The *rath* moves slowly through the overcrowded streets in accompaniment of loud music from an electronic sound-system atop a van that precedes it. It is heavily guarded by the police to prevent any accidents or, perhaps, the fringe devotee looking for a shortcut to salvation from 'diving' under the wheels. Of course, as Ujaan Ghosh (2018) shows, sacrifice, suicides and accidents were almost entirely figments of the colonial imagination that caricatured the rath yatra at Puri for British consumption.

At this point, we must turn to the public, a large share of whom might not declare themselves to be Vaishnavites but attend the rath yatra nonetheless. How many of them would testify to what the changing British narrative once called a 'native predilection for tamasha or sightseeing, or by a restless desire for religious excitement'? (*Fraser's Magazine*, February 1873, 179, quoted in Ghosh 2018: 81). To what extent, also, can it be meaningfully stated that the average believer is strictly Vaishnav, Shakta or Shaiva? It is quite usual for most practising Hindus to believe in and pray to multiple deities. Not many are versed in the dense exegesis of the Vedantic literature, nor do they particularly feel a pressing need to rationalise their religious universe. As the conditions of modernity shape their public engagement with the deities, sectarian lines are often the first to come under siege. The popular faith, in fact, is what Daniel H. Smith calls 'omnipraxy', which is democratic, fluid and unmediated by experts (1995: 36). And this lays the foundation of shared memories, symbolic histories and myriad meanings of identity and belonging. This is also how the goddess Tripureswari, whom Gautam Bera argued to be 'central to the life and culture of Tripura' (2017: 21), has emerged as an emblem of the state and its people.

Archives, monuments and celebrations, as Pierre Nora shows, can all become *lieux de mémoires* (sites of memory) in crystallising collective remembrance and crafting a cultural history. The *lieux*, for Nora are 'places, sites, causes—in three senses—material, symbolic and functional' (1997: 14). I argue, therefore, that while Jagannath might not be the symbolic *lieu* of public memory, he can very well emerge as the functional *lieu*. In performing the act of rath yatra, he literally comes out of the imposing shadow of his alter-ego and creates what Guy Debord (1995) would call a spectacle.[11] And in so doing, he sparks a transformation of the internal bhakti that is figuratively incarnated by the devotional bodies in the temple into an external bhakti that is literally performed with the senses of sight (in the act of *darshan*) or touch (in pulling the *rath*) by the public at large.

In other words, I argue that bhakti evolves from being an act of embodiment to one of *bearing witness*. The spectacle of bhakti calls for a new form of participation. This, it must be said, is not consonant with Diana Eck's understanding of *darshan* as 'to see' and 'be seen' (1996: 6–7), since it is traditionally believed that during the rath yatra, the mere sighting of Jagannath is sufficient for salvation. With the exceptional meaning accorded to the act of *darshan* during the Chariot Festival, it is only reasonable that the lack of the intimate reciprocity that devotees can enjoy in the sanctum of the temple will not come in the way of their liberation. Also, as Puja Sahney has shown in the cases of popular pilgrimage spots such as Shri Venkateshwara at Tirupati, when *darshan* is not possible, 'even a small glance of the deity is supposed to have the power to bless the individual' (2016: 282).

Returning to the transformation of bhakti into one that bears witness, it must be remembered that the act of witnessing includes an implied audience. Christian Novetzke has argued that all forms of bhakti are performances that create 'publics of reception rather than communities that imply a single cohesive issue or idiom' (2007: 255). While he does not deny the possibility of private devotion, bhakti in his view is inseparable from its social milieu. Given the public nature of *sankirtans* and *nagar-kirtans,* one cannot but see Novetzke's point. Bhakti, of course, could imply several means of devotion and not all of them quite fit his notion (who stretches an interesting point connecting bhakti with an audience to the baffling—and self-defeating—claim that 'if no one else, one can be sure that at least God is always watching') (Novetzke 2007: 256). Surely, for the non-monistic believer, God is always watching and the point makes no useful contribution to our understanding of an implied (human) audience for the social performance of devotion. The undeniable absence of an audience in certain forms of bhakti is thus niftily tackled.

Despite the logical overreach in Novetzke's zeal at universalising his point to include all forms of bhakti, the initial part of his argument—that bhakti is performative (and hence anticipates the possibility of an audience)—deserves attention. Keeping in mind that the theory of *bhakti-rasa* was drawn from the secular literary tradition whose primary thrust was upon the implied aesthete, it seems reasonable that during the *sankirtan* in the temple the devotee also becomes the first audience (*rasika* or aesthete) of his own performance of bhakti which, as we have earlier seen, is directed inward. The difference, however, is that he is only figuratively looking within his mind as he embodies the *Radha-bhava* (as noted earlier) while the rath yatra is an external spectacle to which one literally bears witness. This, however, is patently not the situation with all kinds of external bhakti. The humbling act of *darshan* is awe-inspiring to the devotee and it is quite possible to be alone in the sanctum. Nor is there any reason to suggest that *darshan* involves a secondary separation where the devotee watches himself, as a *rasika* or otherwise, having a *darshan.* The personal *japa,* too, comes under this category. Not all forms of bhakti then necessarily need an audience.

The aesthetic problem, for the Vaishnava devotee, is, in fact, something else. The songs sung during the rath yatra are not all about the glory of Jagannath, Balaram and Subhadra. The shadows of Radha and Krishna linger on through the chants and the devotional songs. It holds importance since in Vaishnavism, 'every musical speech-act is considered a performative utterance which makes Radha-Krishna and their location in the sacred place apparent' (Sarbadhikary 2015: 181). This, to the secular audience, might present no great difficulty but how does the Gaudiya devotee experience the secularised spectacle of an image of Krishna that is at odds with his affective union with Radha-Madhav? An even more pertinent question is the function played by the presence of devotional bodies in a predominantly secular space. Nonetheless, the primacy of Jagannath during the Car Festival remains beyond doubt. He comes out in public and is not only visible but also is he palpably 'present'. This is quite a reversal of what usually occurs within the precincts of the temple. And it is through this semantic capsizing that the festival performs the crucial role in keeping Jagannath in circulation through the excitement in strikes in the media, in the informal public spaces, and specifically among the non-devotees long after he has returned to the inner sanctum.

Conclusion

The blurring of the sacred into the secular public space is far from being unique to the rath yatra. Every year, after the Durga puja, there are massive processions for immersing of the *murtis* (images of clay) in lakes and rivers. The *nagar-kirtans* initiated by Chaitanya is another instance. Every day, a band of devotees from the temple of Jagannath go to the streets dancing and loudly singing the name of Krishna. The *nagar-kirtan* may not embody the image of Jagannath but the public mind certainly registers a devotional performance in the secular public space. The chapter has followed Jagannath in his eastward voyage to Tripura and has noted how this journey has been attentive to regional sensibilities. In situating him within the Gaudiya Vaishnava canon, this essay has sought to dispel a palpable silence in its otherwise rich scholarly literature. If it has grappled with two competing images of the same deity, it has also looked into a mystifying phenomenon in the very act of embodied devotion—the aesthetic of Jagannath's 'disappearance' and its affective implications.

The larger historiographical and methodological questions, however, continue to linger. If Chaitanya was constructed as a symbol of Bengali nationalism in the nineteenth century, how do the indigenous communities of Tripura respond to Gaudiya Vaishnavism? What role does Jagannath, within the ambit of Vaishnavism, play in the constitution of a regional identity in Tripura? Given the longstanding Shakta heritage of the state, how seamlessly do the sects overlap or, more importantly, how consciously can they be told apart? I would, therefore, like to end this discussion by briefly touching upon, first, the scholarly critique of the phenomenological approach in unpacking religious experience and, second, the emerging intellectual debate on 'post-secularity'.

Robert Sharf (2000) has drawn our attention to the pitfalls of placing religious experience beyond the purview of empirically-grounded inquiry. While Sharf's intervention in debates on a certain rhetoric of experience remains salutary and valid, it does not convincingly explain away—as we have seen with *bhakti-rasa*—the very existence of all private experience, spiritual or illusory. If anything, it invites us to engage with competing discourses on the experience of religion (for new directions in the field, see Taves 2009). It is not purely by chance that the ruthless rationalising of our lifeworld often disproportionately harms the weak and the marginalised who, lacking the training and the sophisticated skills in logic and rhetoric, often have no other recourse but to voice their non-rationalised lived experience. Stephen Bush, thus, suggests that experiences can be spoken of 'without thereby assuming that they are immediate, absolutely private, and universal' (2012: 222).

Practised religiosity appears to be responding to and adapting with rational and modern secular ideas. It no longer appears inevitable that with increasing secularisation, the social relevance and importance of religion would be on wane. How emphatically can it be said that places like Tripura have ever made a distinct separation between the sacred and the secular when the public space is always teeming with evolving modes of religiosity? In other words, does the public consciously confront the emptying of religion from certain spheres of their experiential reality? Jürgen Habermas, referring to the loss of the explanatory power of the secularisation hypothesis, coined the term 'post-secularism' (2003). To be sure, he specified that his use of the term was confined largely to the affluent West since 'a "post-secular" society must at some point have been in a "secular" condition' (Habermas 2009: 59). Notwithstanding the storm generated by the coinage, it should be recalled, as Coviello and Hickman (2014) insist, that 'post-secularism' is neither a return to a form of theocracy nor a denial of the secularisation process. It 'refers to an epistemological and methodological reorientation from which history might look different' (Coviello and Hickman 2014: 646).

In reorienting the normative understanding of religious piety in Islamic societies, critics like Saba Mahmood (2005) have sought to show how emergent subjectivities among women in the Egyptian 'Mosque movement' is not a simplistic submission to patriarchal servitude, but an active reclaiming of agency within the exigencies of their circumstances and beliefs. The 'politics of piety', then, is not a rejection of the forces of secularisation but a careful, concerted response to refashion oneself in their wake. Post-secularism, to move beyond the territorial confines outlined by Habermas, is then a process of modernising the religious consciousness as much as it is about promoting tolerance in the political space. The pressing question then is how persuasively it can speak to us in a remote corner of Tripura. More pertinently, how does bhakti transform the public space in the light of insights we glean from the debates on post-secularism? What performative role, if any, does the rath yatra play in the rapidly transforming public space?

Future research could look into what the rath yatra means to those who merely consume it as a secularised festival, with no soteriological or affective investment in it. It could be asked how specific sites of memory refashion the religious subjectivities of the people and how these debates sharpen our inquiry into the interstices of the sacred-secular continuum. Carl Schmitt, after all, once presciently remarked in *Political Theology* that 'all systematic concepts of the modern theory of the state are secularised theological concepts' (2006: 36). In the post-secular worldview, bhakti as total devotion may blend seamlessly into embodied piety which, expanding on Mahmood's formulation of 'political piety' (as the exercising of individual agency but having little to do with the politics of statecraft), can turn into an instrumental navigator of political theology in blurring religious bhakti with 'profane' bhakti (as in the case of *desh bhakti*).[12] This, while modernising forms of religious consciousness, embroils aesthetic forms and political forms in an evolving state of interlocking *Kulturkampf.*

Acknowledgements

I would like to express my gratitude to Debananda Dam and Rembert Lutjeharms for giving me access to materials that would, otherwise, have been beyond my reach.

Notes

1. In his study of bhakti and the public, Novetzke locates the genealogy of the *public sphere*, the parameters of its debate and its dialectic within the works on Habermas as indicating modern technologies, civil society, nation, political life, et cetera. He contrasts it with the idea of 'public culture' which he says is a 'study of modern, urban cultural forms in interstitial spaces' (2007: 260). I will, therefore, use the neutral term 'public space' unless I am referring to either of those two specific meanings.
2. It is an institutionalised monastic organisation that emerged out of the late-nineteenth century Vaishnavite reformist movement started by Kedarnath Datta Bhaktivinoda, leading to the birth of the Gaudiya Math in 1920, Chaitanya Gaudiya Math in 1953 and ISKCON in 1966.
3. It ought to be noted that it was not until the partition of British India, with the influx of Hindu refugees from erstwhile East Pakistan, that the Bengalis became a clear majority in the state, leading to inevitable contestations of power and backlash (see Ghosh 2003: 230, Ghoshal 2010: 1208–1215).
4. That Jagannath indeed commands lesser focus compared to Radha-Krishna was confirmed by Srila B.K. Baishnav Maharaj, a senior monk of the Chaitanya Gaudiya Math at Agartala during a telephonic interview on 28 December 2018. The term used by him was *pradhanyo kom* ('lesser significance'). Although he also clarified that in the Chaitanya theology, Jagannath's is the *aishvarya* self while Krishna's is the *madhurya* self and they are one and the same.
5. And while gender is beyond the purview of this article, it must be noted that a strong majority of the lay devotees who frequent the Jagannath temple at Agartala appear to be women, even though monastic Gaudiya Vaishnavism has no provision for them to renounce.

6. The traditional *yogas* (roughly 'methods of union') for salvation in the Vedic religion were, initially, *karma yoga* ('rituals') and, later, *jnana yoga* ('knowledge'), to which the age of the Epics (as summarised in the *Bhagavad Gita* from the *Mahabharata*) added *bhakti yoga* ('faith')—together termed as the three *yogas* for salvation (union with the absolute Brahman). In the nineteenth century, the Vedantic revivalist Swami Vivekananda equated Patanjali's *ashtanga yoga* with *raja yoga* (the path of meditation). *Bhakti yoga*, however, did not champion rejection of the other paths as the post-Chaitanya view of bhakti as total devotion does.
7. Interestingly, references to *Utkala-khanda* of the *Skanda Purana* exist which, purportedly to bolster the Vaishnavite claim on Jagannath, explained the unique physical features of the Puri deities as a result of the siblings being ecstatic about the intimate pastimes of Krishna in Vrindavana. In other words, Jagannath, Subhadra and Balaram themselves, in this version, were implied to have embodied the *rati bhava* of Krishna worship. Its textual history, location and the time of its composition might help illuminate this contradiction further.
8. Except for the occasion when the image of Jagannath was allegedly burnt after the invasion of Kalapahad in 1568. The *brahmapadartha* (the inner essence), however, is said to have remained unscathed and was subsequently installed in a new image in 1575.
9. Rupa Goswami classified *bhakti-rasa* into twelve forms, viz. (1) *santa-bhakti rasa,* (2) *priti-bhakti rasa,* (3) *preyan-bhakti rasa,* (4) *vatsala-bhakti rasa,* (5) *madhura-bhakti rasa,* (6) *hasya-bhakti rasa,* (7) *adbhuta-bhakti rasa,* (8) *vira-bhakti rasa,* (9) *karuna-bhakti rasa,* (10) *raudra-bhakti rasa,* (11) *bhayanaka-bhakti rasa,* (12) *vibhatsa-bhakti rasa.* As Krishna Sharma points out, Goswami further divided the first five into primary (*mukhya*) and the rest into secondary (*gauna*) *rasas* (Sharma 1987: 288–289).
10. In fact, ISKCON has been, among others, organising its own rathyatra in Agartala since 2016 and might soon challenge the pre-eminence of that of the city's Jagannath temple in scale and popularity.
11. Quite literally, in ontological terms, the manifold images of Jagannath everywhere except in Puri are spectacles. Devoid of the *brahmapadartha* that is believed to animate the Puri Jagannath, his icons elsewhere are what Guy Debord would call the inversion of reality and the circulation of 'representation' (1995).
12. See, for instance, Aniket De (2018) who points out that

    > the rallying cry of the swadeshi movement was… *Bande Mataram*, 'I hail the Mother'. The swadeshi years were replete with Shakta symbolism: revolutionary ideologues worshipped Kali, the Durga Puja emerged as a national festival and the nation was conceived as *Bharat Mata* or Mother India. (451)

References

Behl, A. 2007. 'Presence and Absence in Bhakti: An Afterword'. *International Journal of Hindu Studies*, 11(3): 319–324.

Bera, G.K. 2017. *A Cultural and Religious History of Tripura*. Guwahati: Spectrum.

Berger, J. [1972]2008. *Ways of Seeing*. London: Penguin.

Bhaduri, N.P. 1988. 'Bhakti (Devotion) as an Aesthetic Sentiment'. *Journal of Indian Philosophy*, 16(4): 377–410.

Bhatia, V. 2017. *Unforgetting Chaitanya: Vaishnavism and Cultures of Devotion in Colonial Bengal*. New York: Oxford University Press.

Bourdieu, P. 1977. *Outline of a Theory of Practice*, edited by J. Goody, translated by R. Nice, Cambridge: Cambridge University Press.

Bush, S.S. 2012. 'Are Religious Experiences Too Private to Study?' *The Journal of Religion*, 92(2): 199–223.

Coviello, P. and J. Hickman. 2014. 'Introduction: After the Postsecular'. *American Literature*, 86 (4): 645–654.

Dash, G.N. 1986. 'Jagannatha and Oriya Nationalism'. *The Cult of Jagannath and the Religious Tradition of* Orissa, edited by in A. Eschmann, H. Kulke and G. Tripathi, 359–374. New Delhi: Manohar.

Dash, K.C. 1996. 'A Study of the Origin of Ratha Yātrā in the Puruṣottama Kṣetra'. *East and West*, 46(1/2): 117–125.

De, A. 2018. 'Review of *Unforgetting Chaitanya: Vaishnavism and Cultures of Devotion in Colonial Bengal* by Varuni Bhatia'. *South Asian History and Culture*, 9(4): 449–452.

Debord, G. 1995. *The Society of the Spectacle*, translated by D. Nicholson-Smith. New York: Zone Books.

Eck, D. L. [1981]1996. *Darśan—Seeing the Divine Image in India*, 2nd edition. New York: Columbia University Press.

Edelmann, J. 2015. 'The Cause of Devotion in Gauḍīya Vaiṣṇava Theology: Devotion (*Bhakti*) as the Result of Spontaneously (*Yadṛcchayā*) Meeting a Devotee (*Sādhu-Saṅga*)'. *Journal of the American Oriental Society*, 135(1): 49–69.

Frazier, J. 2012. 'Ritual and Practice in Hindu Studies'. *The Journal of Hindu Studies*, 5(1): 1–9.

Ghosh, B. 2003. 'Ethnicity and Insurgency in Tripura'. *Sociological Bulletin*, 52(2): 221–243.

Ghosh, U. 2018. 'Chariots of the Gods: The Many Histories of Jagannath, "Juggernaut", and the Rathayatra in the Nineteenth Century'. *History of Religions*, 58(1): 64–88.

Ghoshal, A. 2010. 'Survival Question of East Bengal Refugees: The Case of Tripura (1946–71)'. *Proceedings of the Indian History Congress*, 71: 1208–1215.

Habermas, J. 2003. 'Faith and Knowledge'. In *The Future of Human Nature.* Cambridge: Polity Press.

Habermas, J. 2009. 'What is Meant by a "Post-Secular Society"? A Discussion on Islam in Europe'. In *Europe: The Faltering Project*, translated by C. Cronin. Malden, MA: Polity Press.

Holdrege, B.A. 2015. *Bhakti and Embodiment.* Oxford: Routledge.

Lutjeharms, R. 2014. 'An Ocean of Emotion: *Rasa* and Religious Experience in Early Caitanya Vaiṣṇava Thought'. In *Caitanya Vaiṣṇava Philosophy: Tradition, Reason and Devotion*, edited by Ravi M. Gupta. Farnham: Ashgate.

Mahmood, S. 2005. *Politics of Piety: The Islamic Revival and the Feminist Subject.* Princeton: Princeton University Press.

Nora, P. 1997. *The Realms of Memory: Rethinking the French Past.* New York: Columbia University Press.

Novetzke, C.L. 2007. 'Bhakti and Its Public'. *International Journal of Hindu Studies*, 11(3): 255–272.

Prentiss, K.P. 2000. *The Embodiment of Bhakti.* New York: Oxford University Press.

Sahney, P. 2016. '*Darśan*, Decoration, and Transnational Hindu Homes in the United States'. *Asian Ethnology*, 75(2): 279–302.

Sarbadhikary, S. 2015. *Place of Devotion: Siting and Experiencing Divinity in Bengal-Vaishnavism.* University of California Press.

Schmitt, C. 2006. *Political Theology: Four Chapters on the Concept of Sovereignty*, translated by G. Schwab. Chicago: Chicago University Press.

Sharf, R.H. 2000. 'The Rhetoric of Experience and the Study of Religion'. *Journal of Consciousness Studies*, 7(11–12): 267–287.

Sharma, K. 1987. *Bhakti and the Bhakti Movement: A New Perspective.* New Delhi: Munshiram Manoharlal.

Smith, H.D. 1995. 'Impact of "God Posters" on Hindus and their Devotional Traditions'. In *Media and the Transformations of Religion in South Asia*, edited by L.A. Babb and S.S. Wadley, 24–50. Philadelphia: University of Pennsylvania Press.

Staal, F. 1989. *Rules without Meaning: Ritual, Mantras and the Human Sciences.* New York: Peter Lang.

Stewart, T.K. 1991. 'When Biographical Narratives Disagree: The Death of Kṛṣṇa Caitanya'. *Numen*, 38(2): 231–260.

Taves, A. 2009. *Religious Experience Reconsidered: A Building-Block Approach to the Study of Religion and Other Special Things.* Princeton and Oxford: Princeton University Press.

11

A SCHOLARLY COMMUNITY AROUND THE LORD: THE ORISSA RESEARCH PROJECTS

Uwe Skoda

'In all parts of the world, in all of human history, there are and have been little communities.'

—Redfield (1955: 1)

Introduction

To start with two brief personal vignettes, as an anthropology student at Freie Universität Berlin I remember entering the office of Prof. Georg Pfeffer in the 1990s and noticing the papier-mâché trinity of Jagannath, Balabhadra and Subhadra adorning the walls together with a large *tala pata chitra* (or palm-leaf engraving) depicting the Lord, his rath yatra, etc. But my understanding of the history behind these artefacts and their status as metonymic symbols of Odisha was limited and I was not familiar with the specific history of an Orissa Research Project (ORP) that had focused precisely on these deities in the 1970s and whose second avatar I joined in 2000.[1] Many years later in 2019, while visiting the splendid Museum Rietberg in Zurich, I met Johannes Beltz, Deputy Director and Curator India and Southeast Asia, whom I incidentally knew through ORP. After flipping through some Odisha related publications displayed in the museum shop he introduced me to the staff as somebody who also did research on Odisha. 'Are you also a "Puri-ksi"?' asks the Lady at the counter knowing about the Odisha and Puri connection of Beltz and seemingly projecting it onto me as well.

Starting from such interactions and symbols around ORP, this chapter explores community formation among scholars working on Odisha and Lord Jagannath that is with reference to two major academic projects known as ORP I (1970–1975) and ORP II

(1999–2005) funded by the Deutsche Forschungsgemeinschaft (German Research Council or DFG)—an agency that carries the term community (Gemeinschaft) in its name. Both projects involved a broad range of institutions and scholars at different academic levels. Some like Pfeffer, H. Kulke, H. von Stietencron were full-time members of both projects, while others like Beltz only joined for a shorter period before finding his position at the museum.

Taking into account this diversity of scholars, the focus on interviews[2] and the work that emerged from the ORP, the chapter traces the history and dynamics of these two closely linked projects that indicate a sustained engagement and remarkable evolution of a scholarly community over decades. It focuses especially on the collaborative, yet constantly negotiated framework and goals, scholarly genealogies as well as the shared privileges—all contributing to a sense of community. The scholarly practices of publishing and creating resources further prolonged and added to a certain group consciousness, while the project simultaneously had its spill over effects from an academic sphere into the homes of the involved scholars. Including this popular culture domain hints at an affective dimension and a profound bonding with the Lord in and beyond the professional realm.[3]

A Scholarly Community

Without rehearsing debates around the concept of community general here,[4] it is rather argued that a scholarly community evolved around the ORPs. Including academics from Germany and India engaged in the projects, it shared characteristics with classical notions of community, for example regarding intellectual bonds (Tönnies 1922[1887])[5] or anthropological notions of small scale groups based on more or less harmonious face-to-face interactions (Hillery 1959; Redfield 1955).[6] More importantly here, this kind of community can be understood as a 'community of practice' (CoP) (Wenger 1998; also Agrifoglio 2015).

A CoP typically involves core members and those in peripheral roles, newcomers and experts, etc. and is defined as a 'group of people who come together to share common interests and goals, with the aim of sharing information, developing knowledge and developing themselves both personally and professionally' (Agrifoglio 2015: 26). Wenger (1998: 72–73) stressed three dimensions of such communities: (a) mutual engagement, that is how it functions with reference to norms and social interactions; (b) a joint enterprise, that is what it is all about—with reference to a joint purpose or common goal of joint actions; and (c) a shared repertoire, that is what has been produced—with reference to artefacts, styles, vocabularies or an outcome.

Membership, according to Wenger, is not primarily about a formal social category. Rather, 'what it takes for a community of practice to cohere enough to function can be very subtle and delicate' (Wenger 1998: 74) and a community's productivity might benefit from diversity, not homogeneity, that is from explicitly including different statuses, specialisations such as supervisors and novices while it is understood that some have more power than others. Like Tönnies, Wenger does not project an idyllic picture of a community, that is shared practice does not mean harmony or may not lead to emancipation (1998: 85). He underlines that the enterprise is often defined in the process and collective negotiations speak of an intensive engagement while including (productive) disagreements (1998: 77–78). CoPs may be established with a mandate, but then to prioritise elements, earmarked areas of knowledge have to be explored which produce their own practice—though under the institutional influence (Agrifoglio 2015: 35; Wenger 1998: 80). Moreover, Wenger stresses the creation of shared 'resources for negotiating meaning' which 'reflects a history of mutual engagement' (1998: 82–83). 'Any community of practice produces abstractions, tools, symbols, stories, terms, and concepts that reify something of that practice in a congealed form' (Wenger 1998: 59) but this repertoire remains rather ambiguous and open for contestation.[7]

Joint Enterprises: The Orissa Research Projects I (1970–1975) and II (1999–2005)

Historically, the project emerged out of a broader interest in temple cities and Kulke's Ph.D dissertation on Chidambaram at Freiburg in 1967 (published in 1970) expressing this research focus. In contrast to Tamil Nadu (Stein 1980) though, the extent of the research on Odisha's temple cities appeared still relatively more limited and rather evolving, leaving more scope for a larger project like ORP I. On a formal level, ORP I, after the application of the Department of Indology at Freiburg University for a study of the Jagannath cult at Puri had been rejected twice in 1967 and 1968 with the argument that it was too small and that temple entry was problematic, it received funding for a pilot project at Puri. It was conducted by Kulke and G.C. Tripathi from March to May 1969.[8] Both paid intensive visits to Odisha's great temple cities such as Bhubaneswar, Puri and Konark.[9] The pilot project was timely because it was followed in July by the grand Navakalevar ritual of the renewal of the wooden images of the Jagannath trinity, performed irregularly always after about 18 years—regarded not only as most sacred but also as a secret. Their positive results augured well for the project that was finally granted in 1970. While initially ORP I was conceived to have a comparative focus on Puri and Bhubaneswar, but the first group was not impressed by a guided tour of temples in Bhubaneswar (for instance, Mukteswara Temple) and the focus was quickly narrowed down to one city that is Puri and its Jagannath cult.[10]

Subsequently, from 1970 to 1975 ORP was funded as SFB 16, that is as 'Sonderforschungsbereich' or 'special research area'—SFB being the highest funding category of the German Research Council—and it became the only 16th project within this category.[11] Institutionally, ORP I was a collaborative venture between three German Universities (Heidelberg, Freiburg and Tübingen) and the three Indian partners (Utkal University in Bhubaneswar, University of Udaipur and Santiniketan).[12] It included a broad range of disciplines such as Indology, religious studies, art history, history, economics, anthropology and sociology as well as other scholars and their topics.[13] The researchers, however, were not all present in Odisha at the same time, but rather stayed in different groups, that is a first group with A. Eschmann, H. Kulke, U. Schneider, H.v. Stietencron and Tripathi, also being Field Director of ORP I, stayed between 1970 and 1971, while a second group with J. Rösel, G. Pfeffer, R. Geib and others arrived subsequently and members of the first group returned to Odisha to complete their studies. Simultaneously, some Indian members also spent time in Germany for instance G.N. Dash stayed in Heidelberg from 1971 onwards.

An academic environment emerging in Odisha turned out to be very conducive for the project. Looking back in 2001, Kulke and Schnepel (2001: 3) listed contributions in this regard: H.K. Mahtab (1960; a chapter titled 'The Cult of Jagannath' his book *History of Orissa*); especially K.C. Mishra in 1965 (his 1965 Ph.D thesis published in Calcutta in 1971 was also titled 'The Cult of Jagannatha' and was the first scholarly monograph on Lord Jagannath); the publication of the 'Madala Panji' or the chronicles of Jagannath temple that were republished in 1969 by A.B. Mohanty. All of them raised awareness of not only of this pivotal text but also added to scholarly debates around Lord Jagannath, his origin and temple which helped the project.[14]

Moreover, the foundation stone laying of the Lord Jagannath temple in Delhi in 1969 was accompanied by small souvenir volumes containing research papers. Their authors such as S.N. Rajguru, K.N. Mahapatra and P. Mukherjee also contributed to the growth of the 'Jagannath consciousness'.[15] After the previous dominance of Bengali scholars working on the history of pre-colonial Odisha, these three scholars may be regarded as the first generation of Odia historians devoting their studies to Odisha's cultural history. As Kulke explained, the latter three were considered by the scholars of the ORP as their *'gurus'* who paved the way for the success of ORP I which was swimming on a wave created by their work (Kulke: personal communication).[16] The fruitful cooperation of the ORP with its *gurus* was based on reciprocity and with its financial support they contributed aspects of their own studies to the ORP.[17] Apart from building on an existing milieu with local *'gurus'*, the project also benefitted from the presence of a few non-Odia scholars active in Odisha just before or simultaneously with ORP I, for instance, F.G. Bailey or the just wrapped up Harvard Project on Bhubaneswar including Cora Dubois, Susan Seymore and James Freeman.[18]

Theoretically, ORP I focused on a 'regional tradition' as its final volume, *The Cult of Jagannath and the Regional Tradition of Orissa* (Eschmann, Kulke and Tripathi 1978: xiiiff), clearly stated. So far largely neglected, it was actually 'not only literally the "central portion" of India's traditions, but also the true melting pot of the local and the all-Indian tradition' (Eschmann, Kulke and Tripathi 1978: xiii).

The region or regional dimension was located by the project research between the Sanskrit tradition, often considered as 'unspoiled' and a village life equally idealised as 'pure' (Eschmann, Kulke and Tripathi 1978: xiii). While both Indology and anthropology may have relegated the regional or 'provincial' level to the background, ORP I focused precisely on one such tradition, namely the Odia regional tradition which historically evolved between the eighth and the eighteenth century and has left its mark in language, architecture and dance styles. The theoretical framing responded critically to Redfield's dominant concept of 'the great and the little tradition' by stressing the crucial middle layers in Indian history and society. It highlighted the role of sacred centres of regional traditions, first and foremost Puri, both as a 'nucleus' of such a tradition and as a 'transmission belt' between the higher and lower level (Eschmann, Kulke and Tripathi 1978: xv). Furthermore, inspired by Srinivas' theory of 'Sanskritisation' and social mobility with an orientation towards a greater tradition, a Hindu-tribal continuum was postulated rather than a Hindu-tribal dichotomy (Eschmann, Kulke and Tripathi 1978: xv). Thus, Puri's sacred complex became the sole focus for ORP I dedicated to understand the origin, development and organisation of this regional 'cult'.[19]

While this approach was related to the theoretical premises of those years, several members felt increasingly uncomfortable with this approach and Pfeffer (2007: 2) reflected critically on its unintended side effects.

> Over the years, we began to question our initial hypothesis, doubtlessly born out of ignorance, proposing the existence of a neat, centrally administered religious, economic and political system which, during the course of a millennium, had been organized in the delta of the Mahanadi. A certain feeling, not altogether uncommon among ethnographers all over the world, indicated that our 'centre' had achieved such a status simply because we had engaged ourselves on a rather conspicuous spot without much information of the world beyond, thus projecting our own conventional religious, administrative and economic criteria of a system upon an unknown socio-cultural entity or mode of integration.

Such increasing questioning of the approach of ORP I contributed to the emergence of a new ORP. However, a continuity of both ORPs was clearly expressed in terms of project membership, first of all, Hermann Kulke as coordinator of ORP II, but also Georg Pfeffer, H.v. Stietencron, G.N. Dash together with Burkhard Schnepel became members of the managing committee.[20] At the same time, projects conducted after ORP I were included especially through a conference titled 'Jagannath Revisited: Studying Society, Religion and the State in Orissa' in Heidelberg in 1997 that offered an opportunity to discuss new concepts or theoretical angles that would later enrich the successful application for ORP II.[21] Unlike ORP I, ORP II lasting from 1999 to 2005 was 'only' a 'Schwerpunktprogramm' (SPP) as a second-rank funding category but included more German universities notably Kiel, Berlin, Heidelberg, Tübingen, Frankfurt/M.—partly because members of ORP I had been offered chairs elsewhere (for example, Kiel and Berlin). After almost 25 years and a few minor projects, many former members of ORP I received funding for another period of deep engagement with the region while many younger scholars, especially pursuing their Ph.Ds, started working on various topics in Odisha—leading to new perspectives and overall a more gender-balanced project by involving more female scholars than ORP I.

When ORP II started, the society in Odisha had already undergone a period of accelerated change unleashed by the post-1990 liberalisation of the economy. The rapid change mentioned directly in the title of the project, clearly raised new questions that the project sought to address. At the same time, it was influenced by post-modern discourses with a recalibration of research towards processes of contestation, appropriation and decentring. ORP II also benefitted from a new research conducted on Lord Jagannath and his temple which was Ishita Banerjee Dube's (2001) and Yaaminey Mubayi's (2005) work on the temple as a 'space of contestation and legitimisation of authority and as an arena for the enactment of relationship of dominance and subordination' (Kulke and Schnepel 2001: 11). Other new research directions included the subaltern studies that also influenced several Odia scholars like B. Pati, B.P. Sahu or C.P. Nanda—who were also later associated with ORP II.

Thematically, ORP II sought to strike a balance between continuity and change that is a certain focus remained on Jagannath. New sources such as small temple archives, private archives, dynastic chronicles (*raja-vamshavalis*), etc. were accessed and older sources were reinterpreted in the light of new approaches. The 'Cult of Lord Jagannath' was discussed in the broader context of an Odia or regional identity, but also vis-à-vis other identities (local, regional and national). Research on *Mahima Dharma*, almost an 'anti-Jagannath', in direct continuation of Eschmann's legacy continued and supposedly more homogeneous and stable identities (such as the Kondh, Odia and Indian identity, etc.) were scrutinised which were—overlapping with, contradicting or destabilising each other. This went hand-in-hand with a shift away from the (sacred) centre of Odisha to more diverse folk and tribal traditions—from region to subregional identities. Questions of origins turned into questions of contexts of time and place, meaning and agency of diverse actors. Perspectives from the margins and peripheries (socially as well as geographically), earlier not an explicit focus were considered crucial to complement hegemonic discourses and in order to understand centres in their complexity and multi-faceted nature—an approach that included not only Lord Jagannath but also other centres and other deities—especially goddesses. Thus, theoretically, a considerable shift away from the elite or dominant discourse(s) in Odisha was also postulated among Jagannath scholars in order to rectify previous essentialisations of Jagannath cult (Kulke and Schnepel 2001: 13ff).

Engagement and Interactions

Scholarly Genealogies

The inclusion of relative novices in order to improve their skills alongside the more experienced members is visible in various scholarly 'genealogies' ranging from ORP I to II, in which Ph.D students or post-docs were trained, that is they were entrusted with increasingly sophisticated and complex scholarly tasks by their Ph.D supervisors, doctoral 'father-figures' or '*gurus*'. Thus, they became experts through a sharing of knowledge typical for communities of practice (Agrifoglio 2015: 27). This mutual engagement included conversations and joint activities such as field trips involving more formalised systems as departments or relatively more improvised and independent interactions in the field.

Such 'genealogies' of work can be read in the connections between G. Pfeffer and his Ph.D students R. Hardenberg, P. Berger, T. Otten, C. Struempell, U. Skoda and L. Guzy, the latter five being fellow Ph.D students under ORP II, while Hardenberg obtained his Ph.D prior to the ORP II but continued as post-doc and became subsequently Ph.D supervisor of new generations of scholars such as D. Ojha. They can also be seen emerging from U. Schneider, Director and senior-most scholar of ORP I, who taught Pfeffer and became 'revered *guru* and mentor' of G.C. Tripathi, H. Kulke and R. Geib at Freiburg University (1962–1967).[22] Kulke, in turn, inspired and supervised scholars of another generation including G. Berkemer, M. Brandtner, S. Arp, H. Frese and others, while—more indirectly—he also influenced other ORP II members such as B. Schnepel or U. Skoda and interacted closely with younger Indian scholars like B. Pati, B. Sahu, C.P. Nanda (all in the ORP network) or K.C. Dash. Similarly, H.v. Stietencron as a senior colleague worked closely with C. Mallebrein and A. Malinar, cartographers in Tübingen and many others.

A special case is A. Eschmann whose 'pioneering work' remained incomplete due to her sudden death in 1977 (Guzy 2002: 31). Eschmann's research, especially on *Mahima Dharma*, was continued by several scholars including Ishita Banerjee and during ORP II particularly, L. Guzy and Johannes Beltz (with Bettina Bäumer) but also B. Pati. As Guzy (2002; translated by the author) argued that the strong interest in *Mahima Dharma* leading to three projects in ORP II 'can be understood as an attempt to ensure academic continuity of Eschmann's research' but also as a form of mourning (Trauerarbeit).[23]

While some Indian scholars started as research associates of (former) ORP scholars and went on to become professors and Ph.D supervisors on their own, for example, D.K. Behera who was also associated with ORP II as a local counterpart, the story of Purna Chandra Mishra is certainly special. As the introduction of his book on pottery published with L. Cort (Cort and Mishra 2012) states, Purna Chandra Mishra began his career as a research assistant of Kulke in ORP I, who acknowledged his contribution in his monograph (Kulke 1979). At the same time, he also assisted Eschmann, Pfeffer, Rösel and Stietencron. The pottery project (1979–1981) started shortly after ORP I and after *The Cult of Jagannath and the Regional Tradition of Orissa* (Eschmann, Kulke and Tripathi 1978) had been published. The authors, clearly familiar with it, refer extensively to Kulke, Eschmann, Pfeffer, Stietencron, Tripathi, P. Mukherjee and Rösel, etc., while Jagannath's trinity adorns a DVD included in the volume. Later, P.C. Mishra was also involved in Williams' (1996) project on Orissa's palm-leaf manuscripts which began in 1979.[24] Facilitating also Frederique Marglin's research, he was involved in almost every major research project in one way or another, in more or less visible roles, while Marglin, in turn, was invited as a keynote speaker to one of the annual ORP II conferences at Salzau.

In the Introduction to *Jagannath Revisited*, published in 2001, Kulke and Schnepel (2001: 4) argued that one can speak of groups of scholars or perhaps even 'schools' evolving prior and around ORP I.[25] Whether 'schools' were formed or not, one can see that colleagues worked together, supported each other in multiple ways for example when ORP I scholars like Rösel learned Odia from another ORP colleague, namely Gagan Dash. Individual careers were often interwoven within ORP networks and at times also included role reversals—for example when Rösel became one of the reviewers in ORP II and, thus, was involved in decision-making processes about the funding or extensions. The pursuing of careers and more broadly the collaborations between colleagues during the projects was never without conflicts and the ORPs had their share of individual or institutional disagreements or perhaps even clashes. For example, the interim report submitted in 1973 stated that two anthropological–sociological contributions co-authored by Pfeffer and Rösel were controversial within ORP (Zwischenbericht 1973: Vorwort). At times such discussions were tinged with institutional affiliations, namely Freiburg/a 'Freiburg group' versus Heidelberg/a 'Heidelberg group'.

Interdisciplinary projects more generally are, as Rösel (1974: 247–248) pointed out, commonly characterised by complicity and competition—the former perhaps more visible in the application process, the latter arguably more linked to claims to specific 'sub-fields' or topics but also with reference to the presented empirical and theoretical ideas as outcomes. The different status of members with permanent or precarious short-term positions (leading to a higher fluctuation) entailed different logics to deliver, that is, the latter are often under more pressure to present novel and unique results by accessing new fields, data, etc. in order to gain employment.[26] The processes of collaborating and competing occur on various levels—institutional or personal—and collegial relationships may be influenced by the politics of referencing, that is forming syndicates or excluding others, in turn, aggravated by institutional rivalries.

'We Were Outsiders'—Space, Status and Privilege

'We were outsiders', Hermann Kulke exclaimed, in an interview in 2018 (personal communication), when discussing the conditions of ORP I scholars working in Odisha. His words, it seems, echo a consciousness among the group of German scholars that they were in a distinctive position which they shared vis-à-vis others in the field and which contributed to group consciousness. This sentiment is expressed by Rösel in his book *Tempelstadt Puri* (Temple city Puri) in 1988. Written in a somewhat lighter vein to reach out beyond academic circles, he looks back at his research in Puri including the eight months he lived in a *dharmashala* just opposite the temple's main gate, while he, like non-Hindus generally, was not allowed to enter the temple—being so close, yet remaining outside the temple offered an almost tangible experience of being an outsider. He wrote

> The fact that access to the temple was denied to us turned out to be a grave and insurmountable obstacle. Local staff, brahmanical colleagues did it for us.... Sitting in front of the temple, but being excluded from visiting the temple, I could only see a painted image of Lord Jagannath, the Patitapabana or 'Saviour of the Fallen', which was placed in a niche of the temple gate for the heathens and untouchables. (1988: 19, translation from German by the author)

Thus, he had to be content with a glimpse of Lord Jagannath that was offered to a foreign non-believer. Already in his dissertation monograph, Rösel (1980: XI) described that he experienced a certain xenophobia in the early 1970s and saw Puri as 'a town with an almost legendary hostility towards strangers'—especially but not only regarding temple entry. Suspicions regarding his stay may have arisen because according to him no other 'white stranger' had spent longer stays so close to the temple and his hosts made sure that nothing else than a kerosene stove for preparing tea was kept in his room in order to comply with rules of ritual purity (Rösel 1980: XI). Though with a servant, he did not fit neatly into the role of a 'foreign science-sahib', his exotic character ('Fremdartigkeit') vis-à-vis his hosts constantly made him an object of marvel presented to others (Rösel 1980: XII). Ironically, he also thanked his hosts in the preface of the book for accepting a white 'untouchable' (Rösel 1980: XIV).

While the temple entry was denied to scholars of both projects and served a visible boundary marker between 'us' and 'them' in constructions of identity in a broader sense and here particularly in a conservative environment, ideas about purity and pollution at times also separated colleagues within the project. For example, Tina Otten during her Ph.D in ORP II was asked to assure her hosts that she did not belong to the community or jati of her fellow Berlin Ph.D scholar living nearby, because, as per the assumption, he would eat beef and pork with his hosts of another community. If she would have been closely associated with him, she would not have been able to settle down in the village as intended (Otten 2006: 22). While some division as in the case of the Jagannath temple in Puri were basically non-negotiable and also regretted by the affected scholars, other boundaries were shifting over time and Peter Berger, another ORP II Ph.D scholar from Berlin, argued that, though an integration into families and communities occurred, this integration, not only in his case, remained ambivalent and he felt more like an 'integrated outsider' (Berger 2007: 502).

The gaze that affected researchers in both projects is also expressed in an anecdote, Jakob Rösel (personal communication) remembered while going through old photographs of the project days. Experimenting with studio photography in Bhubaneswar he had his photo taken with studio props especially Gopis—sitting or standing—while he himself wore an attire that could easily be understood as 'hippie'. After the photograph had been taken the owner of the studio used it as an advertisement for his windows—presumably to highlight the fact that he had a 'western' or 'white sahib' customer and to attract more customers in this way. He succeeded in the sense that the photo caused considerable attention with a lot of people stopping and looking at the window. A combination of a novelty factor with an exotic outsider status that is the 'Hippie sahib' with a gopi deviated from the familiar modes of representation. It turned into a kind of an attraction, but also caused worries within ORP because some colleagues were concerned with the reputation of the project which may suffer in turn.

However, during ORP I, rather than ORP II, a sense of belonging was apparently not only negatively framed through acts of exclusion and exoticisation, but also spatial inclusion—especially within the project house or rather a compound-like set of neighbouring houses at Bargarh Road or Badagada Canal Road (near Kalpana St.) that served as a base in Bhubaneswar. In the memory of Jakob Rösel (personal communication) the neighbourhood, also called Paharganj, was a rather deserted place where one had just started to construct houses—a kind of cement desert depicted in Figures 11.1 and 11.2. The ground for this 'base' was prepared by Hermann Kulke who took on the role of a 'Quartiermacher' (person in charge to prepare the residence or literally 'quarter') in October 1970. Here, colleagues shared houses and offices—some also staying with their families. For example, Schneider, Kulke and Eschmann shared a house, next to von Stietencron with family while Tripathi and various persons copying manuscripts stayed around the corner. The occupancy changed with the 'cohorts' of scholars arriving, but the houses were used over a longer project period.[27]

The situation of living together in the project houses in close proximity probably fostered a sense of belonging and of being insiders, even more so in a not entirely welcoming 'outside'. At the same time, the project houses were not exclusively occupied by project members but included, for instance, Thomas Donaldson who worked

Figure 11.1 Project house in Bhubaneswar in a bungalow-like style with a front porch where colleagues arrived and were sent off for field trips to other parts of Odisha
Source: Photo by J. Rösel, adapted by the author.

Figure 11.2 Project house in Bhubaneswar in a bungalow-like style with a front porch where colleagues arrived and were sent off for field trips to other parts of Odisha
Source: Photo by J. Rösel, adapted by the author.

on Hindu and Buddhist art (1986) and moved in with his family after Schneider had left.[28] Yet, there was no general consensus on where the base should actually be—Bhubaneswar or Puri—and given the different disciplinary backgrounds, not everybody agreed that, for example, moving out of the project house and into a *dharmashala* in Puri was a good idea. However, there was a shift to Puri later on where project members also shared a beach house.

In addition to the housing in ORP I, the project members also shared a status of relatively privileged scholars or outsiders—generously funded by the German Research Council—and somewhat echoing Tönnies' dictum (1922[1887]) that community life is often tied to community property and pleasure. The solid financial position of the project enabled team members to buy manuscripts for the research or to have access to a project jeep in order to collect data—at a time when hardly any private cars were used. While the jeep at times might have caused friction when several members planned to use it at the same time, it was clearly a status symbol marking a governmental power position—also interpretable as wealth.[29] Other markers of distinction like cameras or servants were equally part of this specific field situation, though the latter were a novel luxury primarily for Germans not used to their presence in their German households while all the neighbouring houses with Indian families had them too.

Reflecting on the privileges and position the researchers enjoyed, Rösel (1974) saw certain parallels to 'colonial sahibs' as well as the dangers of a self-isolation that go hand in hand with privileges and actually stand in contrast to the idea of a participant observation, though researchers might glorify their presence and supposed hardships in the 'field'. He argued:

> Considering local conditions the project researcher in terms of his salary represents a new '*raja*'—a fully funded member of a research project receives roughly the salary of an Indian minister. This means that the researcher can actually employ every researcher in a mid-range position without worrying about copyright issues of later publications.... The economic superiority of the researcher vis-à-vis the local population of the host country changes his scientific position. The outstanding purchase power of his salary and the immense opportunities, which the project offers, be it in the form of a jeep or an office, as well as the opportunities to get a privileged access, can lead to a shift of his research interests to completely other fields. (1974: 248–249)[30]

However, other ORP-scholars pointed out that, unlike in the case of German consular staff, ORP I did not include allowances (travel or daily allowance) for accompanying families which left considerable strains on their financial situation.[31] In any case, a generous funding continued during ORP II that enabled project groups to invest in a jeep or enabled individual members to buy a motorcycle, etc.—still very considerable status symbols in the 2000s and particularly in villages. Yet, at least from the perspective of a Ph.D scholar in ORP II, the differences were somewhat more levelled—partly because the

German Research council had reduced its funding and most Ph.D scholars worked with a 50 per cent position and partly because due to liberalisation a new and relatively wealthy middle class emerged commanding similar or more resources.[32] Also, in contrast to ORP I, scholars were based in faraway places in Odisha or in archives beyond Odisha and, therefore, did not co-reside to the same extent at one 'centre'. Some colleagues worked in clusters though for instance a group of four to five Berlin anthropologists in southern Odisha and they realised the advantages of having their colleagues nearby (for example, Berger 2007: 492–493). While this group of anthropologists maintained a project hub there, it was not a residential compound and their individual accommodation in villages could be characterised as being very basic. Other researchers of the highly decentralised ORP II hardly met other colleagues in the field, but instead met them in Germany—first and foremost during the annual project conferences in 2000–2003 in the relatively remote Salzau manor (and finally in 2004 in Civita Castelana in Italy) where all project members were supposed to assemble and discuss outcomes regularly.

Precarious Position as Enforced Bonding?

While the 'outsider' team members enjoyed certain privileges, their position was at other times rather precarious as they were also affected by suspicions and accusations. Rumours circulated that in some cases families of people selling manuscripts to ORP were not satisfied with the process or share that they claimed they should also have received.[33] Still other rumours doubted the quality of the purchased manuscripts and argued that only fake manuscripts were given to ORP. In one particular incident ORP was even (wrongly) blamed to be involved in the theft of a Shiva statue from the Loknath Temple (Kulke, personal communication).[34] However, such 'initial complications' were overcome with the help of local colleagues such as G.N. Dash and R. Nayak (Pfeffer 2007: 1).

In 1972, though a concrete police case was registered in the presence of scholars like G. Pfeffer, G.N. Dash, G.C. Tripathi. As Dash (Kulke, personal communication) remembered, nobody was allowed to leave the room when the police arrived in the project house. Legend has it that Tripathi anticipated what was to come and hid the most precious manuscripts he was working on under his bed where his wife was sitting. The 17,000 palm leafs of the Madala Panji (MP) were confiscated in big plastic bags and brought to Cuttack whereas the 195 palm-leaf manuscripts in a backroom remained untouched. In a handwritten letter Tripathi wrote to Kulke at Heidelberg:

> We are passing through a very critical phase of our Project because our MP has been confiscated. According to Police the Deula Karana was not entitled to possess the MP which was the property of the Jagannath Temple. We are blamed to have seduced the Deula Karana to sell the stolen case to us and even helped him to steal the MP. I was supposed to take it in a very short time to Germany and Orissa's cultural treasure would thus have been lost forever. Anyhow, we shall all overcome. Geib and Rösel will soon tell you everything after their return. (translation from German by Kulke)

Due to political circumstances it took more than two years until the ORP got back the MP in 1974 after visas were issued again and after several rounds of negotiations and informing the police of the correspondence between Shri R.K. Rath and Prof. Schneider and his assurance that the manuscripts will be dedicated to the Orissa State Museum (OSM).[35] The episode indicates a precarious and at times rather vulnerable position of ORP I. It also shows that the success of projects depended on legal requirements such as visa and, closely related to it, on a dialogue with the Governments of Odisha and India that continued beyond ORP I, for example, with a meeting between Kulke and Chief Minister Naveen Patnaik (see the Preface).[36] The established relationships certainly contributed to the success of ORP II and the way it was conceived. Last, but not the least, the awarding of Padma Shri as one of the highest honours to a foreign scholar—namely to H.v. Stietencron (2004) and H. Kulke (2010)—and other awards to ORP project members signalled a recognition of their contributions to Odia Studies and added to the reputation of the ORPs.[37]

Creating Resources and Repertoires

Anderson (1983) famously argued that print technologies and print capitalism facilitated an imagining of communities. Without postulating any direct correspondence, the collaborative work of a scholarly community on its printed products appears to have also contributed to the fostering of a sense of community of the ORPs. Over the years the two projects, as a small output oriented, face-to-face community, at times under pressure from funding agencies and at other times enjoying a dose of 'academic tourism', invested substantially into publishing as a central scholarly practice, which, again, does not necessarily mean that all members were involved in all activities.

Manuscripts and Archives

For ORP I, more than ORP II, the collection of manuscripts played a major role in forming an invaluable basis, especially for in-depth historical and Indological research. Following Kulke (personal communication) it was known that ORP buys old manuscripts.[38] Its most outstanding acquisition was the already mentioned Madala Panji including the Rajabhoga manuscript, Odisha's most important chronicle (Dash 2010) which was purchased with the intention to donate it to an Odia institution.[39] Subsequently, several *pandas* (priests) were hired with project funds to copy the acquired palm-leaf manuscripts in Sanskrit or Devanagari and Odia.[40] This process triggered speculations about the purpose of the acquisition or, in rare cases, hard feelings among the selling families culminating in the already mentioned police case that ended in a positive way by the donation of the entire Madala Panji to the Orissa State Museum on 12 August 1974.[41]

Copies of the manuscripts (with English translations) are also preserved in the 'Orissa Archive' at the South Asia Institute or SAI, established at the University of Heidelberg in 1976.[42] Already during the early years of ORP II the idea prevailed that one set of the copied ORP manuscripts and translations which were stored at the

South Asia Institute in Heidelberg and in particular all its original palm-leaf manuscripts were still preserved in the residence of G.N. Dash, including the Rajabhog, should be donated to an institution at Bhubaneswar at the end of the ORP. They were finally handed over to the Record Centre (Eastern Zone), National Archives of India in 2006 combined with a symposium titled 'The Madala Panji and Orissan Historiography'.[43]

Publications and Conferences

Apart from collecting, translating and preserving manuscripts, the ORPs produced edited volumes, often based on conferences, monographs, reports, etc. Many of these publications were completed and released only after the projects in terms of funding were officially over, but clearly had an afterlife and periods of collaboration exceeded the project periods. This holds also true for arguably the best-known publication of ORP I—namely its collective opus magnum published as 'The Cult of Jagannath and the Regional Tradition of Orissa' only in 1978. It displayed the full range of topics covered in the interdisciplinary project with contributions on history, religion, anthropology, economy, etc.[44] The fact that initially a few separate volumes had been envisioned but somewhat merged in one volume again exemplifies the negotiations within this scholarly community, which in this case turned out to be a blessing in disguise because it brought together almost all scholars in an 'omnibus'-like volume. Two notable omissions being R. Geib and J. Rösel, but these lacunae were rectified in a revised and expanded edition in 2014.[45] Its Preface to the Second Edition contains a detailed review and bibliography of the new studies on Jagannath and Odisha's cultural development during the 35 years since its first edition.

ORP I also led to a wide range of monographs based on in-depth research during the project—such as Geib (1975), Pfeffer (1976), Kulke (1979), Rösel (1980), Schneider (1984) and Tripathi (2004) to name a few and more edited volumes such as Kulke and Tripathi (1993). Thus, the production of a shared repertoire in terms of books continued for many years—depending on production cycles of publishing houses, positions at universities and other compulsions. Specifically in ORP I members also invested considerable energy in a reference book published in 1981 by H. Kulke, in collaboration with G. Dash under the title *Orissa: A Comprehensive and Classified Bibliography.*[46]

While some research continued around Lord Jagannath in the 1990s, for instance, Hardenberg (1999 and 2000; significantly under the supervision of Pfeffer), former ORP I scholars and 'novices' reassembled in 1997 for the already mentioned conference 'Jagannath Revisited' which led to another volume (Kulke and Schnepel 2001), the follow-up project and generally another period of productive research and publishing. Subsequently, various ORP II members edited conference volumes based on the annual conferences of ORP II from 2000 to 2003 [in chronological order: A. Malinar/J. Beltz and H. Frese (eds.) (2004); G. Pfeffer (ed.) 2007; A. Malinar (ed.) 2007; H. Kulke and G. Berkemer (eds.) 2011]. Released during and after the project, they focused on different aspects of the overall application and clearly show a work-in-progress, because the conferences were not outlined in the overall application, but rather negotiated in the process with the contributors being asked to relate their work to the overall theme of the respective conference and volume.[47] However, all conference volumes were embedded in a series of books titled *Studies in Orissan Society, Culture and History* and edited by Kulke and Schnepel which started with *Jagannath Revisited* (1997) and included also other monographs (Mubayi 2004; Schnepel 2002; Skoda 2005).

All tangible outcomes mirror, as the editors of the first volume stated, the work of ORP, but apart from members, it included guests and keynote speakers (Malinar, Beltz and Frese 2004: xi). For example, the Salzau Conference in 2003, as the abstract volume but also the later publication document, included guests and associated scholars like A. Tanabe (Japan), Bhairabi Sahu, C.P. Nanda, Shishir Kumar Panda and B.D. Chattopadyaya—all from India—with the latter also delivering a keynote. The conferences in the slightly remote manor of Salzau in northern Germany, however, were not only an annual occasion to present and discuss on-going research, they were equally relevant for networking with international scholars focusing on similar issues thus creating various layers of involvement with regular core members and occasional guests and also with long-term fellow colleagues collaborating in other projects and publication. Besides, they played a role in solving internal administrative issues and were also a way to regularly meet with reviewers appointed by the DFG to evaluate the quality—and therefore were more or less mandatory—and they provided an opportunity for socialising beyond the conference hall for instance by including a Baltic Sea trip in 2003. Additionally, several conferences and smaller workshops were not only held in Heidelberg but also in Sambalpur and Bhubaneswar during and around ORP II and led to more publications (for instance Berkemer and Frenz 2003; Otten and Skoda 2014).[48] Two 'Festschriften' for Kulke (Brandtner and Panda 2006) and Pfeffer (Berger et al. 2010) have distinctive Odisha angles. And while the final ORP II conference in the secluded nunnery of Civita Castellana (Italy) was not meant to lead to a grand opus magnum comparable to *The Cult of Jagannath*, a comprehensive two-volume coffee-table book-set was published later by Kulke as chief editor under the title *Imaging Odisha* in 2013.[49]

Exhibitions

In addition to the publications and manuscripts, the ORPs and particularly ORP II, led to various exhibitions—partly as a visual side of the research within the project that is during the Salzau conference 2003 and partly as outreach beyond the project. First and foremost, the work of Cornelia Mallebrein, often in collaboration with H. von Stietencron, needs to be mentioned here, for example, her exhibitions shown in Heidelberg, Konstanz and elsewhere as well as her catalogues on 'The Divine Play on Earth: Religious Aesthetics and Ritual in Orissa' (2008 together with Stietencron).[50]

Another interesting and close connection emerged from the Museum Rietberg in Zürich, which, in 1980, published a volume titled *Orissa: Kunst und Kultur in Nordost-Indien* [Orissa: Art and Culture in Northeast-India], written by E. Fischer, S. Mahapatra and D. Pathy. It contained contributions from Hermann Kulke but also Thomas Donaldson (among others) and in the 'Preface' E. Fischer, Director of the Museum from 1972 to 1998, mentions that he first travelled to Odisha in 1973 where H.v. Stietencron introduced him to the beauty and importance of antiquities of Odisha (1980: 7).[51]

Fischer's and Pathy's exhibitions not only created further resources in collaboration with ORP but probably also paved the way for other exhibitions at the museum, though they focused less on Lord Jagannath. For example, two scholars from ORP II, namely Cornelia Mallebrein and Johannes Beltz (2012), jointly curated an exhibition and published a catalogue on 'tribal bronzes' from Middle India (including Odisha) in 2012.

Entering Scholarly Homes: The Lord and a Popular Culture Side

As Wenger (1998: 72–73) argued, communities of practice typically create 'a shared repertoire' consisting of various artefacts, etc. Apart from the various 'deliverables' already mentioned, it is proposed that the scholarly community also had a popular culture element in the sense that the Lord entered the homes, was collected, 'consumed', gifted and exchanged in several forms. Icons of the Lord, the trinity or images of the temple may have been purchased as souvenirs, such as *pata chitra* (as mentioned in the Introduction) from Raghurajpur, wooden or bronze statue, as an application work from Pipli, etc. Bought for aesthetic reasons or to be used as table cloths, the transitions between aesthetic object, cultural object and souvenir were clearly blurred. As Guzy (personal communication) explained, these objects—in her case kept both in the private space and in the office space—are a crucial source of inspiration, kept for one's own joy, part of one's biography and everyday life culture. In fact, it was the bonding with these objects that mattered for Guzy rather than the bonding with the other members.

In some cases, especially among ORP I scholars, who stayed with their families in Odisha, a stronger intimacy with the Lord evolved and as Kulke (personal communication) mentioned Lord Jagannath became almost like a 'family deity'. His elder children made drawings of the Lord while being in Odisha and he keeps a part of his study reserved for various Jagannath statues—like a little shrine—and his grandchildren lately showed an interest in them and started to engage with them in a playful way. For instance, a very young grandson once mixed few Lego figures with figures of the Jagannath trinity and his little granddaughter painted an image of Jagannath with hearts around 2010—as Kulke as a proud grandfather noticed. Given the centrality of Kulke in both projects, it may not come as a surprise that the bonding is perhaps the strongest in his family stretching over three generations now. The home of the Kulke family also shows how Lord Jagannath was deeply embedded in gift exchanges. For example, G. Dash gifted LPs with Jagannath hymns to Kulke or Prabhat Mukherjee[52] who was considered an Odishan *guru* by Kulke, became 'Uncle Mukherjee' for Kulke's children and in 1971 presented to him a Jagannath in the form of a wooden rath as a gift to Kulke's daughter—an object still cherished as part of her little Jagannath house-shrine at their home. The daughter presented to her father the same rath in 1979 when he stayed with his family at Bhubaneswar, teaching at the Utkal University. Similarly, Mukherjee's daughter stitched a Lord Jagannath on a frame and gifted it in the early 1980s to the Kulke family—as in Figures 11.3 and 11.4 respectively. While a Maussian establishment and maintenance of relationships involving memorabilia of the Lord as gifts might be particularly strong in the Kulke family, other scholars also gifted Lord Jagannath in several forms to colleagues who would be familiar with the Lord (Guzy, personal communication) or did so indirectly through their books or received representations of the Lord as gifts simply because they were identified with the Orissa projects or Odisha in general.

Figure 11.3 A wooden rath gifted to the daughter of H. Kulke by 'Uncle Mukherjee' around 1971
Source: Author, courtesy H. Kulke.

Figure 11.4 Lord Jagannath stitched by the daughter of P. Mukherjee for the Kulke family around 1980
Source: Author, courtesy H. Kulke.

In rare cases, images were commissioned and tailor-made according to the wishes of individual members. Rösel remembered that he asked the temple painter to paint images for him that were later copied to black and white by Rösel's wife and integrated in his book on Puri (Rösel 1988: 26–27).[53] However, not all members collected icons of Lord Jagannath. For example, J. Beltz (personal communication) reasoned that he was hardly interested in it because of his earlier research on Ambedkar and Dalits, while C. Mallebrein (personal communication) did purchase a few representations of the Lord, but felt closer to goddesses like Ma Tarini—identifying Lord Jagannath with male dominance. Thus, to keep the Lord in private context, it did not preclude that scholars often started extensive collections of other deities in line with the topical shifts under ORP II.

Conclusion

Did a community of scholars or rather scholarly practice evolve around the Odisha projects and Lord Jagannath? The responses of members on the German side differed in many ways. Some simply appreciated the intensive professional collaborations—also in the field—while others did not subscribe to the positive or idealising connotations of the term and referred to existing hierarchies of seniority and gender. Still, others criticised the formation of supposedly close-knit sub-groups that existed during ORP II at several universities (Berlin with anthropology, Kiel with history, etc.)

while arguing that there was only limited exchange between these groups beyond the conferences or publications. In that sense, they felt that there was no 'real' community, though these scholars also highlighted important individual ties to other colleagues. Some considered it more diplomatically as a 50/50 situation—a glass half-full or half-empty depending on the perspective—collaborations and conflicts between institutions, but also senior or junior scholars, over approaches, etc., while acknowledging intensive interactions.

Based on these diverse individual accounts it has been argued that the scholarly community that evolved around the two projects shared features with other 'communities of practice'—namely a mutual and rather profound engagement in pursuing a joint enterprise including the production of common resources and creating a repertoire. The academic goals where outlined in the applications and later publications—with a significant shift from centre to periphery, etc. from ORP I to ORP II, while designing ORP II as a follow-up of ORP I. Project members engaged deeply in both projects in several ways, though co-residential elements remained fairly limited to ORP I. A sense of a distinctive community, it seems, also emerged in interactions with locals in Odisha and also through a relatively privileged position of the scholars, while remaining outsiders in the field. Finally, the work of the project is reflected in its considerable output of tangible deliverables, but also the setting up or supporting of archives, which remain valuable resources. Beyond the professional realm, the ORPs had a spillover effect into the private lives of the concerned scholars and interactions around the projects included a popular culture and affective dimension in which additional ties with Lord Jagannath were established, who in turn was implicated in gift-exchanges, etc.

The chapter offered insights—or perhaps glimpses—into the evolution of a scholarly community and the functioning of two large and diverse projects, which defy any simple generalisation. Arguably, the most relevant shift from ORP I to II concerned the decentring of Lord Jagannath and the engagement with subregional perspectives that broadened or perhaps relativised ORP I. One might even say that the recalibrated ORP II led to new forms of bonding—most notably with goddesses. Thus, it may not surprise that the final volume of ORP II 'Centres Out There?' actually presented Ma Tarini on the front cover (and an aerial view of her temple on the back cover)—indicating a topical shift and deepening of the understanding of Odia-ness, but also supplementing the bonding with Lord Jagannath.

Notes

1. The author was involved in ORP II from 2000 to 2005 that is until 2003 as a Ph.D scholar and afterwards did a post-doc project.
2. Including interviews with Kulke (24 August 2018), Rösel (13 January 2019), Guzy (25 January 2019), Beltz (2 February 2019) and Mallebrein (7 February 2019).
3. Since ORP I dealt more explicitly with Lord Jagannath there is a slightly stronger focus on I rather than II. For details on the projects also see the project webpage https://orp.uni-kiel.de/ which is only accessible through the web-archive: https://web.archive.org/web/20110719105340/http://orp.uni-kiel.de/ORP-Frameset.htm (accessed 8 March 2019).
4. Community or 'Gemeinschaft' as a concept has been used in the humanities and social sciences in many different contexts for at least 200 years, if not longer—entailing various, usually positive connotations (Hillery 1959; Rapport [1996]2004). Perhaps, precisely because it remains a rather vague and elusive concept, it has enjoyed immense popularity—both as an analytical as well as an emic term.
5. Ignoring the evolutionist underpinnings of Tönnies (1922[1887]: 8ff) idea of community here, especially the proposed transition from Gemeinschaft to Gesellschaft (Community and Society), it is still worth noticing that he highlighted three central and often interrelated factors in the formation of a community. He called them (a) 'blood relations' ('Gemeinschaft des Blutes'/'Verwandtschaft') or ties of kinship and affinity; (b) 'locality' ('Gemeinschaft des Ortes'/'Nachbarschaft') or co-residence (in households, villages) and (c) the 'mind' ('Gemeinschaft des Geistes'/'Freundschaft'). The latter is formed independently of kinship and neighbourhood, being conditioned by and resulting from similarity of work or opinion. It grows most easily where people share the same or a similar calling or craft. Such a benevolent spirit is not located in any one place, but dwells in the conscience of its worshippers and accompanies their wanderings in foreign parts (Tönnies 1922[1887]: 15–16).

   Thus, community is about linking and bonding rather than separating and, for example, a comradeship is tied to profession(als), albeit in an 'invisible' location, but also linked to creativity and faith.

6. Later community studies, in the avatar of village community studies, also stressed a certain 'quality of distinctiveness' with reference to boundaries, sentiments including an ethnocentrism, norms, structures and a visibility to others, which is 'expressed in the group consciousness' (Redfield 1955: 4). Apart from that, they also highlighted joint activities and interactions (not necessarily with all other members though)—sometimes rephrased as common interests and face-to-face relations; focused on communities of small scale and localities; and considered them as rather homogeneous and 'slow-changing' as well as self-sufficient (Redfield 1955; Hillery 1959). Deviating from these approaches, symbolic anthropology emphasized markers of communities understood as 'a symbolic construct and a contrastive one' commanding a common repertoire of symbols and meanings and a 'shared vocabulary of value' (Rapport 2004[1996]: 115).
7. Wenger (1998: 125) also worked with indicators such as 'sustained mutual relationships', which maybe more or less conflictual; or 'shared ways of engaging in doing things together' thereby emphasising a certain fluidity or overlap with other forms of organisation, for example, 'formal departments'; 'project teams' (with more specific tasks and periods); fuzzy 'communities of interest' or loose 'informal networks' and pointing to the fact that CoPs may be bigger or smaller, short-lived or long-lived, inside boundaries or beyond; co-located or dispersed, face-to-face or virtual etc. (Agrifoglio 2015: 30–34).
8. Tripathi had joined Udaipur University as a Sanskrit lecturer after having finished his Ph.D in Indology at Freiburg in December 1969.
9. Kulke primarily contacted relevant Government institutions and scholars at the Utkal University, while Tripathi worked in the Jagannath temple and discovered important manuscripts. Subsequently, Kulke wrote a report about the positive response at Utkal University and also mentioned the reaction of the Secretary of Cultural Affairs and Chief Editor of the Orissa Historical Research Journal who emphatically stated: 'we need thousands of hands like yours'.
10. Including also Tripathi's/Mahapatra's work on Navekalevara.
11. By January 2019 the DFG had granted 277 SFB projects.
12. Later also scholars at Berhampur University.
13. As Kulke (1979: IX) wrote in 1979:

> G.C. Tripathi analysed the philosophy of the Jagannath cult; A. Eschmann investigated initially Mahima Dharma and then shifted to the relations between the Jagannath cult and the Adivasi population in Puri's hinterland; H.v. Stietencron looked at the religious aspects and surroundings of the cult; U. Schneider and R. Geib focused critically on the local Sanskrit and Oriya texts (especially the origin myths of the Indradyumma-legend);

J. Lütt contributed with his work on the history of Sankaracharyas in Puri as descendants of Sankara; G.N. Dash studied the most important Madala Panji (MP) temple chronicles Puris with reference to the relations between priests and Odishan kings, which was also the focus of G. Pfeffers research on the Sasana Brahmins as intellectual elite of Odisha in Puri's Hinterland; J.Rösel and E.Hein as sociologists and economists focused on pilgrimage and the temple economy; while, last but not least, Kulke analyzed Hindu kingship ideology and the mutual relations between Odisha's feudatory states and their tribal deities and the Jagannath cult.

14. Mahtab claimed Buddhist origins of the cult, while K.C. Mishra linked the 'cult' to 'indigenous religious, historical and social roots', that is dynasties, tribes, religious movements (see Kulke and Schnepel 2001: 3).
15. S.N. Rajguru was a historian, epigraphist, working for the Orissa State Museum; K.N. Mahapatra was Superintendent of Archaeology of the OSM and P. Mukherjee was Reader in History, Utkal University.
16. All three are also singled out in the preface of Kulke's Habilitation published in 1979. Other historians were growing parallel to ORP I—for example K.S. Behera.
17. In 1971, K.N. Mahapatra, thus, produced for the ORP for the first time a comprehensive manuscript on the thirty Jagannath temples of Odisha, which he published privately in 1978. S.N. Rajaguru translated for the OPR the Jagannāthasthalavṛttātam, an important Telugu version of Puri's chronicle. It had been discovered by Kulke at the Government Manuscript Library at Madras in 1971 and was published posthumously in 1992 by the Shri Sanskrit Vishvavidyayala at Puri. In a joint financial cooperation of the ORP with the Indian Council of Historical Research at Delhi, P. Mukherjee undertook a critical edition of a selection of the official British 'Jagannath Correspondence' at the Orissa State Archives. Before his unexpected death in 1984 he finished only the first volume up to 1850 which was edited by N. Gardner Cassels (2000).
18. Moreover, the foundation stone laying of the Lord Jagannath temple in Delhi in 1969 accompanied by small souvenir volumes containing research papers by S.N. Rajguru (historian, epigraphist, working for State Museum), K.N. Mahapatra (State Museum, in charge of manuscripts, also author of 'Jagannath temples in Eastern India' 1977), and P. Mukherjee (Reader in History, Utkal University) also contributed to a growing 'Jagannath consciousness'. In fact, as Kulke explained later, the latter three were considered by him as *'gurus'* who paved the way for the success of ORP I. All three are also singled out in preface of Kulke's Habilitation published in 1979. Other historians were growing parallel to ORP I—for example, K.S. Behera.

19. As it was presented later on the webpage of ORP II:

> India's great regional traditions form the 'central position' in the literal sense of an uninterrupted cultural continuum which links the world of India's villages with the great all-Indian tradition. Since the last century, the study of these regional traditions has been overshadowed by anthropological and Indological research which usually focusses on the 'outer positions' of this continuum. The first Orissa Research Project, therefore, undertook the study of one of India's great regional traditions with a strong emphasis on the cult of Jagannath and the temple city of Puri. The project revealed vital elements of the Oriya identity as it is particularly known from the dominant coastal region.

Traced from https://orp.uni-kiel.de/ but the link is no longer accessible. Available at https://web.archive.org/web/20110719105340/http://orp.uni-kiel.de/ORP-Frameset.htm (accessed 8 March 2019).

20. The wider Steering Committee included also J. Lütt of ORP I, but also other scholars from Heidelberg, München, Bonn, Greifswald etc.—for details see https://web.archive.org/web/20110719105340/http://orp.uni-kiel.de/ORP-Frameset.htm (access 8/03/2019).
21. In the 1980s and 1990s new dissertations were written on Orissa, which either evolved in the aftermath of and around ORP I or set new focal areas which in turn influenced ORP II. These include E. Schömbucher's (1984) work on the Telugu-fishermen in Puri and their Jagannath-rites; the research of R. Hardenberg (1999 and 2000) on the Nabakalebarar-rites of the Jagannath-cult and the ideology and rituals of the 'Rajas of Puri'; the work of Berkemer on the Little Kingdom of Kalinga using the concept 'little kingdom' relevant for ORP II later and the research of Schnepel based on his long-term field research (1989–1995) on the Jungle Kings in South Orissa which was later turned into a habilitation (1996). The overlapping interests of Schnepel and Kulke, who was familiar with Schnepel's work as a reviewer, led to the idea of holding an Orissa-conference in 1997, which was meant to critically reflect on ORP I and more recent research. Instead of the Brahman-dominated Jagannath-cult in Puri as focal point of ORP I, the conference was also held to focus on 'contested local and subregional identities'. Thus, Berkemer's 'Little Kingdoms' and Schnepel's 'contested identities' became crucial theoretical contributions to ORP II. The 15 participants of the conference in June 1997 included Prof. S.K. Mitra (political scientist, Heidelberg) and five former ORP I scholars (G.N. Dash, H. Kulke, G. Pfeffer, J. Rösel and H. von Stietencron). Additionally, nine participants of the 'post-ORP I - generation' were at least partially integrated into ORP II later (I. Banerjee-Dube, G. Berkemer, M. Brandtner, R. Hardenberg,

C. Mallebrein, P.K. Nayak, A. Schmid, E. Schömbucher). All contributions were published in 2001 as the first volume of a series of books, edited by Kulke and Schnepel and dedicated to the project. It was released by Chief Minister Naveen Patnaik. During the conference, it was decided to apply for a second ORP under the title 'Various Identities: Socio-Cultural Profiles of Orissa in Historical and Regional Perspectives'. 'ORP II' was accepted by the DFG in 1998 for the years 1999 to 2005. It was officially completed in 2006 with the handing over of the palm manuscript collection of ORP I to the National Archives in Bhubaneswar.

22. See 'Preface' of *The Cult of Jagannath*, 2nd edition, 2014.
23. Thus, scholars of several universities—Beltz in Heidelberg, Guzy in Berlin, etc. and worked with Eschmann's bequest and were very much aware of this continuity. Beltz (personal communication) saved and still preserves boxes with Eschmann's hand-written notes, papers, etc. that did not become part of an Orissa Archive as it was established for manuscripts, but not for such written remains of ORP scholars—showing individual connections as much as the limits of archiving discussed below.
24. It continued in 1982–1983 with a Senior Research Grant from the American Institute of Indian Studies. It included a year in Puri for Williams, focusing on this project and participating in the life of one of the great Hindu pilgrimage centres. The project, Williams (1996: xxi) mentions, benefitted from help of established 'Orissa hands' abroad including Hermann Kulke, Eberhard Fischer, Louise Cort, Thomas Donaldson and Frederique Marglin. Purna Chandra Mishra's role 'deserves the title Independent Scholar rather than Research Assistant having been indispensable to many foreign researchers over the years'.
25. Namely (a) a dominant 'Oriya School' of Jagannath Studies; (b) an 'intermediary group' and (c) a 'theory-oriented group' which differed over theoretical approaches. The first driven by the '*gurus*' of ORP I focused on epigraphical and literary sources rather than fieldwork, but engaged in processes of cross-fertilisation with ORP and contributed to a proliferation of Jagannath Studies from 1980s onwards and blossomed in institutions such as the Jagannath Sanskrit University, Sri Jagannath Research Centre Puri, Sri Jagannath Research Institute BBSR, etc. The second with scholars like G.N. Dash, Kailash C. Dash, G.C. Tripathi, also Stietencron, R. Geib, C. Hacker (on silk clothing), Cort et al. took issue with the holistic agenda of the 'Oriya School' and its emphasis on origins and rather shifted to specific issues, though inspired by first generation, while the last 'school' with Pfeffer (sasana religious elite, later tribes), Rösel (pilgrimage), later Hardenberg but also Kulke (state formation and tribal deities) and Schnepel (ethnohistory) pushed the project into altogether new theoretical directions.
26. Rösel calls it the 'Schliemann-Syndrom'.

27. The occupancy or sharing of spaces was not only influenced by the project, but also by ties of friendship existing already before the project, which then had an influence too.
28. Being a keen temple photographer his contributions were also included in joint publications like *Imaging Odisha* (2013).
29. Occasionally, the jeep might have been used for other purposes, though project members made it a point not to use it for private shopping and once a senior member was even criticised to travel with the jeep via the market for shopping on his way for fieldwork. However, as Jakob Rösel (personal communication) remembers it was used once for the wedding of the daughter of the caretaker of the *dharmashala* where he was staying—a goodwill gesture that caused considerable excitement in the bridal family.
30. The original quote in German:

> *Der Projekt-Wissenschaftler stellt sich gegenüber den Landesverhältnissen von seiner Bezahlung her gesehen als neuer Raja' dar; ein Vollmitglied eines Forschungsprojektes bezieht in etwa das Salär eines indischen Ministers. Dies bedeutet: der Wissenschaftler kann praktisch jeden mittelmäßig qualifizierten Wissenschaftler des Gastlandes für sich arbeiten lassen, ohne daß er irgend etwas zu befürchten hätte, was die Urheberrechte seiner später publizierten Studie anbetrifft.... Die ökonomische Überlegenheit des Wissenschaftlers gegenüber den Bewohnern seines Gastlandes verändert auch seine wissenschaftliche Position. Die überragende Kaufkraft seiner Salärs und die gewaltigen Möglichkeiten, die ihm das Projekt zur Verfügung stellt, sei es in der Form des Jeeps, des Büros, und die Möglichkeiten, überall als erster Zutritt zu finden, können dabei bald eine Verschiebung seiner wissenschaftlichen Interessen auf völlig andere Gebiete bewirken.*

31. Flights to Calcutta at a rate of 3,200 DM per person meant a considerable burden at a time for families when the monthly salary was 1,400 DM at German universities. It also meant that some members had to take a loan in order to balance the bank accounts after this expenditure. Thus, their lifestyle, as well as the lifestyle of members of the just ending Harvard-Bhubaneswar Project, was relatively modest compared to 'official' Americans residing in villas in Bhubaneswar (Forest Park). Scholars of the latter project such as the Freemans would rather visit their German colleagues by bicycle and even the field director Prof. Cora Dubois 'resided' in a simple apartment in the State Guest House (Kulke: personal communication).
32. Fifty per cent positions for Ph.D scholars were rather common at German universities by the 1990s.

33. Other rumours stated that local colleagues who did not become associates of the project were unhappy with the way they were not included.
34. In fact, a rumour even stated that statue was already in the air and only brought back after a while. Later on, it turned out that it had been stolen by a man of the locality who had buried it in the sand near the temple.
35. The case started on 23 March 1972 and dragged on till 1974 primarily by two reasons. After all German members of the ORP had returned in 1972, no new research visa was granted to Western scholars. It was Indira Gandhi's retaliation against Nixon's policy of threatening an intervention in the war of independence of Bangladesh by sending an aircraft carrier into the Bay of Bengal. Probably more serious were problems faced by the police. Only soon after their confiscation of the manuscripts they were informed about the above-mentioned correspondence of Shri R.K. Rath and Prof. Schneider and his assurance that the manuscripts will be dedicated to the Orissa State Museum (OSM). To return them immediately to the ORP would have been an admission of guilt by the police. Only in May 1974, when Eschmann, Kulke and Hein returned with their new visa as the last batch of ORP I, Kulke had to go through severe negotiation with the police to organise the ceremony of the dedication of manuscript at the meanwhile fixed date 12 August 1974. It was a sincere problem to prevent the police from transporting the MP manuscripts directly from its depot to the OSM, as it initially insisted. Instead they should first return it to the ORP office which will then transport it itself to the Museum—a procedure of high symbolic value. Kulke succeeded only after quoting the old but valid Anglo-Indian law that confiscated bags were always sealed by two keys and that they can be opened only simultaneous by the two keys, one of them being still in possession of the ORP since 1972. Kulke informed twice police officers that the ORP may not be willing to use its key if the manuscripts may not first be returned to its offices before the ceremony at the OSM will take place. The responsibility for the bundled manuscripts (in plastic bags in the wet basement!) would then remain with the police for years or decades to come. Finally, with the permission of the Asst. Director General (ADG) of the Police, one hour was conceded to Kulke! It was certainly a kind gesture of the police, and most likely of its ADG too, that Eschmann and Kulke welcomed next morning to their surprise and delight three police jeeps with the manuscripts already at 11 AM, six hours before the ceremony at 5 PM. And it was a great pleasure for them to welcome the same officer who had also been in charge of the confiscation the manuscripts two years ago. He congratulated the ORP for having saved the MP by purchasing it and dedicating it now to the OSM. During the donation ceremony at the OSM, Orissa's 'cultural treasure' was dedicated in the name of the ORP by Dr Linser, German Consul General at Calcutta, to Shri J.M. Das Mahapatra, Minister of Cultural Affairs of Odisha. Shri K.N. Mahapatra

delivered an improvised keynote as S.N. Rajaguru, as senior *guru*, was unable to reach in time Bhubaneswar from far off Paralakhemundi in south Odisha (Kulke: personal communication).

36. Generally speaking, this dialogue was going on well throughout the time of both ORPs. The only exception in Odisha was due to the just mentioned temporary confiscation of palm-leaf manuscripts. The general refusal of research visa for German scholars in 1973 by the central Government and the official reluctance of the central Archaeological Survey of India to permit P. Yule's archaeological excavations at Odisha in 2000–2005 were beyond the influence of the ORP in Odisha. But, again at the same time, the fact that Yule was not prevented from undertaking some 'trial excavations' and surveying several hitherto unexplored archaeological sites is a good example of the success to gain the support through local institutions (Yule 2006).
37. In 1996, the Chief Minister Janaki Ballabh Patnaik conferred Hermann Kulke also the Nabakalebara Award of the Shree Jagannath Research Institute at Bhubaneswar.
38. For example, in 1970–1972 G.C. Tripathi purchased systematically nearly 200 original palm-leaf manuscripts, mostly of religious and ritual contents with special reference to the Jagannath cult.
39. On 24 December 1970 Tripathi and Kulke acquired it for ₹ 8,000 from R.K. Samantaray, the official Deula Karana of the Jagannath temple. The MP was stored safely in Tripathi's residence at Bhubaneswar. On 2 February 1971 Prof. Schneider informed Shri R.K. Rath, the Secretary of Cultural Affairs, about the purchase of the MP by the ORP by a letter.

    > The collection should remain in Orissa and be made accessible to scholars interested to work on it. We, therefore, intend to donate the whole collection to any appropriate institution after we have utilised it for our own research work. May we, therefore, approach you with the request to kindly advise us and offer us your valuable suggestion to which institution it should be donate.

    Ten days later Shri Rath suggested to Prof. Schneider 'to make over the manuscripts to the Orissa State Museum which has facilities for preservation. Scholars from within the State and from outside will also have access to these manuscripts. Permit me to thank you for your attitude of cooperation and assistance' (Kulke, personal communication).
40. Thus, until the summer of 1972 about 7,000 palm-leafs were copied and quite a few of them also translated. Of the typed copies, three of each texts were copied, two with the help of blue paper. The third copies, often hardly readable, were distributed to ORP members and to some Odiyan scholars for their personal use. The ORP researchers were thus, as already mentioned, doubtlessly in a privileged position. The funding allowed the

project not only to purchase many manuscripts but also their copying at a time when Xerox copying was not yet available.

41. The most important Rajabhog chronicle was retained and remained to be safely stored together with all the other palm-leaf manuscripts in a specially purchased steel almirah in the residence of G.N. Dash until 2006. After the official end of the fieldwork of the ORP I in 1975, its library (books and other secondary sources) and the sets of all the original handwritten and first typed copies of manuscripts and translations were transported to Heidelberg (temporarily and partly also to Freiburg and Tübingen).
42. As the SAI webpage states: 'While the project proceeded the scholars involved decided to guarantee the public an open access to the complete material. Therefore, it was agreed upon to keep it under the guardianship of the South Asia Institute as soon as the project had been completed.' This means that books were integrated into the main library, but the manuscripts remained in a separate room and were made accessible as 'a special collection in compact storage and easily obtainable during the library hours' using modern digital technologies. Available at https://www.sai.uni-heidelberg.de/saibiblio/bib_orissa.php (accessed 10 February 2019). Similarly, Tübingen developed a web-database of temples in Odisha, which is online accessible. Available at https://www.escience.uni-tuebingen.de/projekte/sakrale-bauten-in-orissa.html (accessed 10 February 2019).
43. In 2004 and 2005 H. Kulke conducted jointly with G.C. Tripathi and G.N. Dash negotiations with Shri K. Jayakumar, Director General, National Achives of India, New Delhi and Dr Lalatendu Das Mahapatra, Acting Superintendent of the Record Centre (Eastern Zone), National Archives of India, Bhubaneswar. It was finally decided to donate the manuscripts and translations to the Record Centre on 28 November 2006. They were handed over in the presence of Günther Wehrmann, Consul General of Germany, by Prof. G. Dharampal-Frick of the South Asia Institute as the representative of both the South Asia Institute and the Federal State of Baden-Württemberg as the owner of the material and by H. Kulke, the member of the first and Director of the second ORP. In the afternoon and the next day, a symposium was conducted as the last act of the two ORPs. It subject 'The Madala Panji and Orissan Historiography: A Symposium', perfectly suited the handing-over ceremony of the MP and the closing of the circle of both ORPs. But even more significant is the fact that out of the fourteen participants of the symposium only three were Germans (Berkemer, Kulke, Skoda) and eleven were Indian colleagues (K.S. Behera, G.N. Dash, L. Das Mahapatra, G. Dharampal-Frick, B.P. Mallik, N. Mohanty, C.P. Nanda, S.K. Panda, B. Pati, B.P. Sahu and G.C. Tripathi). The small number of German participants is certainly not representative for the number

of German members of the two projects. However, the pleasingly high number of Indian colleagues allows a glimpse insight into the inspiring acceptance and contribution of our Indian colleagues.

44. Divided into three sections: (a) The Formative Period; (b) Climax and Crisis and (c) Resurgence and Present Trends.
45. As explained in the preface of the second edition of *The Cult of Jagannath and the Regional Tradition of Orissa* (2014): 'J. Rosel was not supposed to publish an article on this subject before submitting his Ph.D thesis which dealt with this very subject.'
46. As the 'Preface' states, this endeavour started already in 1970 as a collaboration between SAI/Heidelberg, Freiburg, Tübingen and Utkal University and turned into a 'major desideratum for further research on Orissa'. The order of the bibliography, as the list of content shows, followed the needs outlined by ORP and participating scholars, that is a focus on history, religion, art, literature and linguistics, anthropology (Kulke, Dash et al. 1981: viii). The bibliography expanded considerably on the initial 2,000 titles—primarily by adding to the section on 'Language and Literature', which was increased by G.N. Dash from 700 to 2,900 titles. Moreover, other scholars linked to ORP I, such as K.S. Mishra and Kedernath Mahapatra agreed to check the details (Kulke, Dash et al. 1981: ix). Indicating the ground-breaking capacity-building through ORP, the authors also argue that '[t]he bibliographical work in this field proved to be particularly difficult because no library, not even in Orissa, possesses complete sets of the most relevant Oriya journals' (Kulke, Dash et al. 1981: vii).
47. The first volume corresponded to the conference 'Text and Context: In Orissa (and beyond)' held in 2000—just like the others later on. The editors of these volumes present a mix of senior experts in ORP I (Pfeffer and Kulke) or relatively more junior colleagues not involved in ORP I, who often worked on post-doc projects, while Ph.D scholars were also included as authors. Unlike the later volumes, the first volume and conference was initially—thematically and conceptionally—planned by A. Michaels (Heidelberg) and B. Schnepel (Frankfurt), who, however, decided to pass it on to another team of editors after the first round of funding. The change indicates the internal dynamics of the projects, but also the system of funding rounds, that is funds were typically granted for two years and extensions subject to evaluation without guarantees of continuity throughout the project.
48. Other conferences with significant ORP angle included, for example, 2001: Mahima Dharma Reconsidered: New Research Perspectives on Popular Asceticism in Orissa, Utkal University, Bhubaneswar, 23–24 February; 2002: Orissa Panel 17th European Conference of Modern South Asian Studies, Heidelberg, 12 September; 2002: Little Kingdoms

as a Model of the Pre-Modern South Asian State, Heidelberg, 9–14 September; 2004: Bali Yatra in Orissa and Beyond. Regional Variations and Social Identities, Sambalpur University, 20–22 February; 2004: Tribal Society in India and Beyond, Sambalpur University, 17–19 December; 2006: Madala Panji and Orissan Historiography: A Symposium, Bhubaneswar, 18–19 December. See also https://web.archive.org/web/20110719105340/http://orp.uni-kiel.de/ORP-Frameset.htm (accessed 8 March 2019).

49. It assembled 18 scholars from both projects and many other Indian and international Odisha experts in order to showcase the cultural and historical wealth of Odisha, the diverse scholarly contributions in the fields of religion, sculpture, art, music, etc. while trying to reach out beyond the scholarly ivory tower.
50. Mallebrein's projects also included 'Die vertauschten Götter [Conversion in India]' (2011). 'The Divine Play on Earth' had a separate chapter on Lord Jagannath but also the goddesses, while the former included Lord Jagannath only in a peripheral way.
51. In the same 'Preface', Fischer also lauds the work of ORP. He argues, after going through Kulke's, Eschmann's, v. Stietencron's and Tripathi's work:

> Not only have these researchers understood to arouse an amicable appreciation for an cultural-historical documentation by outsiders und to compile an immense material in terms of manuscript-copies, translations, books and the like, in the meantime they have written pivotal studies especially on the religious history of Orissa. (1980: 8, translated by the author)

The original quote in German:

> Nicht nur haben diese Wissenschaftler es verstanden, in Orissa freundschaftliches Verständnis für kulturhistorische Dokumentation durch Aussenstehende zu wecken und ein umfangreiches Material an Manuskript-Kopien, Übersetzungen, Büchern usw. zusammenzustellen, sondern sie haben inzwischen auch äußerst wichtige Studien vor allem zur Religionsgeschichte von Orissa verfasst.

Fischer's only lament was that the Orissa Bibliography had not been released in time for this volume, which in turn served as a catalogue for an exhibition at the same museum—incidentally also with Lord Jagannath on the cover (though sharing the space with Goddess Durga and others). The collaboration between Fischer and ORP continued into ORP II when he delivered a keynote during the annual project conference. Together with Pathy, Fischer published another volume titled 'In the Absence of Jagannatha' in 2012 that related directly to Lord Jagannath, frequently refers to ORP sources and is still sold in the museum shop at Museum Rietberg.

52. Reader in History, Utkal University and author of 'History of Orissa in 19th century' (1964).
53. One image was explained in the caption: 'Square in front of the temple: unconventional subject for a temple painter because it is outside of the traditional motives; scene depicts a family, guided by a *panda*, in front of the Lion's Gate' (translated from German by the author). Other images in this volume include: pp. 62–63: 'Rath Yatra', original produced in Raghurajpur depicting Lord Jagannath during the rath yatra; pp. 72–73: 'Jagannath Mandira: Jagannath, Subhadra and Balabhadra in Ratnavedi in the sanctum' (original by temple painter, then redrawn for the book); pp. 126–127: 'view of temple town' painted by artisans in Raghurajpur and are based on popular culture originals.

References

Agrifoglio, R. 2015. *Knowledge Preservation through Community of Practice*. Cham: Springer Link.

Anderson, B. 1983. *Imagined Communities: Reflections on the Origin and Spread of Nationalism*. London: Verso.

Berger, P. 2007. *Füttern, Speisen und Verschlingen: Ritual und Gesellschaft im Hochland von Orissa, Indien*. Berlin: Lit.

Berger, P., R. Hardenberg, E. Kattner and M. Prager. 2010. *The Anthropology of Values*. Delhi: Longman.

Berkemer, G. 1993. *Little Kingdoms in Kalinga: Ideologie, Legitimation und Politik regionaler Eliten*. Dissertation. Stuttgart: Steiner Verlag.

Berkemer, G. and M. Frenz. 2003. *Sharing Sovereignty: The Little Kingdom in South Asia*. Freiburg: Klaus Schwarz Verlag.

Brandtner, M. and S.K. Panda. 2006. *Interrogating History: Essays for Hermann Kulke*. Delhi: Manohar.

Cort, L.A. and P.C. Mishra. 2012. *Temple Potters of Puri*. Ahmedabad: Mapin.

Dash, G.N. 2010. *Jagannatha and the Gajapati Kings of Orissa: A Compendium of Late Medieval Texts (Rajabhog, Sevakarmani, Deshakhanja and other Minor Texts)*. Delhi: Manohar.

Donaldson, T. 1986. *Hindu Temple Art of Orissa*. Leiden: Brill.

Eschmann, A., H. Kulke and G.C. Tripathi. 1978. *The Cult of Jagannath and the Regional Tradition of Orissa*. Delhi: Manohar.

Eschmann, A. 1978a. 'Hinduization of Tribal Deities in Orissa: The Śākta and Śaiva Typology'. In *The Cult of Jagannath and the Regional Tradition of Orissa*, edited by A. Eschmann, H. Kulke and G.C. Tripathi, 79–98. Delhi: Manohar.

Eschmann, A. 1978b. 'Mahima Dharma: An Autochthonous Hindu Reform Movement'. In *The Cult of Jagannath and the Regional Tradition of Orissa*, edited by A. Eschmann, H. Kulke and G.C. Tripathi, 375–410. Delhi: Manohar.

Fischer, E. and D. Pathy. 2012. *In the Absence of Jagannatha: The Anasara Paintings Replacing the Jagannatha Icon in Puri and South Orissa (India)*. New Delhi: Niyogi.

Fischer, E., S. Mahapatra and D. Pathy. 1980. *Orissa. Kunst und Kultur in Nordost-Indien* [Art and Culture in North-East India]. Zürich: Museum Rietberg Zürich.

Geib, R. 1975. *Indradyumna-Legende: Ein Beitrag zur Geschichte des Jagannātha-Kultes* [Indradyumna-Legend: A Contribution to the History of the Cult of Jagannath]. Wiesbaden: Harassowitz.

Guzy, L. 2002. *Baba-s und Alekh-s. Askese und Ekstase einer Religion im Werden* [Baba-s and Alekh-s. Asceticism and Ecstasy of a Religion in the Making]. Berlin: Weißensee Verlag.

Hardenberg, R. 1999. *Die Wiedergeburt der Götter. Ritual und Gesellschaft in Orissa* [The Rebirth of the Gods: Ritual and Society in Odisha]. Dissertation. Hamburg: Kovac.

Hardenberg, R. 2000. *Ideologie eines Hindu-Königtumes. Struktur und Bedeutung der Rituale des Königs von Puri (Orissa/Indien)* [The Ideology of a Hindu-Kingdom: Structure and Meaning of Rituals of the King of Puri (Orissa/India)]. Berlin: Das Arabische Buch.

Hillery, G. 1959. 'A Critique of Selected Community Concepts'. *Social Forces* 37(3): 237–242.

Kulke, H. and G. Berkemer. 2011. *Centres out there? Facets of Subregional Identities in Orissa*. Delhi: Manohar.

Kulke, H. 1970. *Cidambaramahatmya. Eine Untersuchung der religionsgeschichtlichen und historischen Hintergründe für die Entstehung der Tradition einer südindischen Tempelstadt* [A Study of religio-historical and historical backgrounds for the emergence of the tradition of a South-Indian temple town]. Dissertation. Wiesbaden.

Kulke , H. 1978a. 'Royal Temple Policy and the Structure of Medieval Hindu Kingdoms'. A. Eschmann et al. 125–138.

Kulke, H. 1978b. 'Khurda rājavamsa o Jagannātha dharma'. *Paurusha,* 12 (1):17–28.

Kulke, H. 1979. *Jagannatha-Kult und Gajapati-Königtum* [The Cult of Jagannath and Gajapati-Kingdom]. Wiesbaden: Franz Steiner.

Kulke, H. and G. Dash et al. 1981. *Orissa: A Comprehensive and Classified Bibliography*. Cuttack: Vidyapuri.

Kulke, H. 1984. 'Tribal Deities at Princely Courts: The Feudatory Rajas of Central Orissa and their Tutelary Dieties (iṣṭadevatās) Kings and Cults'. Institute of Oriental and Orissan Studies, Vol 2. Cuttack. Reprinted

H. Kulke 1993. *State Formation and Legitimation in India and Southeast Asia*, 114–136. Delhi: Manohar.

Kulke, H. and B. Schnepel. 2001. *Jagannath Revisited. Studying Society, Religion and the State in Orissa*. Delhi: Manohar.

Kulke, H. and G. Berkemer. 2011. *Centres out There? Facets of Subregional Identities in Orissa*. Delhi: Manohar.

Kulke, H. 2013. *Imaging Odisha*. Ashram Patna: Prafulla.

Malinar, A. 2007. *Time in India: Concepts and Practices*. Delhi: Manohar.

Malinar, A., J. Beltz and H. Frese. 2004. *Text and Context in the History, Literature and Religion of Orissa*. Delhi: Manohar.

Mallebrein, C. and H.v. Stietencron. 2008. *The Divine Play on Earth: Religious Aesthetics and Ritual in Orissa*. Heidelberg: Synchron.

Mallebrein, C. 2011. 'Tutelary Deities at Royal Courts in Orissa'. In *Centres out There? Facets of Subregional Identities in Orissa*, edited by H. Kulke and G. Berkemer, 255–272. Delhi: Manohar.

Mallebrein, C. and J. Beltz. 2012. *Elefanten, Schaukelnde Götter und Tänzer in Trance. Bronzekunst aus dem heutigen Indien* [Elephants, Swinging Gods and Dancers in Trance: Bronze Art from Contemporary India]. Zürich: Museum Rietberg und Verlag Scheidegger and Spiess.

Mallebrein, C. 2011. *Die vertauschten Götter. Religionswechsel in Indien* [The Exchanged Gods: Conversion in India]. Heidelberg: Synchron.

Mubayi, Y. 2004. *Altar of Power: The Temple and the State in the Land of Jagannatha*. Delhi: Manohar.

Orissa-Projekt/Sonderforschungsbereich 16. (1973). *Die hinduistische Tradition und ihre Bedeutung in der gegenwärtigen Entwicklungsphase Indiens/Zwischenbericht*, Sept 1973 [Orissa-Project: The Hindu Tradition and its Meaning in the Contemporary Phase of Development of India/ interim report] (unpublished manuscript).

Otten, T. 2006. *Heilung durch Rituale. Vom Umgang mit Krankheit bei den Rona im Hochland Orissas*. Berlin: Lit.

Otten, T. and U. Skoda (eds.). 2014. *Dialogues with Gods. Possession in Middle Indian Rituals*. Berlin: Weissensee Verlag.

Panda, S.K. 1986. *Herrschaft und Verwaltung im östlichen Indien unter den späten Gangas (ca. 1038–1434)*. Wiesbaden: Steiner Verlag.

Pfeffer, G. 1976. *Puris Sasana-Dörfer. Basis einer regionalen Elite* [Puri's Sasana Villages: Basis of a Regional Elite]. Unpublished D. Litt. thesis. Heidelberg.

Pfeffer, G. 2007. *Periphery and Centre: Studies in Orissan History, Religion and Anthropology*. Delhi: Manohar.

Rajaguru, S.N. 1992. Śrī Jagannāthasthalavṛttānta. Translated into English by S.N. Rajaguru, edited by B.K. Svain. Puri: Shri Jagannath Sanskrit Vishvavidyayala.

Rapport, N. [1996]2004. 'Community'. In *Encyclopedia of Social and Cultural Anthropology*, edited by A. Barnard and J. Spencer. London: Routledge, 114–117.

Redfield, R. 1955. *The Little Community: Viewpoints for the Study of a Human Whole*. Uppsala: Almquist and Wiksells.

Rösel, J. 1974. 'Bemerkungen zur interdisziplinären Entwicklungsländerforschung' [Comments on an Interdisciplinary Research on Developing Countries]. *Internationales Asienforum*, 5(2): 243–253.

Rösel, J. 1980. *Der Palast des Herrn der Welt: Entstehungsgeschichte und Organisation der indischen Tempel- und Pilgerstadt Puri* [The Palace of the Lord of the Universe: History of Origins and Organisation of the Indian Temple and Pilgrimage Town of Puri]. München: Weltforum Verlag.

Rösel, J. 1988. *Tempelstadt Puri* [Temple town Puri]. Freiburg: Hedwig Falk.

Schneider, U. 1984. *Der Holzgott und die Brahmanen*. [The Wooden Deity—daru devata—and the Brahmins. Edition and translation of the Purusottama Mahatmya], 2 vols. Wiesbaden: Harassowitz.

Schnepel, B. 2002. *The Jungle Kings: Ethnohistorical Aspects of Politics and Ritual in Orissa*. Delhi: Manohar.

Schömbucher, E. 2001 'Inviting Deities into Lord Jagannātha's Town: The Religious Practice of the Vādabalija Fishermen of Puri'. In *Jagannath Revisited: Studying Society, Religion and the State in Orissa*, edited by H. Kulke and B. Schnepel. Delhi: Manohar, 49–64.

Skoda, U. 2005. *The Aghria: A Peasant Caste on a Tribal Frontier*. Delhi: Manohar.

Stein, B. 1980. *Peasant state and society in medieval South India*. Oxford: Oxford University Press.

Tönnies, F. 1922[1887]. *Gemeinschaft und Gesellschaft. Grundbegriffe der reinen Soziologie*. Berlin: Karl Curtius.

Tripathi, G.C. and H. Kulke. 1993. *Religion and Society in Eastern India: Eschmann Memorial Lectures*. Eschmann Memorial Fund, Utkal University, Bhubaneswar.

Tripathi, G.C. 2004. *Communication with God: The Daily Puja Ceremony in the Jagannatha Temple*. New Delhi: Aryan Books International.

Wenger, E. 1998. *Communities of Practice: Learning, Meaning, and Identity*. Cambridge: Cambridge University Press.

Williams, J. 1996. *The Two-Headed Deer: Illustrations of the Ramayana in Orissa. Berkeley:* University of California Press.

Yule, P. 2006. *Early Historic Sites in Orissa*. Delhi: Pragun Publication.

ABOUT THE EDITORS AND CONTRIBUTORS

Editors

Jyotirmaya Tripathy is a member of the Faculty of Humanities and Social Sciences at the Indian Institute of Technology Madras, India. His broad areas of interest are cultural development thought and contemporary India, with specific interest in the cultural dimension of development and the way institutional development questions are contested by popular practices. He has published on these topics in various journals. He has co-edited *The Democratic Predicament: Cultural Diversity in Europe and India* (2013) and *Becoming Minority: How Discourses and Policies Produce Minorities in Europe and India* (2014).

Uwe Skoda is Associate Professor for India and South Asia Studies at the Department of Global Studies, Aarhus University, Denmark. Currently, he is working on the one hand on visual culture and on the other in the field of political anthropology—particularly transformations of kingship, indigenous people and domestic politics. His recent books are *India and its Visual Cultures: Community, Class and Gender in a Symbolic Landscape* (2018, co-edited with Birgit Lettmann) and *Highland Odisha: Life and Society beyond the Coastal World* (2017, with Biswamoy Pati).

Contributors

Amarjeet Nayak is Reader in the School of Humanities and Social Sciences at National Institute of Science Education and Research (NISER) Bhubaneswar, India. His primary areas of interest are

Postcolonial Studies, Speculative Fiction and Film Studies. He is also a published short story writer in English and Odia.

Animesh Mohapatra teaches English at Delhi College of Arts & Commerce, University of Delhi. His research interests include book history and modernity studies. He has co-edited with Sumanyu Satpathy a volume of Odia literary criticism in translation, *Natabara Samantaray: A Reader* (Sahitya Akademi, 2017). Currently, he is co-editing with Jatindra Nayak the Odia volume of a series on 'Critical Discourses in India' to be published by Taylor & Francis.

Gautam Choubey teaches English at Atma Ram Sanatan Dharma College, University of Delhi. His research interests include print studies, Hindi literature, popular culture and translation. He has recently finished a Hindi translation of Andre Beteille's *Democracy and its Institutions*, and a screenplay for a period drama on Gandhi. He has also translated satires of Shrilal Shukla, Basanta Kumar Satpathy and Awadhi couplets of eighteenth-century Odia poet Brajnath Badjena. Presently, he is working on a critical biography of Hindi novelist Yashpal and a history of Bhojpuri literature.

Pranay Kumar Swain holds a Ph.D in Social Sciences from the Indian Institute of Technology Kanpur. Presently he is working as the Chairperson in the School of Humanities and Social Sciences at NISER Bhubaneswar. He has significant hands-on experience in teaching, research, consulting and training inclusive of planning, monitoring and management of programmes cutting across quarters of social development. His areas of interest are social development, social transformation and sociocultural lives.

Ranjan Kumar Panda is a Professor of Philosophy in the Department of Humanities and Social Sciences, Indian Institute of Technology Bombay, India. His areas of interest are philosophy of mind and language and philosophy of education. He has edited a book titled *Language, Mind, and Reality: A reflection on Philosophical Thoughts of R.C. Pradhan* (Overseas Press, 2015). He is currently working on a volume tentatively titled *Self-knowledge and Moral Identity.*

Samik Malla is a doctoral researcher at the department of Humanities and Social Sciences, IIT Madras. He has been an Erasmus Mundus IBIES scholar at the Department of Philosophy, Università degli Studi di Milano, Italy during 2015–2016. His research interests include intellectual history, literary theory and political theology. Hailing from the Northeastern state of Tripura, he is keenly interested in its religious and cultural history.

Shaswat Panda teaches English literature at North Odisha University, Keonjhar Campus and is a Ph.D scholar at the University of Delhi. His doctoral research examines the way biography writing was influenced by India's encounter with colonialism and the purposes biographies were meant to serve in post-independence India. His other interests include translation, life-writing and visual cultures of Puri.

Sreejit Datta teaches English, Creative Writing and Cultural Studies at the Mysore campus of Amrita Vishwa Vidyapeetham in Karnataka, India. He is an accomplished vocalist, trained in Hindustani Music and Rabindra Sangeet and has held a prestigious fellowship in the latter, awarded by the Ministry of Culture, Government of India. His research interests include aesthetic philosophy, musicology, literary criticism and comparative cultural studies.

Umasankar Patra teaches English at Ambedkar University Delhi, New Delhi. A recipient of the Christopher Isherwood Foundation Fellowship, he has submitted his doctoral dissertation on the working of the autobiographical in Christopher Isherwood at the Department of English, University of Delhi. He has been published in *The Explicator, Indian Literature* and *The Book Review*, and has translated literary criticism from Odia into English. He is currently working on the interface of pedagogy, modernity and literary marketplace in colonial Odisha.

INDEX

Note: The letter 'n' 'f' following locators refers to notes and figures respectively.

N